RISE
AGAINST
EAGLES

RISE AGAINST EAGLES

STORIES OF RAF AIRMEN IN THE BATTLE OF BRITAIN

CHRISTOPHER YEOMAN & ADRIAN CORK

FONTHILL

In loving memory of Ruth Young
25/07/1959 – 20/05/2011

Fonthill Media Limited
Fonthill Media LLC
www.fonthillmedia.com
office@fonthillmedia.com

First published in the United Kingdom 2012

British Library Cataloguing in Publication Data:
A catalogue record for this book is available from the British Library

ISBN: 978-1-78155-085-4 (print)
ISBN: 978-1-78155-161-5 (e-book)

Typeset in 10.5pt on 13pt Caslon
Printed and bound in England

Connect with us
facebook.com/fonthillmedia twitter.com/fonthillmedia

CONTENTS

Ju 87 Stukas. (*EN Archive*)

Foreword

By Flight Lieutenant Charles 'Tich' Palliser, DFC, AE

Rise Against Eagles is a wonderful book that has brought back many memories for me of those days in the Battle of Britain, especially reading about my dear South African friends, Gerald 'Zulu' Lewis, Terry Crossey and Percy Burton. I have particularly fond memories of Terry because it was through him that I met my wife. I have a painting on the wall in my house depicting Percy Burton's action with a Bf 110, which saw him killed. This painting was sent to me by an artist in England and is a treasured part of my collection. To read about this encounter in this book was truly moving. Due to the wonders of the internet and social networking, I have also been able to connect with the family of Gerald Lewis and, of course, it is always good to read about my dear friend Tom Neil. He was my Flight Commander and we remain friends to this day. This work also pays tribute to the pilots from New Zealand, Poland and Czechoslovakia – a wonderful band of men. Of course, there are many wonderful pilots in this book who I never knew and never met but I very much enjoyed reading about them all. I offer my congratulations to Christopher and Adrian on producing a wonderfully written book.

Authors' Notes

Every summer my family and I make it a priority to visit Duxford, in Cambridgeshire, to attend a spectacular, world renowned air show called Flying Legends. The air show is like no other, bringing history to life with its vast collection of Second World War aircraft on display at an aerodrome enriched with history.

Before the Second World War, Duxford was home to 19 Squadron that reformed at the aerodrome in 1923 and later became the first squadron to be equipped with the most advanced monoplane in the RAF at the time, the Supermarine Spitfire. During the Battle of Britain, Duxford was also the centre for Douglas Bader's famed 'Big Wing' and later in the war was used by the United States Army Air Force.

The most recent Flying Legends air show that I attended took place on 10 July 2011, seventy-one years to the day that the Battle of Britain is noted to have officially begun. Throughout the morning, I spent a lot of time walking up and down the flight line gazing upon a collection of beautiful warbirds that included Spitfires, a Hurricane, Curtiss Hawks, P-51 Mustangs and a B-17 Flying Fortress to name but a few. Just looking at these aircraft on the ground is enough to stir up the imagination, but watching them in the air is something else. The magnificent sight and sound of those legendary aircraft evokes a feeling of remembrance of the past and as beautiful aerial displays take place over the aerodrome, a sense of reverence passes like a wave through the crowds below. Perhaps the most poignant part of the Flying Legends show is the final act known as the 'Balbo' where every participating aircraft soars through the sky in mass formation. It is a spectacle only to be fully appreciated firsthand. The sound is utterly breathtaking.

At the close of the 2011 show, something unexpected suddenly occurred that was heart rendering. To my left I heard a rushed voice scream 'There's been a collision!' I turned my head to the right and saw two large pieces of metal falling from the sky and then an aircraft dived towards the earth until we lost sight of it behind a large group of trees across the aerodrome. The sight was sickening, but relief quickly followed dread as a parachute opened in the sky. The pilot appeared to be worryingly low and it seemed that nobody knew what had happened. It was the end of the show, nothing was mentioned about the incident but two aircraft did not return to land at Duxford.

Later that night I learned that a Douglas A-1 Skyraider's wingtip had clipped a P-51 Mustang called 'Big Beautiful Doll' in mid-air. The pilot of the Skyraider managed to land his aircraft elsewhere despite a damaged wingtip and the pilot of the P-51, after bailing out of his cockpit, descended to safety. 'Big Beautiful Doll' sadly crashed in an adjacent field behind trees which had blocked our vision from where we stood as nervous onlookers. The silver Mustang with black and white checker nose paint was lost, but it could have been worse. It was a huge relief that both pilots were all right, although perhaps shaken up. The accident stuck in my mind for a while as I considered the loss of such an iconic aircraft and how precious all of them really are to the aviation world today.

From a modern perspective it is difficult to appreciate what Second World War pilots went through when they saw their colleagues' aircraft fall from the sky in combat, when they witnessed friends collide with other aircraft and when parachutes failed to open. Such sights occurred on a daily basis as young men from all over the world fought for their respective countries.

As much as I enjoy visiting historic museums like Duxford and watching the great warbirds in flight, my core interest in the Second World War stems from the men that fought in the RAF in the defence of Britain. My passion for military aviation began some years ago after my father became close friends with Wing Commander Bob Doe and his wife Betty. One afternoon while he was visiting the Does at their lovely home in Tunbridge Wells, I nonchalantly picked Bob Doe's book *Fighter Pilot* off my parents' bookshelf just to see who Bob Doe actually was. I initially sat down with the book with the intention of just looking at the photographs within, but I suddenly became captivated by certain pages which presented Bob's combat reports from 1940. At first I read one or two of these reports until I became so engrossed in the content that I began reading from the beginning.

I finished the book that very night, educated for the first time about the Battle of Britain. The next day I asked my father if he could take me to meet Bob Doe on his next visit, which he did a few weeks later. Before meeting Wing Commander Doe I felt both excited and nervous, but upon entering his home I was instantly put at ease by his warm handshake and welcoming smile. We spoke about the Battle itself over lunch and I was later privileged to have been able to spend some time with his original logbooks which were aptly bound together with authentic Hurricane fabric. I knew I was in the company of a true hero and that feeling is one that I will never forget. Since that time I have had an unquenchable interest for everything to do with the Battle of Britain, but most especially for the pilots themselves.

Over the following years I have had the great pleasure of meeting and spending time with many of the surviving men who flew in the Battle of Britain on numerous occasions. These great men who Churchill immortalised as 'The Few' have cemented my desire to continually learn about their experiences and most importantly to remember them and those who sacrificed their lives for a free world. I am grateful that I grew up in a home that remembered the conflict of 1940 because as I reflect upon my education as a schoolboy, I find it infuriating that I never once heard the term the 'Battle of Britain' used, not even in my history classrooms. It was a subject I learned elsewhere. Bearing in mind the impact the Battle of Britain has had, not just on the UK, but also on the world we live in today, I believe that it is fundamental that we remember and celebrate our history in order to keep it alive for future generations.

Rise Against Eagles is a collaboration of personal tributes to a selection of airmen who bravely flew against the Luftwaffe during the Second World War. All of whom epitomise the courageous and selfless spirit possessed by the RAF airmen who fought against Nazi Germany.

This book has been divided into four sections. The first airman to be attributed is Flying Officer Bobby Pearce who served in the Battle of France as a Fairey Battle rear gunner. Bobby is one of the kindest gentlemen that I have had the pleasure of meeting and his love for Second World War aviation was infectious, so I was thrilled to learn about his experiences from those early days in France. Then there are two New Zealand pilots who fought in the Battle of Britain, namely Don Cobden and Wally Churches, both of whom served with 74 Squadron during 1940. Squadron Leader Gerald Lewis' story concludes the first section. I began to research Lewis' wartime service after a conversation I had with Wing Commander Tom Neil several years ago in a hotel bar in Kent. Tom informed me that I shared the same religious membership as an old 249 Squadron friend of his and I later learned that it was Gerald Lewis. After getting in contact with Lewis' son, Mark, I began to collect information about his distinguished wartime experiences which proved fascinating.

The second section of this book is dedicated to the 'Merseyside Few' which will be explained in further detail hereafter by Adrian.

The third section consists of four of 'The Few' whose stories are not widely known, but whose names kept cropping up while I was researching my previous books *Tiger Cub* and *The Battle of Britain: Portraits of The Few*. I really wanted to write about these four men whose stories must continue to be remembered. Lastly, section four contains the story of a Bomber Command veteran, Squadron Leader Benny Goodman, whose experiences with 617 Squadron offer a different perspective into aerial warfare than those airmen previously mentioned.

Since our collaboration, Adrian and I have endeavoured to highlight some of these men's experiences from the resources we have had available. The purpose of this book is to pay tribute to these great men included in these pages, which in turn hopefully pays tribute to all of the pilots they flew and fought alongside in the defence of Britain.

Christopher Yeoman

James Bond is not a name normally associated with The Battle of Britain, but he is the man indirectly responsible for my preoccupation with it. Well, Bond's creator, Ian Fleming, is anyway. In 2008, I visited an exhibition at the Imperial War Museum celebrating the centenary of Ian Fleming's birth. As well as his writing career, the exhibition covered Fleming's wartime experiences as Personal Assistant to the Director of Naval Intelligence and later as a Naval Intelligence Officer. I enjoyed the exhibition and, as is usual at these things, exited into a shop. After looking at the Fleming/Bond items, I started browsing the books that really represent the theme of the Imperial War Museum, those on the First and Second World Wars. My enduring love of history was reawakened as I stood looking at those books.

As a boy growing up during the early 1970s, most of my mates wanted to be footballers, to have the sideburns of Kevin Keegan or the white signature boots of Alan Ball. Of course, I loved football too, but strangely enough wanted to be an archaeologist. I don't remember what history I studied at primary school but I must have enjoyed it. History became my favourite subject at secondary school, but again I don't recall what I studied or why my love of the subject continued. Until my O-Levels in 1976 that is. My history teacher treated his class like students rather than schoolchildren and lectured to us in a way I hadn't been taught before. I remember studying Italian and German Unification and being completely enamoured with the stories. I did well enough to take history to A Level. After this, whatever I was interested in, I bought whatever I could to learn and understand as much as possible about my current interest. So, standing in the Imperial War Museum shop browsing shelves of Second World War books, my old desire to 'get into' a subject was right there with me.

I decided to buy some books about different stages of the Second World War and, as is my way, read them in the order the events occurred. I chose a book on Dunkirk, two on The Battle of Britain, one on the Great Escape, one on The Dambusters, and one on D-Day. After reading Hugh Sebag-Montefiore's epic on Dunkirk, I read Tim Clayton and Phil Craig's *Finest Hour*, Matthew Parker's *The Battle of Britain*, Stephen Bungay's *Most Dangerous Enemy* and Patrick Bishop's *Fighter Boys*. By now I was completely obsessed with the events of the summer of 1940.

What I struggled to get my head round, and still do, is that the young fighter boys of the RAF, 'The Few', were exactly that. Young. Aged eighteen, nineteen and twenty, and charged with the defence of their country and, not to exaggerate at all, the defence of the free world. After that I started buying all the books I could lay my hands on, particularly those by the pilots themselves. One of the books I bought was the hard to find *Men of The Battle of Britain* by Kenneth G. Wynn. This is a book that provides a potted biography of each of the 2,917 Allied airmen who flew operationally in The Battle of Britain.

Dipping in and out of this I was taken aback to find that a number of pilots killed in action were buried in Liverpool and Wirral and three of them less than five miles from my home. I had assumed most pilots would be buried in and around Kent and Sussex. So I went through Wynn's book, pilot by pilot, making a note of those laid to rest, not only on Merseyside, but in the North West of England. I spent much of the summer of 2009 touring cemeteries and graveyards in search of pilot graves and joined The Battle of Britain Historical Society so I could formally adopt any of the graves that did not have a carer. I've visited graves from Windermere to Egton-with-Newland, from Macclesfield, Poynton and Delemere to Marple and St Helen's. But it is Merseyside's connection with The Battle of Britain that has captivated me. My research has shown that the Battle's connection to Merseyside doesn't only extend to pilots laid to rest here, but there are a number who were born and went to school on Liverpool and Wirral.

I met Christopher Yeoman through a shared interest in the Battle of Britain and Liverpool FC. Our first meeting was because of Christopher's great friend who flew in the Battle, Wing Commander John Freeborn DFC*. But that is a story for another book. We have spent many hours discussing the Battle and share the same view. So it is because of Christopher's encouragement that I started to write about it. And so we come to the purpose of this work.

The deaths of Bill Stone, Henry Allingham and Harry Patch in 2009 saw the passing of the First World War generation. This focussed my mind on what I wanted to do, that is to put on record as best as I can the stories of those Battle of Britain pilots who are buried in Liverpool and Wirral. Not just what they did in battle, but who they were, who they loved, who loved them and what their connection to Merseyside is. This work is my tribute to them, The Merseyside Few.

Adrian Cork

Please note that occasionally to remain true to source, there are unavoidable inconsistencies when referring to the same Messerschmitt aircraft regarding the use of 'Me' and 'Bf'.

Introduction

After the First World War, the Treaty of Versailles forbade Germany from having an air force but in breach of the Treaty, German pilots trained under the guise of civil aviation schools using light training aircraft. On 26 February 1935, Adolf Hitler ordered Hermann Goring, a veteran of the First World War and ace fighter pilot, to establish the Luftwaffe in direct violation of the Treaty's ban on German military aviation. As the Luftwaffe developed with cutting edge technology and engineering, a formidable force was evolving in the shadows of Europe.

During the Spanish Civil War of July 1936 to March 1939, the Luftwaffe gained valuable experience by testing aircraft, pilots and tactics when its Condor Legion was sent to Spain in support of the anti-Republican government revolt led by Francisco Franco. The Luftwaffe's aircraft proved superior in combat against its outclassed opponents and its bombing attacks caused devastation to its targets.

At the outset of the Second World War, the Luftwaffe – brandishing the insignia of an eagle gripping a swastika in one of its claws – was modern, battle-hardened and confident in its abilities. When Hitler invaded Poland on 1 September 1939, Britain and France declared war on Germany. Although fewer in number, the RAF was equipped with comparable aircraft to the Luftwaffe unlike the rest of Europe. The durable Hawker Hurricane and the revolutionary Supermarine Spitfire were Fighter Command's protagonists of the Second World War. Both fighter aircraft played definitive roles in clearing the skies of dark tyranny under the command of Air Chief Marshal Sir Hugh Dowding whose ingenuity and preparatory foresight brought Winston Churchill victory in 1940.

The conflict between the RAF and the Luftwaffe first began in France when a small band of Hurricanes were sent to defend ultimately a hopeless cause. When France fell to German occupation in June 1940, Hitler's gaze turned reluctantly to Britain. Between July and October 1940, the most iconic aerial conflict was waged when heavy numbers of Luftwaffe bomber and fighter aircraft relentlessly crossed the Channel seeking to gain air supremacy over the RAF in preparation for a German land invasion. However, by 31 October, it became evident that the Luftwaffe had failed to achieve its aims and Britain remained free from Nazi oppression. During this decisive conflict, RAF fighter pilots from all walks of life flew continuously against unfavourable odds in a most perilous sky, and once Britain was secured from Hitler's grasp they proceeded to fight on the offensive. This work collects the experiences of ten RAF fighter boys who fought against Nazism in their rise against eagles.

The following poem was written in the dispersal hut at Kenley in October 1940 by Wing Commander Paul Farnes, DFM, who was a sergeant pilot at the time with 501 Squadron during the Battle of Britain.

Readiness at Dawn

By Paul Farnes

Night has shed its heavy cloak
And the stars 'ere put to flight.
The dawn is gently breaking
With a pale and misty light.

But we got up some time ago
To herald in the morn,
For our orders of the night before
Said 'Readiness at Dawn'.

We go round to our aircraft
To see they're in good state,
And then there's nothing left to do
But settle down and wait.

When we're sitting round dispersal
To do battle in the sky
I often stop to wonder
If today someone will die.

It may be Bob it may be Bill
It may be Morf or Mac
Because as like as not this day
Someone won't come back.

Some types are reading letters
And some are playing crap

Some are sitting thinking
Some quietly take a nap.

Suddenly the 'phone rings,
It's the operations line
And every man is on his feet
And the same thought's in each mind.

The order comes to 'Scramble'
The engines start as one
We rush out to our aircraft
And the battle has begun.

The squadron soon is airborne
And straight away begins the climb,
For height's the first and foremost thought
In every pilot's mind.

Tail-end-Charlie starts his weaving
To guard our tails and watch the sun,
For she makes a natural cover
For every skulking Hun.

Ground station calls the Leader
And says "There's ninety plus
And they're heading straight for Dover,"
So they're heading straight for us.

Someone switches on his set
And the thought's in each chap's mind
That a warnings going to follow
So each man looks behind.

It's Harry who is calling
He's having trouble with his hood,
He says "I'll have to break away,
Is my message understood?"

We're now at thirty thousand
And it won't be very long
Before we start the battle
In which Mac won his 'gong'.

The R/T crackles once again
And there's a shout of "Tally-Ho,
They're on our left at ten o'clock,
Come on chaps, let's go!"

The C.O. starts a gentle turn
To bring us on their beam,
But we've got to dive through Messerschmitts
That give the bombers fighter screen.

We dive down through the cover
But there are more up higher still
Just waiting till we turn our tails
Before they try to kill.

But the Spitfires up above us
The Hun has yet to face,
And soon there'll be a battle royal
In this great barren space.

The fight is soon at fever pitch,
It's each man on his own
And deeds of courage are performed
Of which nothing will be known.

On the ground down far below us
Our Mothers' younger sons
Are watching us with envy
As they listen to the guns.

But if our prayers be answered
And God grant that they will,
When they've only just reached manhood
They won't have to learn to kill.

The fight is nearly over now
The Hun has turned away
And those of us who're lucky,
Live to fight another day.

The ground crews on the tarmac
Watch our return with anxious heart

And find that three have not come back
Who went up at the start.

It's Hughie, Bob and Johnny
Who're missing from the show,
But they may have baled out somewhere
And be trying to let us know.

Bob rings up sometime later
To tell us he's O.K.
He baled out over Tunbridge
But that is all he'll say.

The news of Hugh and Johnny
Came through to us next day,
They'd crashed in flames near Dover;
There's not much one can say.

But someone takes a long drawn breath
And with unsteady voice
Says "If they'd known they had to go
It would have been their choice."

"To die fighting for their country
Against the bloody Hun
In order that some other folk
May wander in the sun."

And when we sit around again
To go up and fight once more
My thoughts of times stray far away
To my home before the war.

And when I think of peace in England
And all it means to me
Moisture dims my weary eyes
And I find it hard to see.

Prologue

At the tail end of an afternoon patrol between Maidstone and Canterbury on 28 September 1940, Hurricane V6617 fell from the sky in a mass of flames. The Hurricane belonged to 249 Squadron who had spent a frustrating hour perusing their flight line for enemy aircraft that proved elusive as Messerschmitt Bf 109s circled teasingly overhead. While under the impression that the enemy had finally fled back across the Channel, the squadron received orders to return to North Weald aerodrome.

Diving from approximately 30,000 feet, 249 Squadron made way for base with Pilot Officer Lewis and Sergeant Hampshire weaving back and forth behind the rest of the Hurricanes as 'Tail-End Charlies'. Just as Hampshire looked towards the sun to check for bandits, he heard Lewis yell 'Look out!' over the R/T. Hampshire took evasive action as tracers passed over his port wing but it was too late for the Hurricane bearing the code letters 'GN-R'. After such a seemingly uneventful patrol it had come as a complete shock that the squadron had been bounced on its return home. Pilot Officer Tom Neil, who was known for his keen eye, was utterly surprised as he looked out of his cockpit to see a fellow colleague hanging in his parachute straps descending towards the earth. The culprits were two Bf 109s, which after making their attacks, dived down into cloud. Sergeant Bentley Beard gave chase and caught up with one of them in the vicinity of Dover. After opening fire, Beard put the Bf 109 down, forcing it to ditch into the Channel where the Luftwaffe pilot was rescued. Pilot Officer George Barclay, a handsome, unassuming young man, also followed the Bf 109s down into a steep dive, but ultimately to no avail. He did, however, catch sight of the falling airman and later that day recorded in his diary:

As it was I saw one parachute and followed it down to the ground. It turned out to be Lewis who has about 16-18 Huns to his credit, so the 109s were no respecter of persons.[1]

Bf 109 of 3./JG2 in flight. 'Yellow 14' was usually flown by Lt Franz Fiby. (*Erik Mombeeck*)

SECTION ONE
BATTLE ATTACK

CHAPTER 1

Flying Officer Bobby Pearce

At the outbreak of war, a small RAF force was dispatched with the BEF (British Expeditionary Force) to assist France in its efforts to repel a German advance. Initially, four Hurricane squadrons were sent out to assist the brave young men who flew in light bomber aircraft such as the outdated Fairey Battle. One such airman was Bobby Pearce, a Wireless Operator/Air Gunner from Erith, Kent.

Pearce joined the RAF in 1938 as an aspiring Wireless Operator. He began his basic training at Uxbridge and then went on to Cranwell Wireless School to learn his chosen craft. On completion of the course, Pearce had his first taste of wireless duties from the air in a Vickers Valentia aircraft. There were twelve students on board and each was given a different message to send to the Radio Shack. Once the message was sent they would then receive a reply. As a young man with a keen passion for aviation, Pearce found the experience to be a complete thrill.

As the course continued, Pearce soon became a capable Wireless Operator and Air Gunner and was then posted to 63 Squadron stationed at Upwood. Prior to his posting, Pearce and his peers were told that they would be sent to either a Bristol Blenheim or a Fairey Battle squadron. When Pearce realised that he would be going to a Battle squadron, he was assuredly informed by the 'old sweats' that he was extremely fortunate because '...Blenheims could not maintain height on one duff engine'. It was not until Pearce arrived at Upwood that he instantly realised that the Battles had exactly the same problem.

The Battle light bomber was a fairly advanced aircraft at the time of its conception, but was virtually redundant before it eventually went to war in 1939-1940. The immense production effort, involving 2,200 aircraft, engines and spares was largely wasted. This could not have been foreseen when the specification P27/32 was issued in August 1932 and in definitive form in April 1933 or when the first big orders were placed in 1935-1936 for the rapidly expanding RAF. Designed to replace and improve upon the Hawker Hind

Hawker Hurricane with BEF tail markings landing at Rouvres, France, in early 1940. (*Peter Ayerst*)

and Hart two-seat biplane day bombers, the Battle lacked speed and defensive armament necessary to survive attacks even by the monoplane fighters of its own design era. Though accepted as being obsolescent, Battles continued to be ordered and made.

In August 1939, while on leave, Pearce received a telegram that exclaimed 'Report to your unit immediately'. On his return, Pearce and two colleagues were flown to RAF Bicester to join 142 Squadron that was preparing to depart for France. The squadron, along with nine other Battle squadrons, were to form the AASF (Advanced Air Striking Force) to offer support in France to both the British and French armies in the event of a German advance into the Low Countries. On 2 September, 142 Squadron left for France. When they arrived, preparations were quickly underway.

The Imperial crew spent some time with buckets of green and brown camouflage paint and long-handled brooms, concealing the beautiful silver paint with a sombre coating. Our destination was Berry-au-Bac, a small village about nine miles north of Rheims. About a mile from the village was a very large area of agricultural land which had recently been harvested. This was to be our aerodrome which was separated by the main Rheims/Laon road from a more modest field which had a small forest of saplings along its border. After landing the aircraft they were taxied over the road to the periphery of the wood, backed into small clearances, and young saplings were propped against the leading edges of the aircraft. The concealments were quite effective. Later the taxiing paths were covered with metal lattice grids by the Pioneer Corps. The N.C.O's and airman were billeted initially in the village. My group were accommodated in a large barn. A groundsheet and a blanket were issued to each of us and our "adventure" had begun. Everything was fun. Breakfast was served in the open behind the Town Hall. It comprised of a slap of French Rye-bread, very dark in colour and very dense in texture. The bread was accompanied with bacon, decanted from 7lb. tins into large trays, and then heated over Primus stoves. We had the choice of either a rasher of bacon placed on our slice of bread or we could submerge our bread in the bacon fat. This repast was washed down with strong, sweet tea decanted from a vast urn. In these early days we were fed at mid-day by the French army caterers and in the evening we were fed in the village by our own cooks – mostly bread, margarine with bully beef or jam. All of this was very novel and great fun. We had quite forgotten that there was a war in progress.

Once the squadron had organised the aircraft dispersal, the administrative and flight offices, practice began. At first the crews embarked on familiarisation flights in the area and formation flying. The latter was of particular importance because the squadron was expected to fly in close formation with the intention of providing crossfire for its mutual defensive support. In due course, a more exciting form of practice came about when the squadron began practising low-level flying and dive attacks on the gun-pits that surrounded the headquarters tent.

Our confidence in our aircraft was high, our low-level tactics we regarded as invincible.

The novelty of living and working in a foreign country soon wore off for Pearce. In fact, after only a month or two the boys of 142 Squadron became very nonchalant with the supposed 'war' and soon adjusted to their life in France.

We established a very good relationship with the locals and we occupied a farm with all its outbuildings in the small village of Ville-au-Bois, quite near the airfield. We slept in the smaller sheds and the larger barns were used as mess-halls. The Officers were accommodated in a Chateau quite near Berry-au-Bac. The Chateau was occupied by the owner with his wife and many maids and menservants. They were welcomed into the family home and enjoyed a life of luxury. A swimming pool and a tennis court were available.

Bobby Pearce in Paris, December, 1939.
(*Pearce collection*)

As winter approached the weather became severe and all of the squadron's efforts were directed at looking after the aircraft so that they would remain serviceable should a crisis breakout. To protect the Fairey Battles, canopies were erected over the engines of each aircraft and a small oil-burning stove placed below to create some warmth. Due to the extreme conditions of cold weather, the airmen were issued a generous amount of cigarette rations and a constant flow of scarves and balaclava helmets were received from England. With little else happening, leave passes were soon permitted for weekends in Paris. There were even rumours circulating about possible leave arrangements being made for visits to England. Pearce included began to feel a lack of urgency around the squadron.

Any trepidation we may have felt was now a thing of the past. We had not heard a shot fired in anger and the "War" may not have existed. We were all delighted when the Squadron moved down to the South of France for a "Practice Camp". We landed at La Salanque near Perpignan on the Mediterranean. High temperatures, tropical plants and a total lack of snow made for an idyllic situation. We spent days engaged in air-to-air firing at a drogue towed by another Battle and air-to-ground firing. We also carried out dive attacks on targets with smoke bombs. Those Air Gunners who had not qualified as such, were, after a test, awarded the coveted Flying Bullet Air Gunners Badge. This award entitled the Air Gunners to an extra sixpence a

Fairey Battle, Berry Au Bac, France, winter 1939. (*Pearce collection*)

day. We returned to Berry-au-Bac and began to enjoy the advent of spring. We were by now competent with our flying exercises and confident that we were ready for any eventuality.

Finally after what felt like an endless lull in Berry-au-Bac, 142 Squadron was rudely awakened to the war. In the early morning hours of 10 May 1940, Heinkel 111s bombed and machine-gunned the squadron's airfield from 600 to 1,000 feet. The attack left some damage to the airfield and two aircraft, but fortunately there were no casualties. A second attack occurred less than two hours later when a lone bomber dropped incendiary bombs from a high altitude but caused no further harm.

The Hurricane squadrons were also early into action including the RAF's first ace of the Second World War, Flying Officer Edgar James 'Cobber' Kain. Just before 0530 hours, Kain scrambled with 73 Squadron's Flying Officer Harold Paul. Shortly into the patrol, Paul ran into a formation of Dornier Do 17s of 4/KG2 at 18,000 feet, north-east of his aerodrome. Paul attacked a Dornier that was in the rear of the formation. His accurate bursts of .303 ammunition sent the bomber spiralling down inverted.

Kain, flying at 20,000 feet over Metz, took his Hurricane towards nine Do 17Zs of 9/KG3 and opened fire. At first, Kain overshot a Dornier but quickly engaged another. Kain scored direct hits on the bomber's engines and fuselage causing it to burn and descend. Kain followed the machine down firing additional bursts until his ammunition boxes were empty. The Do 17 finally crashed east of Metz and Kain broke away from the attack.

He 111s of Geschwaderstab/KG53. (*EN Archive*)

Dornier Do 17z of 6./KG76. (*EN Archive*)

At approximately 1200 hours, 142 Squadron was briefed to attack a panzer division that was approaching the French border. Eight Fairey Battles took-off, but Pearce's aircraft flown by Pilot Officer I. C. Chalmers had to return as their undercarriage failed to retract. Of the seven aircraft which were able to carry out their low level passes through light anti-aircraft fire, three failed to return. Flying Officer M. H. Roth and his crew were shot down and became prisoners of war, Pilot Officer F. S. Laws and his crew were shot down and killed, and Sergeant A. N. Spear, whom Pearce would later fly with, force-landed his damaged aircraft and returned with his crew back to Berry-au-Bac the next day. Pilot Officer W. H. Corbett and his gunner were wounded and their observer killed. Flying Officer A. D. Gosman's gunner also received slight wounds. Flying Officer A. D. J. Martin and Sergeant V. Heslop returned relatively unscathed. After such an awful ordeal, the dangers of flying in Fairey Battles were all too real for the airmen.

During the following days, 142 Squadron's airfield continued to be bombed by German aircraft. On 12 May, a morning raid scored a direct hit and destroyed one of the squadron's aircraft – K9259.

On 14 May, four Battles of 142 Squadron left Berry-au-Bac to bomb a pontoon bridge that was located between Sedan and Mouzon; however, at 1300 hours, the four aircraft were shot down by friendly fire. The unfortunate culprits were French Morane fighter pilots who mistook the Battles as Henschel Hs 126s. One Battle pilot was badly burned, another was injured and five men were tragically killed.

Shortly after this horrendous incident, the squadron was back in the air at around 1330 hours. Once again, Pearce was flying with Pilot Officer Chalmers alongside eight other Battles with orders to destroy the bridges at Sedan. The squadron was met by intense anti-aircraft fire from the ground and Bf 109s, but the target was bombed and several hits successfully struck the bridges. Once again Sergeant Spear's aircraft came under attack and he was shot down by Bf 109s. Both his crewmen were killed but Spear managed to bail out of his aircraft before landing behind enemy lines. He was able to evade capture and later returned to the squadron. For this, Spear was awarded the DFM. Out of the eight aircraft that originally set off only four returned to base.

In the days that followed, the Squadron's losses were severe. There was however an apparently inexhaustible supply of replacement aircraft and crews. Most of the sorties required a total flying time of about 40 minutes. We had become very aware of our vulnerability to attack from below and from behind and we therefore tended to keep as close to the ground as possible. This was an exhilarating experience for the air gunner standing in the open rear cockpit. Quite small changes in height would cause the feet to leave the floor when he became "weightless" for a moment, the next instant he was forced to the floor when the

Bobby Pearce manning his position in a Fairey Battle, 1940. (*Pearce collection*)

aircraft gained height. This zero gravity effect alternating with a positive gravity situation necessitated a constant check on the "monkey chain" by which we were tethered to the floor of the aircraft. Our bomb-load at this time comprised of 4 x 250lb bombs, fused for low level attacks with an 11 second delay. We sometimes added a further 2 x 250lb bomb on external racks, one on each wing. It may be of interest to know that the cruising speed of the Battle was about 210 mph. With a bomb-load of 4 x 250lb bombs the speed was reduced to about 180 mph and with the Air Gunner's canopy open (which was necessary in order for him to fire his gun, but acted as an airbrake – speed was reduced by a further 20 mph). It can be appreciated that the Battle with a speed of 160 mph was no match for a ME 109 with a speed of 360 mph and a cannon firing through his propeller hub with a range of 600 yards. The rear gunner had to maintain a very tight grip on his Vickers K gun. The loaded ammunition pens were stored on "pegs" on the side of the cockpit. When it was necessary to change a drum (each drum held 40 rounds), the empty was tossed on to the cockpit floor and the replacement quickly removed from its peg and fitted to the gun. At this period the guns were fitted with a ring and bead sight, later we had reflector sights which were more efficient. Each gunner was responsible for filling his own ammunition pans. Most of us favoured the idea of using predominantly tracer bullets. We considered that the enemy would be more discouraged by bullets which he could see approaching him. Anyway it seemed to work for me.

On 15 May, the Luftwaffe continued to mount aggressive attacks on Berry-au-Bac. In the afternoon, a raid of Heinkel 111s bombed the airfield leaving thirteen craters in their wake.

The squadron soon moved to Faux-Villecerf, salvaging what equipment they could from Berry-au-Bac. On 19 May, further devastation hit the squadron when out of the three serviceable Battles that went on a morning raid none returned. It was a desperate and sorry affair for 142 Squadron. After being urgently re-equipped at Pouan, the squadron soon found themselves with twenty-five aircraft. Operations continued.

When the time arrived to attack German troop columns, the troops were not in the least intimidated by either the noise of the attacking aircraft or by the Browning gun mounted in the leading edge of the starboard wing. Neither did they seek shelter from the rear gunners bullets as the plane climbed away. Instead, in an orderly manner, they left their vehicles, made their way into the adjacent fields or verges, lay on their backs in serried ranks and, with their rifles pointing skywards, awaited the arrival of their attackers. Thus the final run was through a hail of bullets. It was no comfort to remember that the radiator beneath the Merlin engine, would very quickly lose its coolant if hit. Our attempts to slow the German advance were also hindered by the steams of refugees who were fleeing westwards.

On 20 May, Pearce was back in the rear cockpit of a Battle with Chalmers flying and Sergeant Howard as observer. Their orders were to make a photographic reconnaissance sweep of the Troyes area, which was successfully carried out. That same night, four Battles were detailed to take part in a late sortie, but on preparation a flare ignited and set one of the aircraft ablaze. The bomb load exploded and tragically killed five of the squadron's ground crew.

Three days later, the squadron switched to night operations due to the impossible loss of both men and machines.

In June 1940, the Fairey Battle squadrons were kept actively involved in a range of various operational sorties against the rapidly advancing German army.

7 June saw the tragic and untimely loss of one of the RAF's greatest fighter pilots – Flying Officer 'Cobber' Kain of 73 Squadron. By this time the New Zealander had claimed an impressive amount of victories against the Luftwaffe with seventeen enemy aircraft destroyed and two damaged. Kain was due to go on leave but accidently crashed his Hurricane and was killed after 'beating up' his aerodrome for the final time. Sometime after the unnecessary tragedy, Pearce and a few of his friends investigated the Hurricane wreckage and each took a souvenir to remember the high scoring ace by. Pearce retrieved Cobber's oxygen mask connector.

On 12 June, 142 Squadron continued to play their part in the defence of France. In the morning, Pearce was involved in an operational raid that consisted of four aircraft attacking a bridge at Le Manoir. Pearce's Battle, flown by Sergeant Spear, scored a direct hit on the target as did a Battle flown by Pilot Officer L. H. Child.

> On 15 June we had orders to fly back to England. In addition to my pilot and observer, we were to take with us the Squadron Intelligence Officer, all Squadron records and his large black Labrador dog. Having decanted our passengers at Shoreham airport, we made our way to RAF Waddington, where having been supplied with uniforms, we were sent on leave. Those of us that survived were indeed fortunate. Outnumbered and outgunned, the inadequacy of the Fairey Battle was all too manifest. The total loss of aircrew of the AASF in the period of 10 May until our evacuation on 15 June exceeded 650 killed or missing and more than 230 Prisoners of War. While our contribution to the campaign was difficult to assess, we undoubtedly acted as guinea-pigs in the new concept of modern air warfare. Hopefully lessons were learned from our endeavours which were of benefit to those that followed on.

The men that flew in Fairey Battles during this period of history will always be remembered for doing their part to hinder the German advance in the Low Countries, despite working in obsolete aircraft. After participating in fourteen operational sorties in Battles with 142 Squadron, Pearce was indeed fortunate to have survived such a volatile and desperate campaign that ultimately failed. Pearce then went on to complete a tour of twenty operational sorties in Vickers Wellington Mk.II bombers that the squadron was equipped with when the Battles were withdrawn. After completing his tour, Pearce was then posted to an Operation Training Unit as an instructor, during which time he was able to participate in two of the first 1,000 bomber raids. When Pearce was finally invalided from the RAF at the end of 1944 due to tuberculosis, he continued to harbour an affectionate love for aviation, but in particular that unfortunate aircraft called the Fairey Battle.

After the war, Pearce became a dental surgeon, retiring in 1980. He was a dedicated supporter of the RAF Benevolent Fund and served as Secretary to the Friends of the RAF museum, Hendon, for many years. Pearce passed away on 24 April 2008, aged eighty-seven.

CHAPTER 2

Kiwi Tigers

Pilot Officer Don Cobden

Donald George Cobden was born in Christchurch, New Zealand, on 11 August 1914. As a young man, Cobden took a keen interest in rugby while attending the Christchurch Boys' High School. It was between the years 1927 to 1931 that Cobden developed into a fine rugby player, earning himself a place in the first XI. With a passion for rugby still burning brightly, Cobden joined Canterbury in 1935 where he played on several occasions. Cobden's impressive pace and strength as a wing soon caught the right attention. Standing approximately 1.85 m and weighing 84 kg, Cobden was selected by the All Blacks.

Cobden's first match for the All Blacks was played against South Africa's Springboks at Athletic Park, but unfortunately his leg was injured in a heavy tackle just twenty-five minutes into the match and was forced off the field. Despite this disappointing start for Cobden, the All Blacks went on to win thirteen points to seven. Due to his injury and a difficult time with team selection, Cobden moved on but continued to play the game he loved in England. Whilst in England, the New Zealander played for Catford Bridge Rugby Club, the Barbarians and the Royal Air Force.

On 2 July 1938, Cobden applied to the RAF for a Short Service commission and was duly accepted. His training began on Tiger Moths in August 1938 at the Civil Flying School Perth. With his training completed, Cobden was awarded his wings and posted to 3 Squadron the day before war was declared in September 1939. After a brief stay, Cobden was posted to 615 Squadron, but was then moved on 6 October to join 74 'Tiger' Squadron stationed at Hornchurch.

By time the New Zealander arrived, the squadron was equipped with Spitfire Mk.Is, but a month after his arrival, Cobden wrote off the first Spitfire (K9860) the Tigers had received when he force-landed at the satellite airfield of Rochford. Apart from this early hiccup, Cobden soon adjusted to squadron life and developed into a first-rate fighter pilot.

The German advance through France and the Low Countries had forced troops of the British Expeditionary Force to retreat to the beaches of Dunkirk. While the troops waited for sea vessels to evacuate them to Britain, they were constantly exposed to terrible air attacks from the Luftwaffe. It was a desperate time that urgently demanded the presence of RAF fighters.

On 21 May 1940, 74 Squadron's rigorous training exercises would finally be put to the test. In the early evening, Sailor Malan led A Flight on a patrol over Dunkirk at approximately 21,000 feet. It was here that the Tigers would meet the enemy for the very first time. Undoubtedly apprehensive, Cobden kept in steady formation as Yellow 2 with Flying Officer Tink Measures leading the section as Yellow 1 and Pilot Officer Ben Draper flying as Yellow 3. As the squadron passed over the North Foreland and approached Dunkirk in line-astern formation, Malan caught sight of two He 111s and gave the order to attack. As Red Section made for the bomber to port, Yellow Section broke off to attack the other. Measures closed range to 300 yards and opened fire with a steady burst that caused the enemy aircraft to wobble violently before turning in a spiralled dive towards cloud. Yellow Section continued to watch the damaged aircraft while Measures sustained his attack until they finally lost sight of the Heinkel as it fell through cloud.

Cobden's first combat report recorded what he witnessed on this encounter:

Report of Yellow 2 – P/O. D. G. Cobden.
I was in line astern with Yellow 1 when we attacked starboard enemy aircraft. Before we closed range enemy aircraft went into left hand turn followed by Yellow 1. I observed Yellow 1 fire a 3-4 second burst at, approximately range 300-100 yds. Enemy aircraft then dived quickly to right into cloud followed by Yellow 1 who reappeared shortly after.

Throughout the following days, the Tigers continued to fly operations across the Channel towards Dunkirk where they were repeatedly met with anti-aircraft fire and skirmishes with the Luftwaffe.

On 24 May, Cobden would once again be part of the action. While flying over the East of Calais on a late morning patrol, Red Section caught sight of a Dornier Do 17 cruising at 3,000 feet. Cobden's combat report explains what happened next:

I was Red 3 in 'A' Flight, No. 74 Squadron, when a Do.17 was intercepted East of Calais at approximately 1135. I attacked after Red 1 and Red 2 had broken off and from the line astern position fired a burst of 4-5 seconds. I broke off as I considered the machine was disabled. When No. 1 was attacking I noticed fairly big flashes from the top turret amidships which seemed to indicate a large calibre gun there. E/a was last seen going down to the ground in a flat dive. Markings and camouflage were on the underside of the wings outside the engines, which gave an impression of a four engine aircraft in the distance.

Two days later, Cobden, Ernie Mayne and Harbourne Stephen shared a probable Henschel Hs 126 that was attacked in the Bourbougville – Bergues region. The following day would be perhaps the most intense yet for the Tigers.

It was 27 May when 74 Squadron opened the day with an offensive patrol over Calais – Dunkirk. Cobden was amongst the eleven Spitfires cutting through the morning air as focused pilots scanned their surroundings for enemy aircraft. The New Zealander's tall, burly frame left little room for movement in the Spitfire's snug cockpit, but constant checks around the canopy was absolutely vital for a fighter pilot's survival. Soon enough the search was over and four Bf 109s were sighted at 12,000 to 15,000 feet to the rear of Blue Section.

To counteract the attacking Bf 109s, Blue Section turned into them while Red and Yellow sections climbed for height. As Red Section ascended, Cobden saw three Bf 109s dive into cloud. Then suddenly the sky was full of enemy fighters. Acting fast, Red 1 ordered his section to break into pairs, so Pilot Officer Freeborn as Red 2 broke off with Red 4 and Cobden as Red 3 followed Red 1 into combat. Within moments gun buttons were pressed and bullets zipped through the air. Freeborn attacked one of the fighters with Red 4, giving it several accurate bursts before it broke away trailing black smoke and licking flame.

Cobden followed Red 1 who attacked a Bf 109 at close range scoring direct hits. The Bf 109 was forced into a dive and Red 1 followed. Cobden looked up and observed two Bf 109s flying approximately 500 feet above his position, so he attacked from astern firing three deflection bursts which appeared to hit the tail of one of the bandits. The damaged Bf 109 went into a steep dive before spiralling into cloud. Cobden then spotted another Bf 109 coming towards him, slightly above and to his port side, so he manoeuvred into a quick climbing turn and ended up on the enemy's tail. Cobden thumbed the gun button and fired two short bursts before it escaped into cloud. After a stressful battle, the Tigers returned to Hornchurch, but they would soon be back across the Channel patrolling dangerous skies.

It had been an intense introduction to the war for Cobden, but during the evacuation of Dunkirk he had proven himself to be a capable flyer and a vigilant fighter pilot. Respected in the air, the big New Zealander was also respected on the ground by the rest of the squadron. Some of his colleagues described Cobden as a man with a good sense of humour and as someone who enjoyed a good night out.

Freeborn remembered Cobden as a playful character:

He was a charming bloke and he'd do anything to upset me. He would get into my aircraft and I'd soon shout, "You're not using my bloody aeroplane!" "Oh yes

I am," he'd say. "I've got to fly something and yours will do." But being 6 foot odd he would put the pedals right forward so that it was more comfortable for him and when I'd get into it, I couldn't even reach the pedals. Don would have the greatest pleasure when he came back from a trip in saying, "That aeroplane of yours does fly well!"

At the end of May, the exhausted Tigers were withdrawn from operations and sent to Leconfield to rest and to be re-equipped.

The squadron returned to active duty on 6 June, but life was seemingly less eventful than the previous month of constant patrols and dogfights with the Luftwaffe. This small respite was the calm before the storm for on 10 July 1940 the Battle of Britain had official been ushered in and Cobden and the Tigers were back in the thick of it.

At 1100 hours in the region of Ramsgate, Cobden led Yellow Section into action. At approximately 10,000 feet, the squadron intercepted a formation of enemy raiders. Cobden's combat report states the following:

I was Yellow leader patrolling with Red Leader off Deal when we saw a formation of 10 -109's above us. We climbed to attack them from astern. The enemy aircraft split up when we attacked and I got on to the tail of one enemy aircraft who immediately turned and headed off and down. I followed and fired a number of bursts at close range. When I broke off the attack he had black smoke coming from his starboard side and white smoke was coming from his port wing root, where his radiator was. When I left him he was well out to sea going slowly down. Most of my bursts were full deflection shots.

Later in the day, Cobden was back in the air leading Yellow Section on another sortie. The following combat report makes interesting reading:

I was Yellow Leader with Blue Leader patrolling a convoy off Dover when a number of Do.17's were sighted. We went into attack at high speed. As I was going in to attack my Nos 2 and 3 sighted enemy aircraft fighters above and broke off to attack them. I picked out a straggler from the Dorniers and attacked from astern with full deflection shots. As I broke off I noticed black smoke coming from his starboard engine. I attacked again, and as I was breaking off I was attacked by a number of 109's who partly riddled my aircraft. I used the extra boost and broke away successfully by doing a steep climbing turn. As my radiator had been shot I had to make a forced landing on Lympe aerodrome with my undercarriage up as it was made unserviceable in the fight.

Fortunately, Cobden was unhurt from this incident and his Spitfire (P9398) was later repaired.

On 24 July, six Spitfires of 74 Squadron took-off from Manston with instructions to patrol the Channel ports. As the Spitfires began to approach Dover, three Dornier Do 215s were sighted flying at sea level making their way for the French coast. Without hesitation the Tigers gave chase and soon caught up with their prey. Despite the persistent efforts from the Dorniers' rear gunners, Freeborn, Cobden and Douglas Hastings got within range of about 300 yards and sprayed one of the Do 215s with a succession of short bursts. Both Freeborn and Cobden saw their tracer bullets hitting their target before the Dorniers climbed into cloud. Due to being too close to enemy territory the Spitfires broke off from their engagement and made their way safely back to base.

The squadron saw out the remainder of July with torrid patrols and arduous engagements with Goering's air force. By 11 August 1940, the first phase of the Battle of Britain had ended and a new onslaught had begun. Rather than concentrate its attacks on the Channel ports and convoys, the Luftwaffe turned its attention on coastal airfields, hell-bent on disrupting Fighter Command.

At dawn on 11 August, Cobden awoke one year older. It was his twenty-sixth birthday, but it would not be a day for celebration. The first patrol of the day saw twelve Spitfires led by Malan take-off into the bright morning sunshine. In astute formation, the squadron climbed for height and set course for Dover. At 20,000 feet, the Tigers engaged eighteen Bf 109s and claimed eight of them destroyed and damaged an additional four. It was an impressive feat for the squadron, but any elation felt would soon be eradicated.

Just before noon, Freeborn led the squadron from Manston with instructions to cover a naval convoy off Clacton. Once airborne, Freeborn became utterly frustrated due to a controller positioning the squadron over a dense cloud base at 32,000 feet. After several attempts to locate the enemy, Freeborn realised they were in the wrong position and that the enemy was below the cloud base approaching the convoy 'Booty'. With haste the Spitfires dived through the thick cloud and emerged to find a massive formation of twin-engine Bf 110s flying in sections of threes and fours. As the squadron dived towards the Bf 110s, Freeborn noticed an explosion out of the corner of his eye, but due to the intense speed they were travelling at he had no time to access the situation. An eruption of combat ensued and aircraft began to fall from the sky. Several of the boys quickly succeeded in destroying and damaging enemy aircraft, but in return two Tigers were taken from their ranks. During this action, Pilot Officer Denis Smith was killed as was the big New Zealander on his twenty-sixth birthday, Pilot Officer Donald Cobden.

The details surrounding Cobden's death are unclear, but his Spitfire (R6757) was thought to have been shot down. However, to this day, Freeborn wonders if the explosion he saw while diving through the thick cloud base was Cobden colliding with a Bf 110.

The New Zealander's loss was felt deeply by Freeborn and the other Tigers for Cobden became an integral member of 74 Squadron. Well regarded by all who

Don Cobden with No. 74 Squadron, back row, fifth from right. (*74 Squadron Association*)

Don Cobden, fourth from left. (*74 Squadron Association*)

had the pleasure of knowing him, Cobden's tough, but good natured character was certainly missed by those left at Hornchurch.

Cobden's body was later washed ashore on the Belgium coast where he was recovered by the Germans.

After months of intensive combat, the squadron had earned a well earned breather from the front line and was sent north to rest and recuperate. Some of the pilots left Hornchurch begrudgingly, not really wanting to be far from the action. Such was the determined spirit of the Tigers. The squadron spent a brief spell at Wittering and then moved on to Kirton-in-Lindsay where new replacement pilots began to arrive and training commenced. One of the new recruits was a New Zealander called Wally Churches who had previously been at 57 OTU, Hawarden.

Pilot Officer Wally Churches

Edward Walter Gilles Churches was born in Auckland on 17 July 1921. He was educated at Onehunga Primary and Auckland Grammar Schools before working for the Posts and Telegraph Department as a telegraph messenger and postman. He was a member of the Waitemata Rowing Club where he collected many trophies. Churches applied many times for a short service commission in the RNZAF but was under age. His eagerness to serve was later rewarded and as a young man Churches reported to the Ground Training School, Weraroa, on 26 October 1939. He then moved on to 2 FTS, Woodbourne, on 16 January 1940 and was awarded his flying badge in April. In February, Wally was commissioned as an Acting Pilot Officer.

Churches sailed for England on 7 June on RMS *Rangitata* from Auckland to join the RAF's fight against the Luftwaffe. After a two-week spell at RAF Uxbridge, Churches joined fellow 'Kiwi' Bob Spurdle at Hawarden, where, after training on Masters, they converted to Spitfires and both received a posting to 74 Squadron. Spurdle recalled their first meeting with 74 Squadron's CO:

Wally and I stood before Sailor Malan and gazed at our new CO with deep respect. "You pilots will be trained hard in the next few weeks. Your life expectancy will be in direct ratio to your ability to learn. Spurdle, you are being put into 'A' Flight – your commander is Flight Lieutenant Freeborn. You, Churches, are in 'B' Flight with Mungo Park. This is a famous squadron and I expect you both to remember it. In the last war Major Mannock won the VC flying for 74. He shot down 73 enemy aircraft. Soon you, too, will have plenty of targets. I'm sure you'll do well![2]

Both Spurdle and Churches felt delighted to be in the ranks of such grand company, but Wally's war was almost over before it even began. On 30 August, Churches was involved in a mid-air collision with another Spitfire flown by Sergeant Bill Skinner. During the morning, the two pilots were practicing a head-on attack. Churches, flying Spitfire X4027, pulled up and his propeller shaved off the tail of Skinner's aircraft. Skinner was forced to bail out and his Spitfire, X4022, crashed and burned out. With adrenalin pumping through his system, Churches managed to force-land his aircraft that was damaged but later repaired. Remarkably, Churches and Skinner were both unharmed by the hair-raising incident and no hard feelings were harboured by either of the two pilots.

Churches was a likable character: he was a quiet, unassuming individual, but very popular among the other pilots. He quickly began to fit in to squadron life often joining the Tigers at their local haunt The Crown at nearby Knockholt. The pub's landlords, Mr and Mrs Elliot, took a shine to the pilots and their daughter took a particular interest in Churches. It seemed the New Zealander felt quite at home in the squadron, flying an aircraft that was the stuff of boyhood dreams.

In a letter to his sister, Churches wrote:

I am flying the machine I always wanted to handle – the Supermarine Spitfire – and I love it. I wish you could see one. I am sure you would love them as being beautiful pieces of engineering and the fastest means of transport in the world.[3]

During the morning of 11 September, fourteen Spitfires of 74 Squadron landed at Duxford to operate with the Big Wing for the day. At 1630 hours, Malan led the Tigers into the air following 19 and 611 Squadrons. The Tigers positioned themselves at the rear of the formation with instructions to intercept bombers approaching London, leaving the other squadrons to engage the fighter escort. The squadron was flying in three fours in sections line astern when a formation of Ju 88s was sighted 20,000 feet over London. Malan ordered a head-on attack but the squadron was rudely interrupted by enemy fighters.

As Yellow Leader, Freeborn broke off with his section to draw away the fighters and in turn lost sight of the Ju 88s. When over South London, Freeborn spotted a Dornier which he attacked from head-on, hitting its port engine and then, after pulling around in a tight turn, continued to spray the bomber with a succession of bursts until it crash-landed in a field near Dungeness and burst into flames.

Meanwhile, as Red 4, Churches intercepted a Heinkel 111 over South London. He opened his attack with a six-second burst from 150-50 yards range and watched his gunfire rip pieces off its wing-root and fuselage. Again, Churches attacked with another accurate burst from his eight machine guns that knocked pieces off the Heinkel's tail. He then turned his Spitfire away from the engagement, leaving the enemy with a dead engine and trailing black smoke. When Churches returned to base he claimed the bomber as a probable.

In the evening, Churches left Duxford with the squadron and returned to their station at Coltishall. Freeborn's Dornier was confirmed as destroyed and an additional ten aircraft were claimed as probable during the sortie.

Churches' next claim occurred on 14 September after his section had scrambled to intercept a raid north of Ipswich. Leading Green Section at around 1500 hours, he observed a lone Ju 88 at 8,000 feet headed in a northerly direction. Churches called for a line astern attack over the R/T and manoeuvred his Spitfire into position. Churches opened the proceedings from 300 yards range but the enemy aircraft dodged in and out of cloud and Churches was forced to circle. Once in position he delivered his next attack, this time firing from a closer range of 250 yards, closing to 150, but the Junkers continued to elude his efforts by hiding in cloud cover. The bomber was out of sight for some time having ducked into heavy cumulus, but Churches spotted it again through a break in the cloud and watched it jettison its bombs. Churches chased the Junkers one last time and fired another burst, but frustratingly the bomber disappeared from sight into cloud trailing black smoke. The chase had left Green Section low on fuel and they landed at Watersham at 1530 hours before returning to base.

Another similar 'hide and seek' encounter took place ten days later, when flying as Green 2, Churches intercepted a Dornier at around 1620 hours. Attacking with Green Section, Churches thumbed his gun button five times as the enemy aircraft went in and out of cloud cover. Churches circled and waited for the Dornier to emerge in a clear patch of sky and when it did he dived to attack the bomber at sea level. Heavy haze swallowed the Dornier from view and Churches had little choice but to climb and head for home. Back at base the New Zealander reported that he had experienced return fire from the Dornier, but it was erratic and out of range.

During the evening of 29 October, Churches reported:

I was No. 2 in Yellow Section Dysoe Squadron, sent off to patrol Biggin Hill at 30,000 ft. at approximately 1630 hrs. 29.10.1940.

Whilst flying in line astern at 30,000 ft. and turning N.E. down-sun Dysoe leader gave the 'Tally-ho' and I saw a ragged formation of Me.109's heading east at about 27,000 ft. The leaders half-rolled into the enemy aircraft and I just caught a glance of a big twin-engine machine flying alone and heading S.E. at about 10,000 ft. over Tunbridge Wells.

I dived vertically on the twin enemy aircraft and identified it as a Heinkel 111K. When within 250 yds. I opened fire and immediately saw my burst entering the fuselage and wing roots. Passing the tail of the aircraft at nearly 350 m.p.h. and about 20 yards astern I saw pieces flying off the enemy aircraft.

When I pulled out of the dive I blacked out completely and momentarily lost sight of the enemy. On next sighting him he was in a gentle dive several miles ahead and making straight for the south coast. I gave chase but was unable to catch him even after passing Dungeness.

When last seen he was at 5,000 ft. and still in a gentle dive.

Not one shot was fired at me and I firmly believe the rear gunner, at least, was disabled.

After passing the coast I returned to Biggin Hill and landed.

The Tigers also claimed three Bf 109s as destroyed during this patrol – two shot down by John Mungo Park and a third by an American Tiger, Willie Nelson.

By the end of October, 74 Squadron, having fought long and hard since Dunkirk and throughout the Battle of Britain, had helped Fighter Command to thwart the threat of Hitler's invasion. Be that as it may, the fight against the Luftwaffe was far from over.

On 2 November, 74 Squadron was ordered to patrol Biggin Hill with 92 Squadron. Malan led the squadrons up to 15,000 feet and then climbed to 24,000 feet. A large number of Bf 109s were sighted around 4,000 feet below their patrol line over the Isle of Sheppey. Malan gave the order to attack and dived into action.

On this occasion, Churches was flying as Yellow 2. During the melee he chased a Bf 109 that was diving in the direction of Boulogne, France, and managed to fasten on to its tail. A short but accurate burst pierced the enemy fighter and caused white smoke to bleed into the morning air. Closing in on the enemy fighter at seventy-five yards, Churches pressed his gun button briefly and watched large pieces fall off the Bf 109's wing and fuselage before it lazily half-rolled and dived into the sea. Due to the strong presence of enemy aircraft above, Churches made way for base 'at zero feet', claiming the Bf 109 as destroyed.

During the afternoon of 14 November, Churches flew as Blue 4 with the squadron after being detailed to patrol Maidstone at 15,000 feet. The Tigers swept the area for some time and then approached Dover where thirty-plus Ju 87s were sighted flying west at 12,000 feet along the south coast. The squadron dived on the formation but Churches broke off from the attack as he came under fire. He turned his head and found that two Bf 109s were attacking from above. He also noticed more Bf 109s about 1,500 feet above and ahead of his position. Immediately, Churches began to take evasive action to elude the two fighters as they continued to chase him. Churches endured two more attacks by the Bf 109s before finally shaking them off. He searched the area and caught sight of another Bf 109 flying just below some high cloud base at 16,000 feet. Churches took his Spitfire 200 yards away from the Messerschmitt and delivered a lengthy burst from his machine guns. No hits were observed but the German fighter took poor evasive action that allowed Churches a prime opportunity to latch on to its tail and fire a four-second deflection burst. The doomed Bf 109 flew into a hail of bullets and pieces flew off its wings. Issuing black smoke, the Bf 109 rolled over and went into a vertical dive before bursting into flames. Churches followed the Bf 109 down to 10,000 feet and then broke off to evade a further two fighters. Once again, Churches succeeded in escaping from the Bf 109s and then returned to base.

On 22 February 1941, Churches took-off from Manston with Sergeant Neil Morrison to relieve two Spitfires escorting a convoy north of Whitstable. As Green 1 and 2, Churches and Morrison settled into position over the convoy at 17,000 feet when Churches was warned of fifteen-plus enemy aircraft approaching. Churches led Morrison up to 20,000 feet and patrolled across sun. A single Bf 110 was seen flying over North Foreland, 2,000 feet below the Spitfires. Churches gave the order to attack and Morrison went into line astern. The Spitfires dived at terrific speed but so did the Bf 110 and they lost it in a cloud bank at 1,000 feet. A second Bf 110 was soon spotted and the Spitfires engaged. Churches fired two short deflection bursts at the enemy machine and Morrison delivered two four-second bursts. Pieces fell off the Bf 110's twin engines with white smoke pouring from them. The nose of the heavy fighter rose slightly and then slowly rolled it on to its back and crashed into the sea. Churches investigated the wreckage that was reported as being thirty-five miles east of Margate. The two Spitfires then set course for Manston sharing the Bf 110 as destroyed.

On 18 March, Churches was credited with shooting down a Bf 109 south west of Folkestone. This was to be his final victory for on 19 April, the gentle 'Kiwi'

Stuka swarm, 1940. (*Erik Mombeeck*)

pilot officer failed to return from a patrol. Wally Churches was later presumed killed in action. Wally's good friend and fellow comrade Bob Spurdle sorrowfully remarked:

> Wally's death was hard to take. We'd flown together some eight months – a long, long time by a fighter pilot's reckoning. I remembered the good times, the wild parties, the pub crawls, egging expeditions; but most of all, the shared ecstasy of watching soft dawns creeping over sleeping fields as our Spitfires circled higher and higher to greet the golden sun.[4]

Having left their homes in New Zealand to fly for the RAF, both Cobden's and Churches' contribution to Britain was of great worth and the cause they fought and ultimately died for would have lasting effects for both Britain and their homeland.

Today, Don Cobden is buried in Belgium at the Oostende New Communal Cemetery with Denis Smith and Harold Gunn, plot 9, row 2, grave 24. Edward Walter Gilles Churches is remembered on the Runnymede Memorial, Panel 63.

CHAPTER 3

Zulu Lewis

Squadron Leader Albert Gerald Lewis, DFC and Bar

Albert Gerald Lewis was born on 10 April 1918 in Kimberly, South Africa. As a young man, Lewis took a keen interest in aviation and when he reached the age of eighteen, was fortunate enough to join a private flying school to realise his ambition of learning to fly. Two years later, Lewis left South Africa and took the long journey to Britain where he joined the RAF on a four-year Short Service Commission in October 1938. For several months, Acting Pilot Officer Lewis increased his flying hours substantially at various training schools, flying aircraft such as the Blackburn B-2, the Hawker Hart, Audax and Fury.

At the outbreak of war, Lewis had successfully completed his training and was posted to 616 (South Yorkshire) Squadron stationed in Doncaster on 18 September 1939. On arrival, Lewis discovered that the squadron was equipped with Gloster Gauntlets, Avro Tutors and the obsolete Fairey Battle. During the following months, the South African continued to increase his flying hours while gaining invaluable experience piloting different types of aircraft. But it was in December 1939 that Lewis was acquainted with the machine that would soon take him to war. Now stationed at Debden with 504 (City of Nottingham) Squadron, Lewis took Hawker Hurricane L1944 up into the cold winter sky on Boxing Day. His first flight in a front line fighter aircraft that travelled faster than anything else he had previously flown was undoubtedly a thrilling experience for the young man from Kimberley. Following this memorable occasion, Lewis continued to fly the Hurricane Mk.I on practice flights over Duxford, Debden and Martlesham Heath.

On 11 February 1940, Lewis comprised part of Green Section flying Hurricane L1957 on a shipping patrol. During this flight, he sighted the enemy for the first time in the form of a Blohm und Voss seaplane. The coming weeks would prove to be fairly uneventful, but Lewis was kept busy flying Hurricanes with fixed-pitch two bladed propellers. This dreary spell called the 'Phoney War' was

Right: Gerald Lewis in 1936 when he was a South African Air Force Apprentice, Springs, South Africa. (*Mark Lewis*)

Below: Gerald Lewis (far right) with pilots of 249 Squadron, 1940. (*Tich Palliser*)

a frustrating time for a fighter pilot, but it would soon come to an end for the South African.

In early April 1940, Lewis was posted to 87 Squadron but was promptly transferred to 85 Squadron in France. It was here that Lewis would make his mark as a fighter pilot in the RAF.

On 3 September 1939, Neville Chamberlain announced that Britain was at war with Germany. Peace talks with Adolf Hitler had been exhausted and Poland was in a hopeless state of affairs. The following day, Squadron Leader Johnnie Hill of 85

Squadron flew a Magister to Rouen, France, where he would meet an assemblage of airmen travelling by rail the next day. On 9 September, sixteen Hurricanes led by the squadron's Commanding Officer David Atcherley left Debden and touched down in Boos, France, via Thorney Island. The next morning they were declared operational. To begin with the pilots of 85 Squadron flew cross-Channel convoy patrols, but on 22 September, they were moved to Merville where they remained at a state of readiness in rotation with 85's sister squadron, 87.

The following weeks proved trying for both squadrons as its eager pilots continued to endure the lacklustre traits of the so called 'Phoney War'. The living conditions were tiresome, the weather was mostly miserable and the airfields were in a dreadful condition for the airmen and ground crews. A succession of unnecessary accidents occurred as a result of such poor runways. On 22 December, the starboard leg of Hurricane L1653 collapsed on hitting a rut on landing. Fortunately, Sergeant Faulkner was unhurt and the aircraft repairable, but the following day two Hurricanes were write-offs. At 0715, Flying Officer Boothby crashed on take-off due to icy conditions at Le Touquet. Half an hour later, Pilot Officer Marshall also crashed his aircraft upon take-off, but both pilots escaped unscathed. On 27 December, yet another Hurricane was written-off after Flight Lieutenant Lormier crashed on a night flying exercise at 0015. It seemed luck was on 85 Squadron's side for the time being as Lormier walked away from the accident unharmed.

On 1 November 1939, 85 Squadron was moved from Merville to Lille-Seclin aerodrome where it continued to concentrate its efforts on Channel patrols to protect shipping convoys from possible air attack. Thus far the enemy had proven elusive, but on 21 November, Flight Lieutenant Richard Lee would claim the squadron's first victory of the Second World War. Whilst on patrol over Boulogne, Lord Trenchard's godson, 'Dickie' Lee, spotted a He 111 and made a successful attack against the Luftwaffe bomber. The He 111 crashed into the Channel and burst into flames. Lee's success naturally lifted his colleagues' spirits, but the monotony of chasing the Luftwaffe's contrails soon returned. During this tedious phase in France, it appeared to most pilots that a war was not even on. Due to a lack of radar technology and organisation that would later prove essential for Britain, it was extremely difficult for them to make contact with enemy aircraft that appeared to be content just probing their defences.

Another morale boost arrived at Lille on 6 December when King George VI visited 85 and 87 Squadrons accompanied by the Duke of Gloucester and Viscount Lord Gort. Both men and machines were lined up on the tarmac to greet His Majesty the King for inspection.

In January, the weather conditions became even more unbearable for those stationed in France. The freezing conditions made flying impossible except in the case of emergency where many tail-wheels were damaged due to snow-covered mole hills. The drastic drop in the temperature also caused the airmen to

Gerald Lewis conversing with Major General Frank Palmer, USA (retired), at North Weald, 1941. (*Mark Lewis*)

suffer from colds, flu and bronchitis. It was a woeful time to be fighting a war. In February, the snow began to melt but the grass airfields only became soggy and caked in slush. Yet again more aircraft became unserviceable while attempting to take-off.

On 24 February, a plot was received that enemy aircraft were approaching the squadron's aerodrome at 20,000 feet. Three aircraft were ordered off to intercept the attack but Pilot Officer David Mawhood's Hurricane nosed over when its wheels bogged down in soggy ground and the remaining fighters sank up to their axles in slush. As fortune would have it, the enemy aircraft turned for home and the aerodrome was immediately dubbed unserviceable.

A notable day for 85 Squadron occurred on 3 March when Lee was awarded the DFC for outstanding brilliance and efficiency as a Flight Commander and for destroying a He 111 bomber in November. Lee was a popular member of the squadron and reputed for his prolific flying abilities.

In April 1940, the squadron welcomed the arrival of a handsome South African by the name of Albert Gerald Lewis. Pilot Officer Lewis' endearing nature and infectious grin soon won his peers over and he soon settled in to squadron life in France.

It had been a difficult time for 85 Squadron who had endured a cold winter with infrequent skirmishes against the Luftwaffe, but in May, things were about to change. On 10 May 1940, Germany finally unleashed its lethal blitzkrieg assaults on the Western Front. German forces and parachute troops soon charged into the Low Countries and in the early morning hours, Holland, Belgium and Luxembourg suffered heavy air attacks that were concentrated on communication stations and airfields. Those of 85 Squadron stationed at Lille-Seclin were all too aware of the dawn offensive as the squadron diarist recorded:

10/5/40. 0410 hours. At the marginally noted hour the Blitzkrieg started, and the first intimation the Squadron received was the sound of innumerable

Hun aircraft overhead and the sound of anti-aircraft fire both light and heavy. Within a few minutes one section of "A" Flight and one of "B" Flight were in the air after the Hun, and inside 40 minutes the two Sections had landed to refuel and re-arm.

Leading A Flight was Flight Lieutenant Bob Boothby with Pilot Officer David Mawhood and Flying Officer Ken Blair in tow. The three Hurricanes sighted two enemy aircraft at 12,000 feet and engaged them near Grammont. On approach, Boothby watched the enemy aircraft, reported to be Ju 88s, turn into the sun before giving the one on the left of his position a long burst of ammunition. The enemy aircraft's engine stopped and oil was seen pouring out into the air and onto Boothby's aircraft. Boothby broke away but returned for a second attack that caused the enemy machine to shudder and descend in a steep dive. After expending the remainder of his ammunition, the Section Leader broke off from the attack. Mawhood witnessed the engagement but his Hurricane was subsequently hit by return fire. Despite Perspex splinters blinding one eye, Mawhood followed the second Ju 88 and retaliated by firing four bursts of .303 ammunition. Mawhood broke away due to his damaged aircraft and serious injury. Blair also attacked the Ju 88, firing three decent bursts which caused heavy smoke to issue from its starboard engine. Blair lost sight of the Ju 88 in the ground mist and turned for home. At 0445 hours, Mawhood managed to force-land his aircraft at Mons-en-Chausse.

85 Squadron's B Flight was led by Lee who was accompanied by Flying Officer Derek Allen and Pilot Officer Patrick Wood-Scawen. They attacked a formation of Hs 126s but the engagement was inconclusive. Later that morning, Lee was back in the air with B Flight when they caught up with a bomber at 15,000 feet between Armentieres and the Foret-de-Nieppe. Lee's combat report for this encounter reads as follows:

> After being sighted, e/a dived to very low height. I could only overhaul from astern very slowly. From 500 yards to 700 yards enemy rear gunner fired continuously. I fired short bursts and finished ammunition on closing to 200 yards. No apparent results except black smoke from one engine. My own aircraft shot badly.

Following on from Lee's attack, Flying Officer Allan Angus closed in on the enemy aircraft and opened fire at fifty yards. After two bursts, the Canadian silenced the rear gunner and put the enemy's starboard engine out of action. The enemy aircraft was last seen diving towards ground near Ghent. During the attack, Angus' aircraft had been hit by return fire and with no oil pressure was forced to land his Hurricane at Celles where it was abandoned. Angus returned to the squadron a few hours later. The aerodrome 85 Squadron was operating from came under attack on two occasions on 10 May, but bombs were inaccurately dropped, hitting the north and south-east sides of the squadron's headquarters.

It was apparent that the 'Phoney War' was well and truly over and the pilots unmistakably knew it. From dawn till dusk they had flown constant patrols, only stopping to rearm and refuel. The next morning, Pilot Officer Woods-Scawen and Flying Officer Allen returned from a patrol and landed their aircraft at Lille-Seclin without their section leader. The likable Lee was missing.

In the afternoon, the Luftwaffe bombed the aerodrome once again and this time scored a direct hit. The Adjutant's driver, W. J. Bolton, was killed in his car and a cook in the Officers' Mess was wounded. The squadron moved to Lesquin village in the evening where billets were found to house personnel. Squadron Leader 'Doggie' Oliver returned home slightly wounded and went straight to bed, but before he retired, Oliver said he would go up again on the dawn patrol. However, in spite of his determined spirit, the squadron knew that his current state of exhaustion would lead to certain death, so a guard was placed outside his quarters to ensure he would not be disturbed until he woke naturally.

On 12 May 1940, Lewis awoke early and found himself walking across the airfield towards a Hurricane code lettered 'VY – E'. After fixing a leather flying helmet over his flaxen mop of hair and squeezing his six-foot, three-inch frame into the snug cockpit of his aircraft, the South African was on the edge of battle.

The obstinate German advance was cutting deeper into Holland and Belgium with alarming speed. Consequently, Belgium troops began to withdraw, prompting British and French forces to take up defensive positions further back. It was soon apparent that in order to thwart German mobility, two key structures must be destroyed if the Allies were to hinder the advance of the Wehrmacht's panzer divisions and approaching German columns. It was decided that the Vroenhoven and Veldwezelt bridges, located south-west of Maastricht, were to be bombed at 0915 hours by volunteer crews of 12 Squadron equipped with Fairey Battles. The area surrounding the bridges was heavily defended by anti-aircraft batteries and the sky was a hot zone for enemy fighters. The mission was exceptionally dangerous, practically suicidal for the obsolete light-bomber aircraft and their crews.

At 0820 hours, eight Hurricanes of 1 Squadron led by Squadron Leader 'Bull' Halahan set off from Berry-au-Bac to make an advanced sweep of the target area for the five Battles that were detailed to bomb the bridges. Once over the target area, the Hurricanes were soon engaged in mortal combat with enemy fighters and the vulnerable Battles were left to claw their way through a hellish sky. One Battle was shot down by a Bf 109 as it attempted to reach the Vroenhoven bridge. Another was badly damaged by flak and had to force-land in the target area as did another that was set alight by ground fire during a low-level attack on the Veldwezelt bridge. Both crews were captured unhurt. At 0915 hours, Battle L5227 was shot down by flak at low-level as it attacked the Veldwezelt bridge over the Albert Canal and Battle P2204 suffered the same fate. Of the fifteen Battle crewmen who courageously flew on this raid, seven were captured and six were killed. Flying Officer Donald Garland (who led the attack) and his Observer Sergeant Tom Gray were both posthumously awarded the Victoria Cross.

After the Battles had made low-level attacks on the bridges it had been determined that twenty-four Blenheims of Bomber Command would carry out a follow up attack. In the early morning hours, four formations of six Blenheim aircraft took-off from RAF Wattisham and made way for the coast where they were to rendezvous with 85 and 87 Squadrons. The Hurricanes were instructed to act as fighter escort on route to the bridges but yet again the Luftwaffe drew the British fighters into combat leaving the formations of Blenheims to their own devices.

In this chaotic arena amongst the clouds, Lewis, flying Hurricane 'VY-E', managed to latch on to a Bf 109 over the target area. Once the Bf 109 was in his gunsight, Lewis thumbed the gun button on his control column that awoke the eight .303 machine guns in his wings. During this busy skirmish with the enemy, Lewis claimed the Bf 109 as destroyed as well as a Heinkel 111 of KG54. On an individual level, Lewis had performed exceptionally well in the heat of battle. Two fellow pilots of 85 were also able to stake claims from this engagement. Squadron Leader Oliver reported shooting down a He 111 and a Do 17 and Sergeant George 'Sammy' Allard claimed two He 111s destroyed.

Despite the individual successes of Lewis, Oliver and Allard, it had been a disastrous morning for the RAF. The Fairey Battles had been massacred during their early morning attack on the bridges and the Blenheims that followed suit also suffered heavy losses. The intense anti-aircraft fire had proven destructive and the enemy fighters were confidently proficient in their duties. Although 85 Squadron returned to base unscathed, 87 Squadron lost two Hurricanes, most likely to JG27 led by Hptm. Adolf Galland. Sergeant F. V. Howell bailed out of his aircraft after being attacked but was injured upon a heavy landing caused by a damaged parachute. Flying Officer J. A. Campell was killed after being shot down by Bf 109s west of Maastricht.

It had been a stressful day for Lewis and his weary colleagues, but the mood was brightened by the return of Flight Lieutenant Lee. The squadron's diarist explained what happened to Lee during his absence:

He had been shot down and had to bale out - he was only slightly wounded. He descended by parachute in or near a village in Belgium which was in the process of being re-occupied by German mechanised forces. He borrowed a peasant's smock and walked through the German lines and reported all he had seen to the first English unit he met; the information proved of the greatest value.

Lee later revealed further details of the incident to those close to him. After he had shot down two enemy aircraft, Lee's Hurricane had apparently been hit by flak, so he was forced to bail out. After hanging in his parachute straps, Lee landed in a field where he spotted a passer-by. He asked the man which direction he should travel in and was told to head towards Belgian tanks that were nearby. Lee took-off in the directions of the tanks and as he approached them he suddenly realised that they were not Belgian tanks, but German. With his uniform concealed in the smock or overcoat he had acquired, the German's believed Lee to be a peasant and locked him in a barn with other refugees. Ever the optimist, Lee climbed up to a window to look out and noticed a ladder beneath the window perched against the outside wall. He duly climbed out, walked several miles and then hitched a ride with some Belgians before returning to his unit.

The situation in France progressively worsened as the blitzkrieg continued to expand in the Low Countries and the Luftwaffe harassed Allied airfields. Fighter pilots were called upon to fly seemingly endless patrols against superior numbers and ground crews worked diligently around the clock to ensure that the aircraft were suitable to fly. An example of the exhausting strain Lewis and his contemporaries were under as a result of these constant patrols is aptly described by A. J. Brookes in his book *Fighter Squadron at War*:

> Sergeant "Sammy" Allard for instance destroyed ten enemy aircraft in a week but only by flying four and five times a day with little or no rest in between. This had to take its toll on both the mind and body. On 16 May, after only an hour and a half's sleep the previous night, Allard took-off on the first of four sorties that day. Bombs were bursting on the aerodrome as he and his section took-off on their second patrol and on the third patrol Allard fell asleep three times over German-occupied territory. As he taxied in from his last patrol of the day, the ground crew were surprised not to see him jump out after the aircraft shut down. A mechanic opened the canopy only to find that Allard had finally succumbed to sheer weariness and fallen asleep where he sat.

On 19 May 1940, the British War Cabinet met to decide whether British forces should join the French that were retreating south towards Paris or to head north towards the Channel ports. The situation in France was becoming desperate as illustrated in part of Churchill's first broadcast as Prime Minister:

> The Germans, by a remarkable combination of air bombing and heavily armoured tanks, have broken through the French defences north of the

Maginot Line, and strong columns of their armoured vehicles are ravaging the open country which for the first day or two was without defenders. They have penetrated deeply and spread alarm and confusion in their track. Behind them are now pouring infantry in lorries, and behind them again large masses are moving forward.

On this day, Churchill determined that no more British fighters should be sent to France and that the RAF units already stationed there were to return to Britain. Now at 60 Wing HQ, Squadron Leader Oliver sent the following instructions to 85 Squadron:

> To judge from our patrol lines the Huns are close to Douai. I have received nine extra lorries and am sending four to Lille/Marcq who I believe are very short. I want you (Molony) and Martin (the Intelligence Officer) to supervise the packing up of the *whole* Squadron except Flight personnel who must remain to start aircraft. Draw the convoy up in the village of Ennetierre amongst the by-roads at the back. All airmen are to keep in vicinity of lorries but under cover until I send word to move. Move NW to Merville and report to 63 Wing. Report to me by Hillman Van on completion of preparations to move.

While all of this was in motion, the pilots continued to fly patrols throughout the day, including Lewis who would sign off from the Battle of France in a most spectacular way. At around 1000 hours, Lewis was airborne in a former 213 Squadron Hurricane code lettered 'AK-A' when he claimed two Bf 109s shot down. His wingman, Flying Officer Jerrard Jeffries, claimed a Bf 109 as a probable. Pilot Officer Patrick Wood-Scawen was also involved in the morning melee as his combat report illustrates:

> At approx 10.00 on 19th May I was on the aerodrome when I saw 3 Hurricanes engaged in combat with several E/A. I took off and shot down 1 E/A in flames 5 miles E of Seclin after bursts of 2 secs; the puff of smoke when this E/A crashed was seen from the aerodrome. I climbed to 5,000 ft and engaged a second ME 109 which dived emitting smoke to the ground after several bursts of 3 secs from 100 yds. I was unable to see where this E/A crashed because I was attacked from the rear by 2 E/A. My ammunition was exhausted so I broke off the engagement and landed.

At midday, Lewis was on patrol once again in Hurricane 'AK-A'. In his own words he described what happened next:

> Our instructions were to carry out an offensive patrol and land at Merville. I was flying in a section of three, led by Flying Officer Stephenson, when the left-

hand gun panel came loose and made formation flying difficult. On reporting to section leader, was ordered to break off and land at Lille. It was probably due to lack of sleep over a period of days that I was unaware of three 109s, which had become interested in me as I headed for Lille/Seclin. The first inkling was tracer over the wings, much too close for comfort. A tight turn gave me a look at the attackers, the leader coming head-on and opening up with his cannon. Within what seemed yards, he flicked over on to his back and presented his belly as he broke away in a steep dive. I remember my head hitting the top of the cockpit cover as I rammed the stick forward and gave him all I had at point-blank range. Fuel streamed out as he dived into the deck and blew up. The other two – possibly less experienced pilots – made a half hearted pass at me, formed up and headed for the Belgian border. At first my inclination was to leave well alone, but there they were, just above and a little ahead. Out came the booster and the Hurricane surged forward, placing me in an ideal position to squirt at one and, as the fuel streamed out, the remainder of the bursts into the other. Neither made any attempt at evasion, giving me the idea that they had been on a training flight, and once their leader was accounted for, they headed home. All three crashed within a fairly close distance of each other. Landing at Lille, I was escorted in by the mechanics grabbing the wingtips and giving me the thumbs-up sign. I was able to indicate three fingers. They flung their caps in the air, grinning like Cheshire Cats. Squadron Leader Oliver came over to see why I had not landed at Merville, as agreed. The mechanics were quick to inform him that three planes had been bagged by me. The CO said that he had had a grandstand view. Needless to say he was delighted and I was told I would be recommended for the DFC.[5]

In the short duration of just two patrols, Lewis had shot down five Bf 109s becoming an ace in a day. It was truly an exceptional feat that was soon publicised in the *London Gazette* on 25 June 1940:

Pilot Officer Lewis has, by a combination of great personal courage, determination and skill in flying, shot down five enemy aircraft, single-handed, in one day. He has destroyed in all a total of seven enemy aircraft, and by his example has been an inspiration to his squadron.

That evening, the squadron left Seclin and moved on to Merville but not before destroying most of its equipment and unserviceable aircraft. Even when the squadron was not in the air, the Luftwaffe continued to be a nuisance by bombing the aerodrome and strafing its brand new variable-pitch propeller Hurricanes. Two days later, the men of 85 finally made way for Britain where storm clouds were beginning to rumble.

It was 21 May when Lewis flew one of only sixty-six Hurricanes to make it out of France. After crossing the Channel, Lewis touched down at Gatwick, which was little more than a grass strip, due to engine trouble. Instead of feeling relieved about landing on friendly soil, the South African became irritated by several guards who drew suspicion from his accent. When they tried to interfere with him taking-off again, Lewis' short fuse ignited into some colourful words which caught the attention of a senior officer who was nearby. The senior officer stood the guards down and then helped Lewis get the assistance he needed to get his aircraft back in the air. The engine trouble was caused by a damaged oil line and Lewis was extremely lucky to have made it across the Channel without the engine seizing. Soon enough, the Hurricane was repaired and he took-off from Gatwick, setting course for Northolt. When he arrived at the aerodrome, he was greeted by Wing Commander Harry Broadhurst and granted forty-eight hours leave. After a strenuous few days, Lewis was glad of the respite. While at the Paddington Hotel, Lewis fell asleep at a table and later awoke to find people staring at him. The Battle of France had truly taken its toll.

On 23 May 1940, Squadron Leader Peter Townsend DFC arrived at Debden, Essex, to assume command of 85 Squadron. His initial task was to reform the squadron and to bring it up to operational efficiency. Before the war, Townsend had trained as an officer at Cranwell and went on to serve with 43 Squadron stationed at Tangmere. He was an experienced pilot who had earned the respect of many of his comrades both in the air and on the ground. Townsend was a true gentleman and a fine example to his men. He would naturally evolve into a proficient leader.

During the evacuation of Dunkirk, 85 Squadron flew convoy patrols over the east coast. After its most valiant efforts in France, the squadron was rebuilding itself with both men and new machines, so the fighter boys were not directly involved with the skirmishes taking place high above the smoky beaches of Dunkirk. Townsend was aware of the inexperience of the new recruits and therefore conducted training exercises that would help prepare them for what lay ahead. As well as drawing from his own knowledge of aerial tactics, Townsend was grateful to have the experience of Lewis, Lee, Allard, Woods-Scawen and others that served in France to offer their guidance to the young fledglings. Lewis was soon christened 'Zulu' by the new squadron leader, a nickname he had also given to Caesar Hull, another South African in 43 Squadron.

While stationed at Debden, Townsend organised training exercises that consisted of mock dogfights between the new recruits and those that had fought in France. Townsend was keen for the green pilots to learn that they should always remember to search the sky for the Hun, to watch their tails, and to understand that when duelling with Bf 109s, their aircraft could out turn the German fighters. However, the Hurricane, in comparison to the Messerschmitt Bf 109, was outclassed. It was certainly a robust aircraft that could withstand a lot of punishment in battle and was a steady gun platform, but the Bf 109 and Spitfire far surpassed its performance capabilities. Perhaps the most worrying flaw about the Hurricane's design for a fighter pilot was the positioning of two of its three fuel tanks. There was an exposed tank on the left and the right of the pilot's feet making a fire risk in the cockpit extremely likely when damaged in combat.

Shortly after Townsend had arrived at Debden, his friend, Flight Lieutenant John Simpson of 43 Squadron, wrote a letter to his intelligence officer after hearing about the exploits of Lee. Simpson, who coincidently often flew with Patrick Wood-Scawen's younger brother Tony, remarked the following:

> I hear that Dickie Lee has done wonders. You see how those boys, who were always looked upon as being the naughty ones, are doing so well. They needed a war to convince the old gentlemen in Whitehall. Do you remember that Dickie was almost given his bowler hat for low flying? That same low flying has apparently stood him in good stead.[6]

Lee's reputation as a tough fighter pilot and daredevil was growing. He was a sociable, handsome young man who was popular with the girls, especially of the blonde variety. Lewis had become good friends with Lee while serving alongside him in France and now trained together in the south of Britain. He once remarked that Dickie Lee had '…that magic quality to evoke unquestioning loyalty, which tolerated the sometimes hair-raising demands he made of those who flew with him'.[7]

On 26 June 1940, Lewis and Lee shared a memorable experience when they flew to an investiture in a Miles Master (N7546). Lee received a DSO and a DFC for his service. Lewis later remarked how proud he was to have been asked to fly his Flight Commander and good friend to his investiture. Two days later the *Daily Mirror* published the following about Dickie:

> He has displayed great ability as a leader and an intense desire to engage the enemy. On one occasion he continued to attack an enemy aircraft after his companion had been shot down and his own machine hit in many places. His section shot down a Junkers 215 in flames one evening in May and another in an engagement next day. Flight-Lieutenant Lee, aged twenty three was educated at Charterhouse in 1935 and was commissioned from Cranwell in 1937. He was awarded the D.F.C in March.

The Ju 215 claimed in the above report was most likely the Ju 86 that was shared by Lee's section on 10 May 1940.

10 July 1940, now known as the first 'official' day of the Battle of Britain, began in earnest for the squadrons stationed in the south of England. Thus far the Nazi war machine had conquered or dominated Europe with unparalleled force. Despite the British Expeditionary Force's best efforts, it could do little else but

Above left and right: Gerald Lewis at Castle Camps, July 1940. (*Mark Lewis*)

retreat back across the Channel or suffer captivity or utter destruction at the hands of German forces. By the summer of 1940, Britain stood totally alone as the last bastion of European democracy and the German leader, Adolf Hitler, knew it. With an utter determination to bring Britain to its knees, Hitler put in place an operation that if successful would ultimately lead the way for a German land invasion of Britain. If Hitler was to achieve such an end then the Luftwaffe would need to secure air superiority so that German bombers, shipping vessels and invasion barges could cross the Channel unmolested by the RAF. At this moment in time, everything depended upon the aerial battles that were about to be fought between the Luftwaffe and the RAF. In short, the mammoth task of securing air supremacy over Britain was left in the young hands of men like Pilot Officer Lewis and his fellow comrades throughout Fighter Command. Throughout the opening phase of the Battle of Britain, the Luftwaffe, who vastly outnumbered the RAF fighter squadrons, crossed the Channel in large formations and concentrated its attacks on shipping convoys and coastal targets before turning its attention on populated towns and cities. On 10 July, Debden was bombed in the early morning hours by a Do 17, but damage was limited to several broken windows around the station. 85 Squadron would be kept extremely busy during the following weeks operating from Castle Camps, which was situated a few miles north-east of Debden and Martlesham Heath. The latter of the two bases was ideally positioned near the south-east coast where the squadron could easily patrol the shipping convoys in the Channel.

On 11 July, Townsend was forced to evacuate his Hurricane after it was disabled by return fire from a Do 17 when bullets exploded in his cockpit and glycol tank. Townsend continued to fly his aircraft for as long as he was able to, but was miles away from the coast and so reluctantly bailed out over the cold sea. He was soon rescued by a mine-sweeper vessel named HMS *Finisterre* and returned to the squadron. The following day, 85 lost Sergeant Leonard Jowitt who was shot down when protecting convoy *Booty* from He 111s. His aircraft crashed into the sea off Felixstowe and Jowitt was not seen again. It had already been a testing few days for the squadron that continued to fly consistent convoy patrols from dusk until dawn during the first month of the Battle.

In August, the Luftwaffe launched a major offensive against the coastal airfields in Britain. Wave after wave, the seemingly endless formations of Luftwaffe bomber and fighter aircraft crossed the Channel to bomb the RAF into submission and claw its fighters from the sky. It was during this frenzied period of conflict that Lewis found himself flying daily patrols among the chaos.

18 August 1940 was a fine summer's day that would eventually be dubbed as 'the hardest day' of the Battle of Britain. The Luftwaffe and the RAF fought fiercely throughout the day and by the end both sides would sustain its heaviest losses of the battle. In the evening, Lewis would enter the fray when thirteen Hurricanes of 85 Squadron were ordered to patrol Debden at 10,000 feet. At 1730 hours, the squadron received new instructions to patrol Canterbury at 20,000 feet and several minutes later ordered to intercept a large enemy raid that was plotted crossing the coast in the direction of North Weald. By 1740, the enemy was sighted and Townsend led his band of twelve men against 200 enemy aircraft. Owing to the great multitude of German aircraft, the squadron was divided and individual dogfights and engagement ensued.

In the eruption of twisting and turning aircraft, Lewis, flying as Green 3 in B Flight, veered off towards two dozen Bf 110s that were circling at 18,000 feet. On his approach, Lewis saw one of the twin-engine heavy fighters detach itself from the circle and dive down towards a Hurricane. In so doing, the Bf 110 presented itself as an ideal target in Lewis' gunsight. Quick to act, Lewis opened fire from almost head-on at a closing distance of about 150 yards. He thumbed the gun button twice, firing two short bursts of ammunition of three seconds each, but this did not put the Bf 110 entirely out of action. Lewis manoeuvred his aircraft into another position and from line astern he fired a four-second burst that caused his prey to emit smoke as it dived steeply towards the water. Lewis was convinced that the enemy aircraft was done for and climbed for height. Unable to see or contact anyone from his squadron, Lewis steered his Hurricane for home. For a fighter pilot it was most fascinating how the sky could be full of aircraft going in all directions at one moment and then empty in the next. After this encounter, Lewis claimed the Bf 110 as a 'probable' in his combat report but was convinced that the enemy aircraft would not have been able to make it back to its base.

In total, the squadron claimed ten enemy aircraft destroyed, four probable and six damaged. The new squadron leader, Peter Townsend, had led by example claiming two Bf 109s and a Bf 110 destroyed.

On the return to Debden, Townsend spotted Hurricane 'VY- G' limping back to base having sustained serious battle damage. Townsend formed up on the wounded Hurricane to assess the damage and to offer moral support to its pilot who had lost the use of his radio. Townsend communicated to the pilot using hand gestures to help guide him in to land. Slowly but surely the damaged Hurricane approached Debden and landed safely on the aerodrome despite missing its starboard wingtip. Townsend discovered that the pilot was Pilot Officer Jim Marshall who had taken-off without authorisation after the squadron had departed for its patrol. During the scrap, Marshall noticed a He 111 about three miles to the south of his position, so turned towards it and opened fire from a range of 250 yards. A five-second burst of .303 ammunition tore bits off the enemy bomber and presumably silenced the rear gunner. White vapour spewed into the air and completely obscured the enemy aircraft as it dived steeply towards the sea. Consequently, Marshall's starboard wingtip collided with the Heinkel's tail, which fatally sent the bomber plunging down into the drink. When Marshall taxied his aircraft across the aerodrome, the squadron anxiously awaited the return of two Hurricanes. Pilot Officer Paddy Hemingway was one of those that were missing and Lee was the other.

That night, Hemingway would not return to Debden as he had been forced to bail out of his Hurricane after its engine had been hit by return fire from a Ju 88. The aircraft was lost to the sea but Hemingway, after spending an hour and a half in the cold water, was rescued by a ship twelve miles east of Clacton and later returned to his unit the following day. Tragically, Flying Officer Richard Hugh Antony Lee DSO, DFC, would never return. Flying as Blue 1 in Hurricane P2923 'VY- R', Lee was last seen by Townsend and Flying Officer Arthur Gowers ten miles north-east of Foulness Point chasing Bf 109s out across the Channel.

> "Come back, Dicky," I called but he was drawing away. Again and again I called, but he kept on. It was useless to chase Huns out to sea; they would be back again the next day. Something had got into Dicky and there was no stopping him. We were both low on fuel and I was out of ammunition. There was only one thing to do: turn back.[8]

Townsend's last sighting of Lee further illustrates the bold determination that the twenty-three-year-old fighter pilot possessed in protecting his homeland from the formidable Hun. It seems that in spite of Lee's low fuel and the extreme dangers of pursuing enemy aircraft alone out to sea, he would not pass up the opportunity of allowing Luftwaffe fighters to escape his grasp. Although the cause of Lee's demise remains unknown it is tempting to assume that his unrelenting, fearless desire to rid the sky of enemy aircraft no matter what the cost got the better of him. Sadly, Lee's body was never recovered and his loss was wholeheartedly felt by those who knew him. Ever since joining 85 Squadron in France, Lewis had become close with Lee. The sad loss of his good friend only concentrated the South African's further distain of the enemy. Lee would be forever missed.

On 19 August, the Chief of Air Staff, Sir Cyril Newall, sent the following message to Debden:

> Well done 85 Squadron in all your hard fighting. This is the right spirit for dealing with the enemy.

The following day, the squadron was moved to Croydon to relieve 111 Squadron and from here Lewis and his fellow fighter pilots continued to fly numerous patrols and sorties against the Luftwaffe. Like all squadrons stationed on the front line, 85 was finding the battle incredibly demanding. The constant state of readiness and the frequent scrambles brought anxiety and exhaustion to the young pilots who, despite the odds, continued to fly and fight several times a day.

On 31 August, the Luftwaffe raided Croydon just before 1300 hours. As bombs hit the aerodrome, twelve Hurricanes led by Townsend climbed for height towards Bf 110s and Bf 109s. The call to scramble had arrived too late and the squadron found itself in an unfavourable position being directly below the enemy. Townsend's aircraft was hit as he climbed through a horde of diving enemy fighters. His left foot was struck by a cannon shell and petrol poured into his cockpit. There was little else the squadron leader could do but bail out of his damaged Hurricane. Later that night, Townsend was treated in the operating theatre of Croydon General Hospital. The shell was extracted from his foot and his big toe amputated. Pilot Officer Pyers Worrall, a recent addition to the squadron, also ended up in the same hospital that evening after his rudder bar and elevator controls were blown away by cannon shells and his leg was injured. Worrall had shot down a Bf 110 before he was bounced by the enemy and forced to bail out over Benenden.

In the absence of Townsend, Patrick Woods-Scawen took over the squadron temporarily and led ten Hurricanes into action at 1710 hours. During this encounter, New Zealander William Henry Hodgson flying as Yellow 3 damaged a Do 215 and destroyed a Bf 109 before his Hurricane 'VY-G' was hit by a Bf 109 cannon shell. The shell blew up his oil lines and glycol tank which set the engine on fire. Hodgson unstrapped himself and was about to evacuate his burning aircraft when he noticed he was flying over a densely populated area near the Thames Haven oil storage tanks. Hodgson unselfishly stayed with his Hurricane to steer it clear of the area below in spite of the flames licking towards him and the white vapour and black smoke pouring into the cockpit. Skilfully, Hodgson slide-slipped his aircraft through the sky to keep the fire under control, and after a tense struggle to keep the flames away from him, Hodgson sighted a field near Shotgate, Essex, which he approached to land. After narrowly avoiding a series

Above left: Gerald Lewis in the cockpit of his Hurricane at Castle Camps, July 1940. (*Mark Lewis*)

Above right: Gerald 'The smiling South African' Lewis during the Battle of Britain (*Mark Lewis*)

of wires and other obstacles in his path, Hodgson made a wheels-up landing at Fanton Chase. It had been a dramatic flight for the New Zealander, which somehow through his own skill and determination, he was able to walk away from unscathed.

31 August had been a strenuous and taxing day for those stationed at Croydon, but it was not over yet. At 1917 hours, with their aircraft rearmed and refuelled, the boys of 85 Squadron were ordered to patrol Hawkinge. When the squadron arrived at its designated position, they received instructions to intercept an incoming raid. The squadron soon sighted anti-aircraft fire thumping into the air from Dover and spotted nine Bf 109s at 15,000 feet to their port side. With the element of surprise, the Hurricane squadron pounced upon the enemy fighters and unleashed their vehement attacks. Flying Officer Gowers opened fire at one of the bandits, giving it a couple of five-second bursts and then followed with a seven-second burst that blew a large piece out of the Bf 109's port wing. The enemy fighter went into a vertical dive streaming petrol and was confirmed to go down in flames by Pilot Officer Lewis who saw its undoing. Lewis then joined up with Flying Officer Woods-Scawen who had spent a few hurried seconds trying to illuminate his gunsight before latching on to a Bf 109 that was flying slightly above. Lewis watched Woods-Scawen climb into position and then deliver a beam attack that caused the German fighter to dive steeply. Woods-Scawen followed the Bf 109 down and gave it a final burst that set the machine's starboard wing tank on fire. Again, Lewis watched a burning Bf 109 dive towards the deck, confirming the kill. The South African then targeted his own Bf 109 and subsequently carried out a beam

attack from slightly below. Lewis' .303 bullets riddled the enemy aircraft and caused black smoke to stream out from it into the evening air. Lewis followed the Bf 109 down to 5,000 feet and then climbed back up into the vast blue yonder to rejoin his squadron. Pilot Officer Sammy Allard also destroyed a Bf 109 in the melee when his gunfire broke pieces away from the enemy fighter and sent it plunging down towards Folkestone. Lewis landed safely at Croydon shortly after eight o'clock in the evening and then penned the following report:

Combat Report
31/8/40
Contacted approx 9 ME 109s in Folkestone – Dover area. Hydro leader climbed into sun to position for attack. Followed Red 2 (F/O Gowers) who downed 1 ME 109 then attached myself to Blue leader F/O Woods-Scawen who set 1 ME 109 on fire. I closed in on ME 109 and opened fire at about 150 yds delivering attack from beam slightly below. E/A billowed black smoke and I followed him down to approx 5,000 ft diving steeply into haze above sea just off coast near Folkestone. Making sure he was done for climbed up to rejoin Squadron. Returned to base. Burst approx 4 secs fired.

On 1 September, Pilot Officer Allard led the squadron on its second patrol of the day shortly before 1400 hours, but it was to be a disastrous affair. An estimated 150-200 enemy aircraft were plotted near Biggin Hill at approximately 15,000 feet. By the time the squadron sighted the mass formations, their Hurricanes faced a height disadvantage of 5,000 feet below the enemy. Allard led the battle climb towards the Dorniers but were intercepted by diving Bf 109s and Bf 110s. Flying Officer 'Gus' Gowers was forced to bail out of his aircraft after it was shot up by cannon shells. The attack caused Gowers agony as his hands were severely burnt and his foot was wounded. His Hurricane crashed near Oxted, and Gowers, a character known for his first-class sense of humour, was taken to Caterham Hospital to be treated. Sergeant Glendon Booth's Hurricane was also clobbered by cannon shell and he was compelled to bail out of his burning aircraft near Purley. When Booth abandoned his Hurricane, he rapidly descended towards the earth with his parachute horrifying alight. The heavy landing caused serious injuries to Booth from which he would never recover and died of his injuries on 7 February 1941. John Ellis, a twenty-one-year-old sergeant pilot was lost on this patrol after an engagement with Bf 109s in the Kenley area. His Hurricane crashed at Chelsfield.

During this frantic skirmish, Allard was successful in attacking a Do 17 that had strayed away from the main formation heading towards Dungeness. After several attacks, Allard sent the Do 17 down with oil and smoke belching from its engines. Suddenly, Allard noticed that his oil pressure had dropped so he made a force-landing at Lympne with a dead engine. While Allard's Hurricane was being repaired, the aerodrome was bombed and his aircraft received further damage. A mechanic was killed and another was seriously wounded in the raid. Other members of the squadron managed to claw a number of enemy aircraft out of the sky. Sergeant Evans put a Bf 110 down in flames and claimed a Bf 109 as destroyed. Pilot Officer English caused a Do 215 to force-land in a field and Sergeant Howes destroyed a Do 215 south of Tunbridge Wells. Howes then damaged a Bf 109 that he caught attacking a Hurricane.

Lewis' Hurricane 'VY-Y' was damaged after it engaged Bf 109s over Kenley at 1415 hours. Lewis returned to base and performed a wheels up landing as the undercarriage had jammed. He landed unhurt and his aircraft was deemed repairable. It had been a most horrid afternoon for Lewis and his squadron. When darkness finally fell across the aerodrome that night there was a sombre atmosphere around Croydon. Flying Officer Patrick Woods-Scawen was officially missing.

On 6 September, Woods-Scawen's body was found in the overgrown grounds of an empty house in Kenley Lane. Evidence suggested that he was shot down in combat with Bf 109s and although he managed to bail out of his Hurricane, Woods-Scawen was tragically killed due to parachute failure. Less than twenty-four hours after his death, Woods-Scawen's younger brother, Pilot Officer Tony Woods-Scawen, was also killed in combat with Bf 109s. Tony was flying with 43 Squadron at the time when his Hurricane was set alight in combat with Bf 109s over east Kent. Tony attempted to crash-land his aircraft at Fryland near Ivychurch, but was forced to bail out. Regrettably, he bailed out at a low altitude and was killed by the fall. The loss of the Wood-Scawen brothers was a great tragedy not only for their respective squadrons but especially for their loved ones at home.

The Battle for Britain continued to rage on throughout September 1940, but on 5 September, the squadron received some respite from the aggressive fighting when it was sent away from the frontline to recover and re-equip. On this day, Lewis flew Hurricane 'VY-Z' from Castle Camps to Church Fenton in Yorkshire. For the time being, the pilots and their ground crews, who had all worked immensely hard during the conflict, were able to rest. Although away from the heat of battle, Lewis continued to fly routine patrols from the squadron's new station within 12 Group.

In mid-September, the squadron welcomed the return of Peter Townsend after he had recently been awarded a Bar to the DFC. Soon after the squadron leader's arrival at Church Fenton, he was informed that 85, along with 151 Squadron, had been selected to specialise in night-fighting. It would be a brand new chapter in the squadron's history, but one that Lewis – one of the squadron's most esteemed and experienced pilots – would not be a part of, for on 14 September, Lewis returned south to the front line.

Since arriving in France, 'the smiling South African' as Lewis would later become known, had served diligently with the squadron, quickly earning the respect of his fellow airmen both as a pilot and as a person. During the Battle of France and the Battle of Britain, Lewis had formed close friendships within the squadron, but he had also felt the pangs of loss when some of his comrades did not return from battle. Despite the ugly backdrop of war, Lewis continued to be an uplifting force to those around him by finding the strength to smile, laugh and persevere through the lottery of mortal combat.

In reflection of the squadron he once commanded, Townsend later remarked:

> 85 Squadron, like every other, save the homogeneous Czech and Polish units, was a marvellous amalgam of men from Britain and the Commonwealth. Whatever our differences in origin and rank, our view from the cockpit, alone, miles above the earth, was identical. Though we fought wing tip to wing tip, each one of us had to fly and fight and, if need be, die alone. It was this sense of isolation and solitude in the air that united us so closely on the ground.[9]

On 14 September 1940, Lewis arrived at North Weald to join 249 (Gold Coast) Squadron where he was welcomed by Wing Commander Victor Beamish DSO, AFC. Previously, the Hurricane squadron had been stationed at Boscombe Down from where its pilots had operated among the smoke-trailed skies of the south. Not long before Lewis' arrival, Pilot Officer Pyres Worrall and Sergeant Charles Rust were also posted from Church Fenton to strengthen 249's ranks. A sergeant pilot by the name of Charles 'Tich' Palliser also arrived on the same day as Lewis. Palliser had been with 43 Squadron at Tangmere before he was posted to North Weald. He remembers the day he arrived and was introduced to the tall, blond-haired South African:

> When Gerald Lewis joined 249 Squadron, he was truly welcomed. We saw him being introduced to Percy Burton and Terry Crossey, two South African Pilots, as was Gerald Lewis, and Terry introduced him to me. I had always enjoyed reading about South Africa, my grandfather, a maritime captain, had taught me a lot about the country, and I enjoyed talking to Gerald. He was a senior pilot and I learned much about flying from him too.

Lewis, having previously fought in the French campaign and during the opening months of the Battle of Britain, was readily accepted by the other pilots of 249 Squadron for his valuable experience as a pilot and a combatant. He was now the fourth South African to join the squadron and he quickly began to bond with his fellow countrymen who were all openly proud of their origins.

On 15 September 1940, the battleground above the south of England was composed of fine weather with patches of cloud. The morning began quietly enough for 249 Squadron until just before 0930 hours when two Hurricanes were scrambled from North Weald to investigate an unidentified aircraft in their vicinity. However, the Hurricanes were recalled back to base within the hour without sighting the suspected aircraft.

The morning then began to heat up when at around 1100 hours enemy formations congregated in the Calais/Boulogne area. Thirty minutes later, the first wave of at least 100 enemy aircraft had crossed the coast between Dover and Dungeness. A second wave soon followed of about 150 enemy aircraft that were intending on reaching London. In preparation to meet the mass raid, Air Vice Marshall Keith Park, Commander of 11 Group, ordered all of his squadrons to 'Readiness'. By 1130 hours, twenty-one squadrons were ready to challenge the Luftwaffe, including a dozen Hurricanes of 249 Squadron.

In company with 46 Squadron, 249 was vectored to the south of London to disrupt a formation of Dornier 17s of I./KG76. After spotting the enemy bombers, Flight Lieutenant Denis Parnall led the squadron into a beam attack. Pilot Officer Bryan Meaker, flying as Blue 2, attacked a Do 17 that was headed east. He fired a decent burst of ammunition that crippled the Dornier's port engine and caused it to break away from its formation in a gentle dive. Meaker followed up with a second attack, this time concentrating on its starboard engine before three Spitfires joined the fray. The Spitfires continued to bite into the damaged Dornier with their .303 bullets delivering fatal blows. The Dornier crashed in flames north of Canterbury. Two of the five-man crew bailed out of their stricken bomber suffering wounds and were taken prisoner.

Pilot Officer George Barclay also staked a claim against a Do 17 after he approached it from a frontal quarter attack that developed into a beam attack. Barclay opened fire from approximately 300 yards and closing but was forced to break over the oncoming bombers to avoid a collision. Barclay then turned his Hurricane into position and carried out a quarter attack on the same Dornier that he had engaged before. The Dornier broke off from the main formation and dived towards the clouds streaming glycol from one of its engines. Barclay pulled back on the control column and climbed towards the main formation of bombers as Hurricanes of 46 Squadron tore after the damaged Dornier to confirm its end.

249's next order to scramble arrived at 1340 hours. Yet again the squadron's Hurricanes, having been previously rearmed and refuelled, raced across the grass aerodrome at North Weald to meet the enemy. When on patrol over South London, the squadron sighted a formation of Dornier 17s followed by a wave of Heinkel 111s. When the Hurricane squadron carried out a beam attack against the Dorniers, the bombers began to split up making themselves targets of opportunity for the boys of 249.

Flight Lieutenant Robert 'Butch' Barton saw his initial three-second burst rip pieces off a Do 17's fuselage that sent it into a dive before he joined up with

Pilot Officer Meaker, flying as his number 2. Both Barton and Meaker attacked another Dornier that they watched go down into cloud with smoke and oil pouring from an engine. Meaker then whipped his Hurricane round into a left-hand climbing turn as two yellow-nosed Bf 109s dropped down on to his tail and opened fire. Fortunately, the enemy cannon fire missed his Hurricane and Meaker continued to gradually tighten his turn until he was able to return the sentiment by firing a short burst at one of the Messerschmitt's. He saw his bullets hit the Bf 109's port wing but it dived into cloud to avoid further damage.

During this engagement one of the squadron's new recruits, Sergeant 'Tich' Palliser, became separated from his section. After cruising at 14,000 feet, he noticed a Dornier flying in a northerly direction at around 5,000 feet below his position. Palliser rammed his control column forwards, putting his Hurricane into a dive towards his unsuspecting target. At a range of about 350 yards, from a steep quarter attack, Palliser opened fire and held the gun button down for three seconds.

The following extract from Palliser's combat report offers further details of the engagement:

> I observed fragments flying from between starboard engine and cabin. This attack was delivered in the wake of a Spitfire which must have hit the port engine of e/a as I could see thick black smoke coming from engine. Four people abandoned e/a by parachute. No return fire noticed.

Disorientated and out of fuel, Palliser decided to land his aircraft in a farm field at Ingrave near Brentwood. He was then greeted by the farmer's son and taken to their farm house where he was able to use a telephone. Later that evening, an RAF lorry arrived at the farm to refuel the Hurricane and at 1900 hours, Palliser took-off for North Weald after 'beating up' the field for the onlookers.

Other members of the squadron also engaged the Dorniers with great success including Pilot Officer Crossey, Pilot Officer Barclay and Pilot Officer Neil who claimed one Do 17 destroyed and another shared with Pilot Officer Eric Lock of 41 Squadron. Lewis, however, while flying as part of B Flight, encountered the second wave of bombers positioned at 15,000 feet. Lewis' detailed combat report for this engagement continues the story:

Combat Report
15/9/40
Encountered a formation of 18 HE 111s in diamond formation at 15,000 feet, with fighters at 20,000 feet, spread over a large area. I found myself with Spitfires, which split up the bulk of the formation. One became separated from the rest. I attacked from slightly below from beam, gave a three-seconds burst, and from here got line astern: set both motors on fire causing undercarriage to

Above left: Gerald Lewis being helped into the cockpit of his Hurricane during the Battle of Britain. (*Mark Lewis*)

Above right: 'Dickie' Lee and 'Zulu' Lewis. (*Mark Lewis*)

drop and the E/A appeared to spiral down in vicinity of Brentwood. As soon as this was down I engaged formation again, which had by now dropped its bombs and was heading towards south coast. I went in after a Spitfire, which broke away, then I closed and set starboard engine on fire. Wheels dropped out and E/A began to spiral down, circled by Spitfires.

In spite of being in a new squadron and in the cockpit of a new Hurricane, Lewis was the same tough fighter pilot that continued to gain victory in the air. He was also surrounded by a crack squadron of pilots that seemed to be knocking down the Hun left, right and centre. On this afternoon encounter with the He 111s, Lewis claimed one as destroyed and the second as a shared probable. Another member of the squadron to make contact with a Heinkel during this engagement was Flying Officer Keith Lofts of Yellow Section. After cutting through the formation of Dorniers with the squadron, Lofts found himself about 2,000 feet below the bombers and noticed an escort of Bf 109s diving towards him. He broke away from the scene and climbed for height when he spotted a large formation of He 111s on his starboard side. Lofts attacked one of the bombers from about 2,000 feet above, giving it a long burst of gunfire. The He 111 broke away from its formation and began diving. Several other Hurricanes followed up the attack that caused the bomber to crash-land at West Malling. Lofts also force-landed his aircraft after it sustained damage from return fire. He was unhurt but his Hurricane was a write-off. Flight Lieutenant Parnall also claimed a He 111 probably destroyed over Central London and a yellow-nosed Bf 109 as damaged. Wing Commander Victor Beamish, a man Lewis would later hail as '...the most effective fighter pilot of the Battle bar none', also shared in the destruction of a Heinkel that was seen to fall vertically with smoke coughing from both engines.

15 September 1940 had been a long and eventful day, not only for 249 Squadron who claimed six and a half enemy aircraft destroyed, nine and a half probable and four aircraft damaged, but also for the whole of Fighter Command that had fought in a most decisive battle against the Luftwaffe. A wildly exaggerated figure of 185 enemy aircraft destroyed evolved from the day's fighting, but in reality the RAF had shot down a total of fifty-six confirmed. Eighty-one of the Luftwaffe's aircrew were killed, thirty-one wounded and sixty-three taken prisoner. In comparison, British combat losses were twenty-seven with twelve pilots killed, fourteen wounded and one taken prisoner. For this reason, 15 September has become celebrated as 'Battle of Britain Day'.

The following day, 249 Squadron received the following signal from 11 Group:

> Well done 249 Squadron, your success yesterday is an outstanding example of the hard fighting which is frustrating the enemy's attack. Keep it up.

The view from the ground in London was a testament to the heavy fighting that had taken place overhead. White contrails snaked through the sky and thick black smoke caused by the Luftwaffe's bombs bellowed into the evening air. Despite Fighter Command's every effort to stop the bombers breaking through its defences, it was ultimately an impossible task for the bomber would always break through.

Bad weather over the next two days offered a slight breather for the squadrons stationed in the south of Britain, but the Luftwaffe continued to raid London during the night. North Weald was also bombed in the early morning hours of 17 September with insignificant damage.

At midday on 18 September, any respite from the action was over for 249 Squadron when it was scrambled towards an oncoming raid. Twelve Hurricanes led by Canadian Flight Lieutenant 'Butch' Barton left the aerodrome and set course for their patrol line. Once over the Thames Estuary near Southend, the squadron noticed ack-ack bursts exploding in the air and spotted a formation of He 111s with Bf 109s acting as close fighter escort. Barton led the squadron into a direct head-on attack. The rapid closing speed was alarming for all involved, but Barton and Pilot Officer Neil opened fire and each damaged one of the bombers before breaking away to avoid a looming collision with the Heinkels.

Lewis was mindful of the lurking Bf 109s above and went after a yellow-nosed bandit that appeared to be heading back across the Channel. Lewis readied himself as he approached the fighter from head-on and slightly below. At an opportune moment, Lewis pulled the nose of his Hurricane up towards the belly of the Bf 109 and thumbed his gun button. A three-second burst of ammunition cut through the air and struck the Messerschmitt sending it down in a flat spiral. Lewis went down after the Bf 109 to see it crash near a wood, but the perilous practice of following an aircraft down to see its demise would soon be discouraged by Wing Commander Beamish who warned Lewis and his squadron of its likely fatal dangers. At North Weald, Pilot Officer Worrall, who flew as Blue 3 on this sortie, also confirmed Lewis' Bf 109 as destroyed.

Beamish, who had flown behind the squadron on this encounter, had been involved in a vicious scrap with Bf 109s. He claimed one probable and another as damaged before he was bounced by three fighters which sent him back to North Weald with a battered Hurricane. The skilled Wing Commander managed to land his aircraft safely, irrespective of the fact that it was peppered with holes and lacked functional brakes.

By the evening, the squadron began to feel some distress at North Weald as one of their own had not returned to base.

On the second patrol of the day, Flight Lieutenant Denis Parnall took-off with the squadron but had to return due to a problem with his Hurricane's air pressure system and gun firing mechanism. He hurriedly took-off from North Weald in another Hurricane with the intention of joining up with the squadron before they met the enemy, but for a short period he was all alone in a hostile sky. For many days no one at North Weald had any idea what had happened to the squadron's A Flight Commander until a signal was received some weeks later. The squadron's diarist recorded the following entry on 2 October 1940:

> A signal from No. 11 Group giving us serial numbers of some Browning guns which have been found on a crashed Hurricane. On checking up it was found that these guns had been fitted to Hurricane V6685 which was the aircraft Flt. Lt. Parnall had been flying when he was posted missing. This proves, much to the regret of us all, that Denis Parnall had been killed in action. A loss to the service of a very fine regular officer.

The exact details surrounding Parnall's final moments remain unknown, but it is thought that he was probably jumped by Bf 109s and shot down near the village of Margaretting at 1325 hours. Parnall went down with his Hurricane that crashed into the earth at high speed and eventually burned out. The crash site was a ghastly scene.

On 27 September, the squadron embarked on its first sortie of the day when it was scrambled at 0850 hours into a cloudy sky. Twelve Hurricanes took flight from North Weald and set course for Wickford with Wing Commander Beamish following behind like a watchful parent. As previously planned, the squadron was soon in company with Hurricanes of 46 Squadron and together they began a rigorous search for enemy aircraft. Not long after the rendezvous, both squadrons received orders to patrol the Maidstone area where they would meet twenty Bf 110s with a heavy escort of Bf 109s roaming above. The Bf 110s were flying in a defensive circle over Redhill when Flight Lieutenant Barton led a diving attack from out of the sun. Barton opened fire at the nearest Bf 110 he could find and observed direct hits on its port engine.

Return fire struck Barton's Hurricane and he was forced to break away, but Lewis, flying as Blue 2, witnessed the Bf 110 crash in the Redhill area. Barton pulled away from the action and landed his Hurricane at Gatwick unhurt while the Squadron continued to fight. Lewis, also diving out of the sun, opened fire at a Bf 110 that was following a Hurricane down. Two short bursts of ammunition caused the enemy aircraft to dive steeply with smoke streaming in its wake. Heeding the advice of Beamish, Lewis did not follow the aircraft and turned back towards the circle of Messerschmitts and engaged another Bf 110. An accurate burst of his ammunition disabled the aircraft's starboard engine and put it in flames. Lewis pulled back on his control column and guided his Hurricane upwards towards the sun. The sheer speed of aerial combat was disconcerting. Everything seemed to happen in a flash, so it was vital for a fighter pilot to continuously search his surroundings to avoid being bounced. On this occasion the Bf 109s that had initially accompanied the Bf 110s had not come down to engage the Hurricanes, so for the third time Lewis was able to return to what remained of the defensive circle. Another burst from the Hurricane's eight Browning machine guns secured Lewis another claim. The Bf 110 was hit and dropped out of the fight with the intention of making it back towards the coast of France, but its starboard engine was out of action and Lewis was in hot pursuit. The South African forced the Bf 110 down in the vicinity of some hills near Crowhurst. It finally crash-landed on a nearby farmyard and burst into flames.

It had been a successful interception for Lewis and the squadron. A total of eight enemy aircraft destroyed and a further five probable were claimed, but it did not come without a price.

At twenty-three years of age, Flying Officer Percival Ross-Frames Burton died in Hurricane V6683 after he vigorously pursued a Bf 110 piloted by Hauptmann Horst Liensberger of V/LG1 over a distance of forty miles. The South African pilot from Cape Province chased the Bf 110 at low level until his guns fell silent over Hailsham, Sussex. Burton's ammunition was spent, but the Bf 110 would not escape the South African pilot who was flying slightly above and behind the twin-engine aircraft. Suddenly, in an unprecedented manoeuvre, Burton's Hurricane banked and collided with the Bf 110. The Messerschmitt's tail unit dropped out of the sky into a field followed by the remainder of the severed aircraft and Burton's wingtip. The Bf 110 pilot and his rear-gunner, Uffz Albert Kopge, were killed instantly. Burton's Hurricane crashed into an oak tree on New Barn Farm throwing its dead pilot clear. Eyewitness reports indicate that Burton had deliberately rammed the Bf 110 in his final act of valour. On this fateful day, Palliser witnessed the collision and later recalled:

We were vectored to the Usworth area close to Tangmere. A hell of a flight - 109's covering about 20 Messerschmitt 110 twin engine fighters. These were in a huge circle for protection and waiting for help from the 109's about 4,000 feet above. 249 hurled into the circle and the fight. I had shot down two of the twin engine fighters and went for the third, which had broken from the circle and was now diving towards the Channel. While this was happening I watched another of our Squadron chase another 110 which was badly damaged. I witnessed that our pilot had fatally damaged the twin engine Messerschmitt. The Hurricane made an upward turn and I noticed his Squadron number and it was Pilot Officer Percy Burton. He must have been hit and been out of ammunition because he flew into the tail and then pulled away. The 110's tail was completely severed. I later heard that Percy had been nominated for a Victoria Cross. But unfortunately nothing happened.

For his action, Burton was recommended for the Victoria Cross, but much to the displeasure of his fellow pilots he was only 'Mentioned in Dispatches'. In August 1940, Flight Lieutenant James Nicolson of 249 had been awarded the Victoria Cross after he courageously stayed with his burning Hurricane to attack a Bf 110. With one award already issued, it was allegedly considered inappropriate to award two VCs to one squadron, which is a possible reason that Burton's recommendation was rejected. But whatever the reasons, the fact remains the same: another young life had been selflessly given in the service of others. It was a sad affair when the squadron learned of Burton's death. He would be sorely missed by those who knew him, but not forgotten. Lewis' son, Mark, recalls:

My father would remind me whenever the saying "Gone For A Burton" was mentioned , that this came about because of the last heroic action of Pilot Officer Percival Ross-Frames Burton, fellow South African and 249 Squadron member. I visited the memorial cross, placed under the oak tree which Percy's stricken Hurricane struck some years ago, with my mother shortly after she had learnt of its existence. It's great to see that this brave man's last act of valour will not be forgotten; although it saddens me that the link to the iconic saying in the English language and this historical event have been lost.

A humble metal plaque on the memorial cross bares the following fading inscription:

'F/O. PERCY BURTONS HURRICANE FIGHTER CRASHED INTO THE TREE BEHIND THIS CROSS AFTER HE HAD EXECUTED A VERY SKILFUL AND BRAVE ACT TO STOP AN ENEMY FIGHTER ON 27/9/1940.'

Another incident to derive from the morning patrol of 27 September was that of Pilot Officer John Beazley. When attacking the same Bf 110 as Pilot Officer Neil, Beazley was wounded in his left foot by return fire. Notwithstanding the pain caused by a bullet that pierced his foot and lodged in his instep, Beazley was determined to return to North Weald, which he achieved before being whisked off to Epping Hospital for treatment.

In the absence of Barton and Beazley, Lewis was tasked to lead the squadron on its next sortie. When the call came to scramble, seven Hurricanes left North Weald to patrol Maidstone with Lewis leading in front. The squadron rendezvoused with 46 Squadron and began to sweep the sky between Hawkinge and Canterbury. Each pilot kept their eyes peeled, constantly searching the area for enemy aircraft until suddenly Lewis spotted two formations of Bf 109s flying to the north-east of the Estuary. The squadron was at 15,000 feet, so Lewis took them up to 20,000 feet to gain a better height advantage, but in so doing were attacked from above by diving 109s. The adrenaline of combat kicked in and individual dogfights broke out across the sky. Lewis came under attack by two Bf 109s, one of which shot overhead allowing Lewis to get off a quick burst. His bullets clobbered the underside of the Bf 109 and sent it crashing into a wood near Canterbury. Lewis then attacked the second Bf 109, also striking its belly that caused it to go down smoking. Sensibly, Lewis veered away from the engagement and did not observe the Bf 109's decent.

Flying as Red 1, Barclay went after Bf 109s that passed by at about 400 yards to his port side. An extract from his combat report explains what happened next:

> I chased a 109 which dived very steeply. I had to use automatic boost to catch up the 109. I lost the 109 in haze owing to its camouflage against the ground, but it suddenly climbed almost vertically out of the haze. I closed to about 150 yards and fired about four bursts, one almost vertically down on the E/A, and two bursts from the beam. The E/A poured glycol. The cockpit roof flew off. The pilot bales out successfully. The E/A crashed (confirmed by Sgt Palliser, Red 3) on a farm SW of Ashford.

The pilot of the Bf 109 was believed to have been Fw Herbert Hoffmann who bailed out of his aircraft severely wounded. The fighter crashed at Brick House Farm near Tenterden, Kent.

During this flurry with the Bf 109s, Worrall claimed one as damaged and Beamish was awarded a probable after his machine guns raked a fighter's fuselage at close range and sent it earthwards in a spin. When the sky had cleared, the boys safely returned to North Weald where the devoted hands of the squadron's ground crew anxiously awaited them. Doused in sweat and exhausted from the action, Lewis made his way to dispersal to report his claims to 249's Intelligence

Officer. In just two patrols, the South African had made an impressive five claims, but the day was not over yet.

At 1450 hours, eleven Hurricanes raced across North Weald on its third scramble of the day. Once airborne, the squadron was joined again by 46 Squadron near Hornchurch. Over half an hour later, when the squadron was at 18,000 feet, an armada of enemy aircraft was located over South London. This time the enemy formations consisted of Ju 88s, Bf 110s and swarms of Bf 109s. Spurred into action, the Hurricanes engaged. Lewis, leading Green Section, went full throttle towards the Ju 88s. His combat report details the event:

> Combat Report
> 27/9/40
> As Green leader, attacked formation of Ju88s with Blue Section, and one just dropped out with starboard engine damaged. Closed in and carried out two beam attacks from slightly above and put other engine on fire. Kept after it as it went down steeply towards coast near Selsey Bill. Crashed into sea just near coast. Shot down one ME109 which crossed my sights after engagement with Ju88. Went down in flames, then followed a second ME109 down which I attacked from above and it crashed in wood near Petworth. This is confirmed by Sgt Hampshire of Green Section. Fired short bursts of approx two to three seconds at ME109s and a fairly long burst at the Ju 88.

When Lewis landed at North Weald for the third time on 27 September, he had victoriously made it through another gruelling day of the Battle of Britain, claiming six enemy aircraft destroyed and a further two probable.

On this same day Pilot Officer George Barclay recorded in his diary:

> Pilot Officer Lewis, DFC, shot down six Huns today!! Some shooting. He's certain to get at least a bar to his DFC.[10]

Barclay's statement proved to be correct when on 22 October 1940, Lewis was awarded a Bar to his DFC. Once again, Lewis' exploits was praised in the media when the *London Gazette* published the following on 22 October 1940:

> One day in September, 1940, this officer destroyed six enemy aircraft; this makes a total of eighteen destroyed by him. His courage and keenness are outstanding.

249 Squadron's tally for 27 September was twenty-one enemy aircraft destroyed, six probable and three damaged. It was a fabulous achievement for the squadron, but one that would be dampened by yet another tragic loss.

When attacking a formation of five Ju 88s, Pilot Officer Bryan Meaker's aircraft was struck by heavy crossfire and the Irishman bailed out, but in so doing he violently hit the tailplane of his Hurricane and plunged towards the earth. His body was later found near a village called Dallington where he had fallen to his death. Meaker DFC had proven himself to be a prolific fighter pilot since joining the squadron in late June 1940 with eight enemy aircraft destroyed to his credit. Meaker's loss would be keenly felt by his colleagues, some of whom reported seeing a Hurricane fall back in the attack of the Ju 88s and a parachute develop only to become entangled in the tail of the aircraft. It was a horrendous end for another of Churchill's brave 'Few'.

After breakfast the next morning, the squadron was ordered to patrol the Thames Estuary with 46 Squadron at 25,000 feet. Several pilots bemoaned flying at such a high altitude, not only because it was bitterly cold, but also they thought the Hurricane did not operate to its strengths at such a height. As it turned out, the patrol was uneventful although a number of Bf 109s were sighted flying back across the Channel at an unreachable height and distance. The welcomed the order to 'pancake' and the Hurricanes returned to base.

In the early afternoon, the squadron received another stomach churning call to scramble. As always, the pilots hurried towards their respective mounts and minutes later were climbing for height in the direction of the enemy. On this patrol, Lewis was flying Hurricane 'GN-R', the same aircraft that he had claimed six enemy aircraft on the previous day. For about an hour, Lewis and the squadron soared around the skies between Maidstone and Canterbury in search of enemy aircraft. Once again the squadron sighted unreachable Bf 109s above their position but soon lost track of them. Assuming the Bf 109s with their limited fuel capacity had flown back across the Channel, the squadron received orders to return to North Weald. While the Hurricanes made way for home, Lewis and Sergeant Hampshire weaved back and forth behind the squadron as 'Tail-End Charlies'. When suddenly out of nowhere two Bf 109s swooped down like preying eagles and opened fire. 'Look out!' Lewis shouted over the R/T. The warning arrived just in time for Hampshire who took evasive action as enemy tracer fire darted over his port wing. But it was too late for the South African as he later recalled:

At about 30,000 feet I was hit by cannon fire, receiving shrapnel splinters in my legs, and the Hurricane caught fire, burning fiercely at the speed at which we were travelling. When I pulled back the cockpit cover the flames roared up round my face and, having just pulled the release of the Sutton harness, I attempted to get out. The suddenness with which I parted company with the plane caused me to be shaken around like an old rag, then the blissful peace and calm of falling free. I remembered what we had been told: don't pull the ripcord immediately on falling free, allow time to separate from the plane, and also to lose initial speed. Brace yourself for the jerk that would follow the opening of the "chute."[11]

As Lewis hung wounded in his parachute and his Hurricane plunged towards the earth in flames, Sergeant Bentley Beard chased one of the bandits and shot it down near Dover. The pilot of this Bf 109 was Knights Cross holder Hptm. Rolf Pingel who ditched his fighter in the Channel before being rescued by the Luftwaffe's Seenotflugkommando. Pingel later reported shooting down a Hurricane near Maidstone.

Hurricane V6617 crashed at Blacketts Farm, Tonge Corner, near Sittingbourne, at 1420 hours. Lewis was admitted to Faversham Cottage Hospital with serious injuries. He recalled:

> I was hit by cannon fire receiving splinters in my legs and the Hurricane caught fire burning fiercely. Trousers burnt off to the parachute harness; legs burnt, face and neck burnt and third degree burn on trigger thumb. When the wreckage was recovered in 1970 the trigger was in the "fire" position.

After recovering for two months in hospital, Lewis returned to the squadron in December 1940, being promoted as a Flying Officer on 29 November. He had also been awarded a Bar to the DFC on 22 October for his performance in combat. When Lewis rejoined the squadron, the Battle of Britain had been won and operations against the Luftwaffe reversed with the RAF taking the fight across the Channel. Lewis returned to the air in January 1941 taking part in routine patrols and various sweeps.

On 10 February, the squadron flew as escort to six Blenheims of 139 Squadron that was detailed to bomb the docks at Dunkirk. When over the target area, a formation of Bf 109s dived to intercept and the squadron had its work cut out. Pilot Officer Bill Davis' Hurricane was bounced by German fighters and he was forced to bail out of his stricken fighter. He was wounded from the attack and became a POW. As Red 4, Palliser broke away from the melee and circled with Red 3 to pick out enemy fighters. He observed three Bf 109s at 5,000 feet south of Calais and gave chase but could not reach them. Palliser turned back towards Gravelines and saw a Hurricane under attack by a Bf 109. Palliser dived down firing a two second burst that raked the enemy aircraft. The Luftwaffe pilot pulled the Bf 109's nose up, attempting to escape his assailant, but Palliser fired another burst at the cockpit and again as it attempted to turn. The third burst scored hits on the Bf 109's engine and side of its cockpit. The Bf 109 dived towards the coastline and Palliser followed down giving it additional bursts. Palliser judged the pilot to be dead as the Bf 109 made no evasive manoeuvres as it descended. Lewis confirmed Palliser's engagement as an extract from Red 4's combat report tells:

> While preparing to follow e/a right down, I saw a fighter coming down on my tail, so I turned violently away and commenced turning steeply. Aircraft

turned out to be friendly. When I looked for e/a I could no longer see him and judged he had crashed as he was losing height fairly rapidly when I turned. Flg Off Lewis, who was flying as Yellow 2 and who was attacked by same e/a, saw my attacks and substantiates my claim that the pilot was killed and e/a must have been destroyed.

When Tom Neil returned to North Weald, he found a very unhappy South African as he recounted:

When later I taxied onto my hardstanding to stop, I saw Gerald Lewis's Hurricane just ahead of me. He was still in the cockpit as I dropped to the ground and I saw him waving his arms in my direction. When I walked towards him, I could see why. There was massive damage to the left-hand side of his cockpit, as though some demon axe-man had been hard at work. No wonder he was upset; it was a miracle he had not been killed or wounded badly. His voice, when I approached, was shrill with outrage... As I looked up, surveying the damage, Crossey approached. We had been heavily attacked, it appeared. Attacked! By whom? I had seen nothing. They were 109s apparently, Hun fighters seen by both of them, but not by me. We discussed and commiserated together excitedly, the aftermath of battle quickening our speech.[12]

249's pilots were becoming increasingly upset on flying Hurricane Mk.Is against the superior Bf 109 on offensive operations. After losing Davis and almost losing Lewis, Neil vented his frustration to Beamish who sympathised with his concerns. Five days later, the squadron began to be re-equipped with Hurricane Mk.IIs. In June, Lewis bade farewell to his friends and 249 Squadron when he was posted to 52 OTU as an instructor commanding C Flight. Lewis had been an integral part of the squadron and was highly regarded by those he fought by during those trying months over Britain and the Channel.

While at Debden, Lewis flew Spitfires for the first time in his career and was impressed with its performance capabilities but felt its cockpit was too cramped for a person of his stature. His loyalty was, of course, with the aircraft that had saved his life and brought him aerial victory on numerous occasions during the Battle of France and Britain. While at 52 OTU, Lewis also flew Tiger Moths, Masters, Magisters and Hurricanes. In January 1942, Lewis was posted to command 261 Squadron after volunteering for overseas service. On 31 January, he flew Hurricane IIB, serial number 6510, on a local flight around Takoradi in Sierra Leone, West Africa. With the same aircraft, Lewis led eighteen Hurricanes from Takoradi to Lagos, then to Kano, to Maiduguri, Nigeria, and then finally to El Genina. He then flew solo to Khartoum and Port Sudan. Lewis recalled:

We managed to get all our aeroplanes in convoy to destination without breaking any (sandstorms, the lot) covering 3,000 miles in three days.

In Port Sudan, Lewis encountered another South African by the name of Pierre St Quentin who was testing Curtiss P-40 Kittyhawks for the RAF. Lewis took one for a flight but it did not convince him that it was better than his tried and trusted Hurricane.

On 13 March 1942, Lewis flew a Hurricane from HMS *Indomitable* for China Bay, Ceylon, but was forced to return to the carrier as his engine overheated. Ever so skilfully, Lewis took his aircraft in at about 80-85 mph and touched down as near to the edge of the deck as possible. Without the use of an arrester hook, Lewis willed his brakes to bring his aircraft to a halt, which they did, bringing him to a stop halfway up the deck. Lewis climbed out of his cockpit thoroughly relieved to have made it with an audience of impressed naval onlookers. Once his Hurricane was repaired, Lewis took-off once again and arrived at Trincomalee in China Bay without further incident to take command of 261 Squadron.

In April 1942, Lewis would return to action but against a very different enemy. On 9 April, a day before his twenty-fourth birthday, Lewis took-off in Hurricane Z4961 at 0745 hours. Upon take-off, he noticed aircraft climbing and diving over a nearby harbour so decided to climb away from the battle area and over the jungle to obtain a favourable position. A chill ran down his spine as he realised that he was a sitting duck. Lewis recalled what happened next:

I had barely got my undercart up, when a hail of bullets struck the armour plate at my back and the throttle lever was no longer there. I was obviously hit, as the plane was on fire and, at that moment, two planes with blood red roundels slid by, in close formation: I realised with a start – Zeros!! In less time than it takes to tell, I was reaching for the release pin in my Sutton harness and I was out. I caught the tailplane on my left hip as I fell away. The Hurricane nosed into the ground just ahead of me, continuing to burn, the ammunition going off like fire crackers. I landed a split second later, right on the edge of a shallow lagoon.

Our normal dress was khaki shorts and shirt. As a result, the burns I received for the second time of asking, smarted like mad when I fell into a couple of feet of salt water (luckily the burns were minor, compared with those I had received in the Battle of Britain). My left upper arm was aching (the muscles, near the shoulder, had been shot away), but worse still, the lower part of my left hand, below the little finger, was shot away, and I could see the sinews exposed (must have happened when the throttle was shot away). The sight of the injuries and the blood made me feel faint; I dragged off my flying helmet, as I was all hot and bothered, but deemed it wiser to replace the helmet, which had an oxygen tube attached, which I thought might act as a tourniquet to stop the bleeding.

What seemed to be shrapnel, rained down, and I was glad of the leather helmet. A Hurricane passed overhead; the awesome chatter of the 12 guns helped me to realise that the Japs weren't having it all their own way. Another thought struck me: what if my parachute should draw attention to my whereabouts? We had been informed that the Japs fired on pilots when they managed to bale-out so, what with the burning plane a few yards away and a parachute to indicate my position, I knew I must move away from there.[13]

Lewis moved as far as he was able but his injuries prevented him from going much further from where he had landed. After seeing his base being heavily attacked, Lewis lay in shock for about six hours until he was eventually found by villagers that came to his aid. The villagers kindly administered a drink of coconut milk and helped him to a jungle road that led towards Trincomalee where he found a stationary Army lorry. A young Marine lieutenant, accompanied by a local Ceylonese guide, invited Lewis into the cab of the truck and then took him back to base where he received treatment for his wounds.

In June, Lewis returned to Britain via South Africa and was made the Chief Flying Instructor at Tealing in Scotland. After a purposeful and distinguished career, Lewis left the RAF as a squadron leader on 16 February 1946 with eighteen confirmed aerial victories to his credit.

The war had been a horrendous ordeal for those who had been unfortunate enough to experience it. Lewis, like many others had both suffered and endured the hardships, understood only by those who sat at the controls of fighter aircraft during the Second World War. With all that he had been through, Lewis at last found peace in 1953 when he converted and was baptised into The Church of Jesus Christ of Latter-day Saints. He valued his membership as something of great worth and became a very spiritually minded man as confirmed in a letter written by Lewis to Squadron Leader Doug Tidy:

As my mind reflects on the Battle of Britain and on the many wonderful characters who formed a part of that scene and died a quarter of a century ago in order that the world might be a better place to live in, as did those in the First World War and indeed all righteous people from the beginning of time I wonder, have we achieved lasting peace? If we are not to disappoint ourselves and all those who have come from before, we need a plan – one that is practical and embraces all mankind. As a member of The Church of Jesus Christ of Latter-day Saints, I sincerely believe that the Gospel of Jesus Christ is the only plan which can embrace the world so that all who desire to may live in peace.[14]

Albert Gerald Lewis died on 14 December 1982 at Standish Hospital near Stonehouse in Gloucestershire, aged sixty-four. He is buried in a cemetery at the very end of Horns Road, Stroud, Gloucestershire. When Marshal of the Royal Air Force, Sir John Grandy, visited the Lewis family, he offered a Battle of Britain flypast at the burial, but Gerald's wife, Yvonne, elected to keep the service low key, deciding that her belated husband would not have wanted a fuss.

Additional Notes
85 Squadron
'Noctu Diuque Venamur'

Flying Officer Richard Hugh Antony Lee, DSO, DFC, was born in London in 1917. He was educated at the Charterhouse School before joining RAF Cranwell in September 1935. Lee graduated from Cranwell in July 1937 and was posted to 85 Squadron at Debden on 1 June 1938. After serving in France with the squadron, Lee continued the fight against the Luftwaffe in the Battle of Britain until he was killed on 18 August 1940 at age twenty-three. At the time of his death, Lee was an Acting Flight Lieutenant with 85 Squadron and is credited to have destroyed at least nine enemy aircraft. Lee is remembered at the Runnymede memorial.

Flying Officer Patrick Philip Woods-Scawen, DFC, was born in Karachi, India, in June 1916. His younger brother, Pilot Officer Charles Anthony Woods-Scawen, DFC, was born in February 1918. Since 1924, the Woods-Scawen brothers lived at 55 York Road, South Farnborough in Hampshire. They were both educated at the Salesian College at Reading Road, Farnborough. In October 1937, Patrick joined the RAF on a short service commission and Tony followed suit, joining in March 1938. After completing his training, Patrick was posted to 85 Squadron at Debden on 20 August 1938 and at the outbreak of war flew with 85 Squadron in France. Tony joined 43 Squadron at Tangmere on 17 December 1938 and was soon involved in action over Dunkirk. Both of the Wood-Scawen brothers fought in the Battle of Britain until Patrick was killed on 1 September 1940 and Tony was killed the following day. Patrick is buried in St Mary's churchyard, Catterham-on-the-Hill, Surrey, and Tony is buried in Folkestone New Cemetery, Kent. Most tragically, the Woods-Scawen family would continue to suffer further loss when Patrick and Tony's first cousin, Sergeant Gerald Woods-Scawen, was killed on 3 October 1941 while serving with 92 Squadron.

Pilot Officer Geoffrey Allard, DFM and Bar, DFC, was born in York on 20 August 1912. He was educated at the Priory Higher Grade School before he joined the RAF on 3 September 1929 as an aircraft apprentice. In 1936, Allard was accepted for pilot training and was later posted to 87 Squadron. On 1 June 1938, he moved to 85 Squadron at Debden. After seeing action in France and in the Battle of Britain, Allard was promoted to Acting Flight Lieutenant and was given command of 'A' Flight in August 1940. On 31 March 1941, Allard took-off from Debden in a Havoc with Pilot Officer W. H. Hodgson and Sergeant F. R. Walker-Smith as passengers. The aircraft is believed to have crashed because of a loose nose panel that jammed the rudder. All three pilots were killed and are buried in Saffron Walden Borough Cemetery, Essex.

Group Captain Peter Wooldridge Townsend, CVO, DSO, DFC and Bar, was born in Rangoon, Burma, on 22 November 1914. He was educated at Wychwood Preparatory School, Bournemouth, and Haileybury College. In September 1933, he entered RAF Cranwell as a Flight Cadet and graduated in July 1935. Townsend joined 43 Squadron at Tangmere on 27 June 1937. On 23 May 1940, he was given command of 85 Squadron at Debden. On 25 February 1941, Townsend claimed the squadron's first night-fighting victory when he destroyed a Do 17. Later that year, he was posted to HQ 12 Group as Wing Commander Night Operations. In April 1942, Townsend took command of 605 Squadron at Ford and in mid-February 1944, was appointed Equerry to the King. Townsend retired from the RAF on 18 November 1956 as a Group Captain. He died in 1995 and is buried in Saint-Leger-en-Yvelines, France.

249 Squadron
'Pugnis et Calcibus'

Squadron Leader Richard George Arthur Barclay, DFC, was born on 7 December 1917 at Upper Norwood in Surrey. After completing his education at Stowe School and then Trinity College, Cambridge, Barclay joined the University Air Squadron and was commissioned in the RAFVR in June 1939. When his training came to an end, Barclay was posted to 249 Squadron at Leconfield on 23 June 1940. During the Battle of Britain, Barclay fought with coolness and determination and was later awarded the DFC for his labours. He was shot down by a Bf 109 at the end of November 1940 and was hospitalised for two months with injuries to his ankle, legs and elbow. In March 1941, Barclay returned to the squadron before being posted to 52 OTU, Debden, as an instructor. Three months later, Barclay was appointed as a Flight Commander with 611 Squadron stationed at Hornchurch and later moved to 601 Squadron in April 1942. On 17 July 1942, Barclay was shot down and killed by a Bf 109 whilst leading 238 Squadron on patrol. Barclay is buried in the El Alamein Cemetery.

Wing Commander Thomas Francis Neil, DFC and Bar, AFC, BRONZE STAR (USA), was born in Bootle on 14 July 1920. He joined the RAFVR in October 1938 and began his training at 17 E&RFTS. After being commissioned, Neil was posted to 249 Squadron on 15 May 1940 where he served during the Battle of Britain. On 7 November, Neil claimed a Ju 87 and two Bf 109s destroyed but was later involved in a mid-air collision with Victor Beamish. Neil bailed out of Hurricane V7676 unhurt. In May 1941, Neil went to Malta with the squadron and took-off from HMS *Ark Royal* on 21 May leading a group of Hurricanes to the island. In September 1942, Neil took command of 41 Squadron at Llanbedr before moving on to 53 OTU as an instructor. Neil also served in the 9th US Air Force as a Flying Liaison Officer with the 100th Fighter Wing. After an impressive career, Neil retired from the RAF in 1964 as a Wing Commander.

Flight Lieutenant George Charles Calder Palliser, DFC, AE, was born on 11 January 1919 in Cleveland, North Yorkshire. He joined the RAFVR in June 1939 and after completing his flying training was initially posted to 17 Squadron at Debden in August 1940, but joined 43 Squadron at Tangmere shortly after. On 14 September, Palliser was posted to 249 Squadron at North Weald where he served during the Battle of Britain. On 5 December, he was shot down by Bf 109s after a long patrol and crash-landed near Stanford-le-Hope, Kent, unhurt. In April 1941, Palliser was commissioned and continued to serve with the squadron when it was posted to Malta. On 8 January 1942, Palliser joined 605 Squadron at Hal Far as Flight Commander. Palliser later served in various places as an instructor before retiring from the RAF in 1947. Palliser currently lives with his daughter Gill in Melbourne, Australia.

Group Captain Francis Victor Beamish, DSO and Bar, DFC, AFC, was born at Dunmanway, County Cork, on 27 September 1903. An RAF College Cranwell graduate, Beamish served in various appointments abroad and in the UK over the years, becoming an airfield commander of North Weald in early June 1940. During the Battle of Britain, Beamish flew frequently on operations with the airfield's squadrons, claiming a respectable number of enemy aircraft destroyed, probable and damaged. On 7 November, Beamish collided with Pilot Officer Tom Neil's Hurricane when his propeller sheared off Neil's tail. Beamish force-landed at Leeds Abbey. On 28 March 1942, Beamish was killed while leading the Kenley Wing over France. His Spitfire was seen to be hit and damaged by a Bf 109. Beamish was last seen entering a cloud near Calais. The legendary Beamish is remembered on the Runnymede Memorial, Panel 64.

SECTION TWO
THE MERSEYSIDE FEW

CHAPTER 4

Flying Officer John Fraser Drummond, DFC

It was a quiet morning in Blundellsands. An autumn wind coming off Liverpool Bay cleared the last remnants of overnight fog and blew the yellow oak leaves from their trees and along the deserted streets. The air raid siren had sounded in the night but thankfully Liverpool had not been a target for the Luftwaffe. This time. Still, Will Drummond had slept fitfully, but he was not needed in work today having been given compassionate leave by his employer, timber merchant's Vincent Murphy and Co. Ltd, after the death of his mother and sister in an air raid three weeks earlier. He went downstairs to make a drink for himself and his wife, Nellie, when he was stopped in his tracks by a knock at the door. As soon as he opened it and saw a man in uniform standing there, he knew what was to come. The postman handed him a manila envelope with Air Ministry pre-printed on the front. Will thanked him, took the envelope then went and sat in his favourite leather armchair. He stared at the envelope for a while before opening it. The telegram inside was timed at 0929 that morning and addressed to him personally. It read 'Deeply regret to inform you that your son Flying Officer John Fraser Drummond is reported as having lost his life on 10th October...' He could read no more.

Will sat there numbed. In the space of three weeks he had lost his mother, sister and now his only son. A veteran of the Great War with the 10th (Scottish) Battalion King's Liverpool Regiment, he and his brothers Harold and Bert had fought with distinction on the Western Front and survived. His thoughts began to drift back to those early days.

Will and Nellie had married in the summer of 1916. They had a daughter, Helen, in June 1917 before John was born on 19 October 1918 in a nursing home in Walton. John spent his earliest years at 47 Warbreck Road before the family moved to 34 Cavendish Road, Blundellsands, in 1924. He attended a Church of England Primary School near to his home but the family moved to 4 Far Moss Road, Blundellsands, in 1930.

At the age of eleven, John Drummond attended Deytheur Grammar School as a boarder in the small Welsh village of Llansantffraid, Powys, close

John Fraser Drummond with 46 Squadron at
RAF Digby in late June 1940. (*Drummond family
collection*)

to the English border. In January 1934, Drummond started Wellington School, Somerset, again as a boarder. He was placed in Willows House and went on to represent them at tennis, cricket and cross country. He took part in the school's Officer Training Corps earning his A Certificate in March 1935 before becoming a Lance Corporal in May. He was quickly promoted to Corporal before finishing as a Sergeant. In July 1935, he passed his School Certificates in Scripture, English, Geography, Elementary Maths and Chemistry. He left Wellington in April 1936 with the Senior Prize for divinity.

Upon returning to Liverpool, Drummond took up an apprenticeship with his father's firm. This work simply did not satisfy him and, influenced by a family holiday to Germany around 1936 from which he believed the Germans were preparing for war and not wanting to fight in the trenches as his father and uncles had, was determined to pursue his ambition to fly. So his parents relented and allowed him to apply to join the RAF. His application was successful and he passed his medical on 18 November 1937.

Drummond began his training at The Civil Flying School at Hatfield on 4 April 1938 before moving to RAF 5 FTS at Sealand, Flintshire, in June. The *London Gazette* of 24 June confirmed that Drummond had been granted a short service commission as an Acting Pilot Officer on probation effective from 4 June 1938.

After completing his flying training, he joined 46 Squadron at Digby, Lincolnshire, on 14 January 1939. Originally equipped with Gloster Gauntlet

Mk.II single-seat biplane fighters, the squadron was re-equipped with Hawker Hurricanes in February 1939. They were to see action just six weeks after the outbreak of the Second World War when, on 21 October 1939, Squadron Leader P. R. Barwell and Pilot Officer R. P. Plummer attacked a formation of twelve Heinkel 115s five miles east of Spurn Head, shooting three down and damaging another.

As a result of this action, King George visited Digby on 2 November to compliment the squadron on the role they had played in protecting coastal shipping from enemy action. He spent around ten minutes with the pilots, including Drummond. The next six months though were uneventful, consisting in the main of providing air cover for the shipping convoys steaming along the east coast. There followed a brief move to Acklington on the Northumbrian coast from December to mid-January 1940 where Drummond carried out anti-aircraft co-operation flights, playing the part of enemy planes so coastal guns would be ready for the inevitable raids.

In May 1940, the squadron was selected to form part of the Expeditionary Force in Norway that had been invaded by the Germans on 9 April. Their Hurricanes were embarked on HMS *Glorious* and arrived forty miles off the Norwegian coast on 26 May. The Hurricanes had to take-off from the deck of HMS *Glorious*, but as the sea was flat and calm, there were doubts that they could do so. Air Ministry figures suggested a 30-knot wind was necessary. The ship's engineers managed to get HMS *Glorious* up to a speed of 30 knots so enabling all eighteen Hurricanes to take-off successfully. 46 Squadron assembled at Bardufoss in the far north of the country and began operations on 27 May.

Drummond saw action shortly after his arrival when, on 29 May, he took-off from Bardufoss in Hurricane L1794. He sighted four enemy aircraft at 12,000 feet south of Narvik and moved into attack the nearest, a Heinkel 111. Although Drummond hit the starboard engine, he had been hit by return fire causing his cockpit to fill with smoke. He attempted to return to Bardufoss but his engine failed. Drummond had no choice but to bail out. He landed in the near freezing waters of Ofotfjord and was picked up by HMS *Firedrake*, an F-Class destroyer later to take part in The Battle of the Atlantic. Drummond had scored his first kill, a He 111 of 2/Kampfgeschwader 26 and described this engagement in his combat report as follows:

> I took off from Bardufoss at 0005 hrs. in formation in No. 2 position with F/Lt. Jameson. I sighted four aircraft south of Narvik, at 12,000 ft. and climbed to attack the nearest, a Heinkel 111. As I started to attack the Heinkel did a steep turn to the left and opened fire with his rear gun. I did a deflection attack becoming an astern attack as the Heinkel straightened out and fire broke out in the starboard engine. The Heinkel started to lose height rapidly and at the same time my cockpit filled with smoke, and I was forced to break of the

attack. I turned to go back to Bardufoss but my engine failed and white smoke poured from my exhausts. I jumped out at 5,00 ft. (sic) and made a parachute descent. I was picked up by H.M.S. FIREDRAKE in UFOT FIORD (sic). Confirmation from commander of H.M.S. FIREDRAKE, who stated that an enemy aircraft disappeared behind Narvik and one to dive into the sea.

Four days later in the early afternoon of 2 June, Drummond took-off in Hurricane W2543 with Sergeant Taylor for a routine patrol over Narvik. An hour or so into the sortie he spotted two Junkers Ju 87s attacking a destroyer in Ofotfjord. He went after the first firing around five four-second bursts. Smoke belching from the starboard mainplane confirmed he had scored a hit. Drummond watched as it force-landed and burst into flames.

7 June was certainly Drummond's busiest day during his time in Norway. It was also the day he cheated death by an inch and earned his DFC. He was patrolling the Narvik area at 0400 hours when he spotted three He 111s flying in formation. He attacked the first bomber but it disappeared into a cloud, so he attacked the other two, hitting the starboard Heinkel. The other returned accurate fire causing Drummond to disengage and seek cover in a cloud. On emerging, Drummond observed the damaged Heinkel heading towards the border with neutral Sweden and so returned to Bardufoss claiming this as a victory.

After some rest, Drummond was in the air at 1715 hours patrolling Narvik with Flight Officer Mee. They sighted four He 111s at around 10,000 feet. Mee attacked the port enemy aircraft and Drummond the starboard. Drummond hit his target causing it to turn for cloud cover whereby he went after another bomber. Spotting two he attacked one, hitting the rear gunner but was also hit by return fire. A shell pierced his windscreen, clipping his goggles and helmet before ricocheting out of the cockpit hood, making a large hole in the process. Drummond returned fire but lost the enemy planes in cloud. He claimed one victory and two damaged.

On landing, Drummond learned that Operation *Alphabet* had been activated and the squadron had been ordered to evacuate Norway immediately. They were to fly their Hurricanes back to HMS *Glorious*. Perhaps because of the day he had had – two sorties in fourteen hours – Drummond was not chosen for the task. Instead, he went with the ground crew of 46 Squadron on the SS *Arandora Star*.

At 0300 hours on 8 June, HMS *Glorious* was detached with the destroyers HMS *Ardent* and HMS *Acasta* to head for Scapa Flow while the other carrier, HMS *Ark Royal*, and the rest of the fleet remained behind to escort the slower main convoy. At 1545 hours, the German battle cruisers *Scharnhorst* and *Gneisenau* spotted HMS *Glorious* and opened fire directly hitting her bridge. HMS *Glorious* returned fire but was hopelessly outgunned. By 1720 hours, the doomed carrier sank taking eight 46 Squadron pilots and their Hurricanes to the bottom. The SS

Arandora Star completed her journey unscathed and Drummond disembarked at Gourock on 13 June then returned to Digby.

Drummond's overall score in Norway was four victories and two damaged enemy aircraft for which he was awarded the DFC. The citation in the *London Gazette* of 26 July 1940 read:

> The KING has been graciously pleased to approve the under mentioned awards, in recognition of gallantry displayed in flying operations against the enemy:— Awarded the Distinguished Flying Cross. Pilot Officer John Fraser DRUMMOND (40810). During operations in Norway, this officer shot down two enemy aircraft and seriously damaged a further three. On one occasion, as pilot of one of two Hurricanes which attacked four Heinkel 111's, he damaged one of the enemy aircraft and then engaged two of the others. Despite heavy return fire, Pilot Officer Drummond pressed home his attack, silenced the rear guns of both aircraft and compelled the Heinkels to break off the engagement.

The squadron reformed at Digby becoming operational at the end of June. The next two months consisted of convoy and defensive patrols. Drummond was posted to RAF 7 Operational Training Unit at Hawarden where he taught Czech and Polish pilots the rudiments of combat flying in Spitfires. He was briefly returned to 46 Squadron where, amongst other duties, he was chosen to lead a flight of three aircraft escorting The Lord Lloyd, Secretary of State for The Colonies, from North Coates to Hendon.

On 5 September, he was plunged into the thick of the Battle of Britain when he was posted to 92 Squadron, first at Pembery then at Biggin Hill. 92 Squadron was already an effective fighter unit thanks largely to its leadership and the strength of character of its pilots. It also had a reputation for indiscipline, having a second home at the White Hart pub not too far from Biggin Hill in the small village of Brasted.

From 1 January 1940, it had been led by Squadron Leader Roger Bushell until he was shot down and captured on 23 May. He would later be executed by the SS for masterminding the Great Escape from Stalag Luft III. Other notables in the squadron included Paddy Green, Bob Stanford-Tuck, Brian Kingcome, Tony Bartley, Johnny Kent, Allan Wright, Don Kingaby and Geoffrey Wellum.

On 6 September, Drummond made his first flight with 92 Squadron and on 8 September, he departed Pembery for Biggin Hill. On his arrival he roomed with Wellum who wrote in his memoirs, *First Light*:

> I share a room with a new pilot. His name is John Drummond. He was waiting at Biggin when we arrived, a quiet retiring sort of chap, a bit of an introvert. As we unpack our kit I get to know a little about him, although he doesn't volunteer an awful lot. It appears he was in a Gladiator Squadron in Norway

and they were, of course, hopelessly outnumbered and virtually decimated. He has a DFC but obviously doesn't want to talk about it so I don't press him. We get on well enough. He's friendly so the arrangement suits me, not that I'm in a position to object. Hardly know he's around anyway.

So the last thirty-five days of Drummond's life were about to be played out defending his country against the imminent threat of invasion.

His first action in the Battle of Britain came in the late afternoon of 9 September when 92 Squadron was scrambled to defend Biggin Hill itself. They lost two aircraft but fortunately no pilots.

On 10 September, Drummond was ordered to fly to Hawkinge as part of an escort for an Avro Anson that was 'spotting' the results from a new fourteen-inch gun firing shells across the English Channel. This proved to be an uneventful flight and he returned to Biggin Hill in the early evening.

On 11 September, after some much needed rest, thirteen aircraft of 92 Squadron were scrambled at 1520 hours to intercept a large formation of bombers escorted by fighters over Dungeness. Drummond was flying as number 3 of Green Section. The squadron split up over Maidstone as pilots carried out individual attacks.

Drummond encountered three Bf 109s at 20,000 feet, attacked number three firing a few short bursts before breaking away. He spotted a Hurricane under attack and hit its assailant hard as it broke away. He pursued the fighter, finishing off his ammunition in the process and causing white smoke to pour from its tail. Drummond looked round to see two Bf 109s diving on his tail and so performed a half-roll and dived sharply to shake them off before heading back to base, landing at about 1730 hours. When reporting to Squadron Intelligence Officer Tom Wiese, Drummond claimed the Bf 109 as a probable.

92 Squadron were kept busy over the next few days defending Biggin Hill, but rain, cloud and unsettled weather hampered enemy action to a large degree. The RAF fighters took some punishment but fortunately the pilots were relatively unscathed. Action escalated on 18 September when 92 Squadron was scrambled to meet the third major attack of the day. At 1555 hours, Drummond flew one of eight Spitfires ordered off from Biggin Hill to rendezvous with 66 Squadron over base. Cloud cover forced them down to 18,000 feet where they observed a formation of sixteen Bf 109s heading toward Rochester. The squadron went in to attack but the enemy aircraft headed for the cloud cover above. Despite losing sight of the Bf 109s, Squadron Leader Kingcome formed up with three pilots and attacked a formation of eighteen Ju 88s and a He 111. By the time the Spitfires returned to base they had claimed one and a half Ju 88s destroyed and two He 111s as a probable and damaged.

Showery weather on 19 September contributed to a day of relative inactivity so Drummond and 92 Squadron were not called into action. That evening, the

Luftwaffe dropped heavy explosive and incendiary bombs over a wide area of Liverpool, commencing their campaign to destroy the city, a campaign that would soon have devastating consequences for Drummond's family.

On the morning of 20 September, 92 Squadron were scrambled to meet the one major attack of the day. A force of a hundred enemy aircraft was intercepted over east Kent, apparently on course for London. In the ensuing melee, two Spitfires of 92 Squadron were shot down (Sgt P. R. Eyles and P/O H. P. Hill both killed) by leading Luftwaffe ace Major Werner Molders (Kommodore of Jagdgeschwader 51) near Dungeness. These victories took his tally to forty making him the first fighter pilot to reach this total during the war.

21 September was a quiet day for Drummond and 92 Squadron as they were only involved in fighter sweeps over east Kent. There was little combat and only one enemy aircraft was reported damaged. That evening, however, the Luftwaffe stepped up their assault on Liverpool with the heaviest raid yet. A bomb smashed into the front of 63 Worcester Road, killing Drummond's grandmother and aunt where they slept.

It is not clear when on 22 September Drummond received the news from Liverpool, but it was perhaps fortunate he was only required to fly a short patrol over Beachy Head as fog and rain reduced activity to a minimum.

By the next morning the weather had cleared sufficiently for the Germans to launch their first major attack of the day at 0930 hours and Drummond, flying Spitfire QJ-T (X4422), and 92 Squadron were scrambled to meet them. Drummond climbed to 20,000 feet and was ordered by Flight Lieutenant Kingcome to attack any Bf 109s he saw. He quickly latched on to the tail of a Bf 109 that was attacking a Spitfire flown by Tony Bartley. Drummond fired a short burst that caused clouds of white smoke to pour from the exhaust. The pilot of the Bf 109, Feldwebel Kuppa of 8/Jagdgeschwader 26, took evasive action but Drummond followed him down firing short bursts until it became apparent that Kuppa would have to make a forced landing. He ended up in a pond near Grain Fort on the Isle of Grain but was captured unhurt. Drummond returned to Biggin claiming it as a victory. The Spitfire that Drummond flew on this particular day, X4422, was shot down by Bf 109s three days later over Farningham, killing its pilot, twenty-year-old Flt/Lt Jimmy Paterson.

On 24 September, the Germans again decided to make their first major attack of the day an early one. Drummond, flying as Blue 1, and 92 Squadron were scrambled at 0845 hours, joining up with 66 and 72 Squadrons over the Thames Estuary. At 16,000 feet they spotted a formation of Ju 88s escorted by a large number of Bf 109s. Drummond led Blue Section through the escort and attacked the bombers. In his combat report, Drummond described carrying out a beam attack on the rear Ju 88 hitting the port engine.

After breaking away from the bomber, Drummond realised he had three Bf 109s on his tail. He turned onto the tail of the rear Bf 109 firing a five-second burst. Clouds of white smoke poured from the exhausts of the German fighter and Drummond turned on to the second Bf 109, again firing short but well-aimed bursts, believing he had damaged his prey. On his return to Biggin Hill, Drummond declared he had expended 2,000 rounds and claimed a Bf 109 as a probable, one damaged and a Ju 88 damaged.

It will never be known how Drummond felt about missing the funeral of his grandmother and aunt that took place on 25 September and the effect it had on him. However, due to decreased enemy action in the London area, he did not fly till 27 September. At 0915 hours, he was ordered to patrol the base as Yellow 1 flying Spitfire QJ-G (X4330) taking two other fighters with him. They engaged enemy fighters and Drummond damaged a Bf 110. He was credited with a third of a victory as it was attacked by Hurricanes, most likely of 46 Squadron, on its way to crash-land in a field just south of Westerham.

After lunch in dispersal, the squadron was scrambled at 1530 hours. Drummond was again flying as Yellow 1. They intercepted a formation of Ju 88s over Sevenoaks and Drummond attacked the outside aircraft at the rear of the formation. The engine of the Ju 88 was smoking when another Spitfire from Yellow Section also hit it. The crippled bomber crashed near High Halden railway station.

Records indicate that 92 Squadron was not in action again until 30 September. At 1700 hours and still flying as Yellow 1, Drummond was on patrol at 27,000 feet north-west of Brighton when he spotted a formation of fifteen bombers escorted by around fifty fighters 10,000 feet below. Drummond dived towards the bombers and encountered two Bf 109s on the way down. After firing a four-second burst at a distance of 350 yards, Drummond observed smoke belching from the Bf 109 as it lost height. He watched it descend towards Beachy Head before returning to Biggin Hill. Drummond claimed this as a probable.

With the coming of October, the Battle of Britain entered its final stage and Drummond was next in action on the morning of 5 October. He took-off about ten minutes after the squadron as 'Ganic 17' and set about finding them. Over Dungeness he saw twelve Bf 109s and decided to carry out a solo attack. He opened fire on the rear fighter, clobbered it and watched it do a half-roll before crashing in the sea. This is likely to have been a fighter from 2/JG 77. Having just seen the Bf 109 hit the sea, Drummond spotted a Henschel Hs 126 flying low above the water. In his characteristic tenacious style, he followed and engaged it, finally bringing it down just two miles from the French coast. Although he could have not known it, the Henschel was to be his last victory. Drummond described the engagement in his combat report as follows:

I took off from Base about 10 minutes after the squadron as Ganic 17, and attempted to find the Squadron. Over Dungeness at 22000 feet I saw 12 Me. 109's. I did a beam attack on the rear two. They turned away from the formation and dived towards the coast. I followed and fired a burst at the rear 109. White smoke came from the 109 and it did a half roll and a long shallow dive towards the sea. I followed and saw it hit the water. As I was following the 109 down I saw a Henschel 126 flying low over the water, I followed it and fired a burst as it turned towards the French coast. I followed it firing short bursts to about 2 miles off the French coast where it force landed in the sea. A Heinkel 111 flew past and watched the Henschel forced land, I also saw a Dornier 215 flying low across the water as I came back. I could not fire at either of these as I was out of ammunition.

The day was further marked by official RAF artist Captain Cuthbert Orde meeting Drummond shortly after he landed and drawing his portrait. Of the nearly 3,000 pilots who flew in the Battle of Britain, GHQ picked less than 200 of the most outstanding for this accolade. Orde's iconic pictures of 'The Few' are always striking. That Drummond's was drawn now, an hour or two after his final kill and with only five days to live, is all the more poignant.

It was three weeks before Will was to learn the full circumstances of John Drummond's death. The weather was showery but bright that morning, Thursday 10 October. No doubt Drummond would see action again today. Since the deaths of his grandmother and aunt he had flown almost continuously, claiming four victories, two probable, two damaged and one shared. He had also seen four colleagues killed in action.

At 0710 hours, he took-off in Spitfire QJ-X with the rest of squadron to patrol Maidstone. After forty uneventful minutes they were vectored on to a Dornier 17 just east of Brighton. All nine Spitfires descended on the enemy aircraft but experienced difficulty in firing as their windscreens were iced up and the reflector sights could not be used. Two of the Spitfires got in close, fired some bursts and got out. The Dornier flew on.

Drummond and Pilot Officer Bill Williams both attempted beam attacks from either side of the Dornier. They missed and continued turning blindly towards each other. Their Spitfires touched, the starboard wing of Drummond's machine striking the tail of Williams. Drummond bailed out but was too low for his parachute to open. He was still alive after hitting the ground so a priest was able to administer the last rites before Drummond died in his arms. His Spitfire crashed close to him, landing on a flint stone wall that bordered Jubilee Field and St Mary's Convent in Portslade.

When his body was examined, Drummond was found to have been wounded in his left arm and leg. Williams, it later transpired, had been shot through the head so was already dead when their machines collided. Censorship meant Drummond's death was noted in the vaguest of terms in the next day's *Brighton Evening Argus*. It simply read: 'Our losses yesterday were five aircraft but the pilots of two are safe.' Will made the arrangements for his son's funeral.

John Fraser Drummond's funeral took place at St Michael's church, Blundellsands, on 15 October 1940. The service was attended by the Mayor of Crosby among other local dignitaries and the chosen hymn sung was Abide With Me. He was buried in Thornton Garden of Rest just four days before his twenty-second birthday. His short life had only known childhood, school, barely a year at the timber merchants and less than three years in the RAF. His death did not go unnoticed in Germany. During his nightly radio broadcast, 'Lord Haw-Haw', aka William Joyce, had this to say about the action that took Drummond's life:

> A single reconnaissance aircraft, returning from photographing the holocaust of London, was attacked today by six Spitfires. Its gallant crew showed great courage in destroying three. The aircraft crashed in France but the photographs have been saved.

In 1940, the war was not only being fought by courageous young fighter boys in the skies above southern England but by ordinary people in the villages, towns and cities of Great Britain as well: the Home Front. This was a period when families were separated, often coping with the loss of a loved one. Cities were being bombed and people had to find new and ingenious ways to keep their lives as normal as possible. One such account of life during these unprecedented times was kept by Brighton schoolteacher Helen Roust in her diary. Her entry for 10 October, the day Drummond died, reads as follows:

> All clear from the night warning at 7am – we were all awake. We heard machine gunning at 8.20am. Time bomb in the Hythe Road district at 12.20, sirens at 2pm, all clear at 2.40. Children have been excitable. Small wonder that we have all felt a little nervy. A Spitfire came down on the Fallowfield Estate. Sirens for the night at 7.20.

The Spitfire she refers to was Drummond's.

The Drummond Family in the Blitz

It was during the first phase of bombing that became known as the Blitz that tragedy first struck the Drummond family. At 1932 hours on 21 September 1940, an air raid warning signalled that the Germans had launched another raid against Merseyside.

The first raids of the Blitz had occurred on 29 August 1940 and they had been almost continual since then. Though much worse was to come, on this night Liverpool endured its worst air raid since the war began. The Luftwaffe unleashed a fearsome barrage of incendiary bombs on densely populated residential areas. As the residents, Air Raid Patrol wardens and Auxiliary Fire Service tried to put the fires out, a second wave of bombers passed overhead dropping high explosive bombs.

At 63 Worcester Road Bootle, John Drummond's grandmother, Mary, and his auntie Edith Drummond were in bed in a ground floor room. As they lay there in the small hours of 22 September, a bomb smashed into the front of the house. The two women had no chance and were killed where they slept. Another of Drummond's relatives, Mary Lang (known as Aunty Polly in the family, who was both deaf and nearly blind), who was asleep in the back of the house, miraculously survived. When the all clear sounded at 0421 hours the next morning the clearing up began.

The *Bootle Times* of 27 September 1940 carried on its front page the news of the deaths of Mary and Edith Drummond. On the inside of the same edition it reported on their funeral. It took place on 25 September, leaving from John's uncle Bert's house at 9 Worcester Road and taking place at Christ Church in Bootle, a few hundred yards away from the scene of the tragedy that still lay strewn with rubble.

The chief mourners that day were Mary's sons William (John's father), Bert and Harold, her brother G. Hamilton, grandson W. F. Drummond, granddaughter Helen Drummond, nephew J. Gibbons and nieces Mrs Nutall and Mrs Salisbury. John's parents sent a floral tribute on behalf of the family. They were interred at Bootle Cemetery in the same grave as John's great grandfather William Sinclair Drummond. The inscription on the gravestone read: '...killed by enemy action on 22nd Sep, 1940.'

John Drummond was on active duty with 92 Squadron at Biggin Hill so was unable to attend the funeral. He had engaged the enemy the day before, claiming a Bf 109 as a probable and damaging another along with a Ju 88. Visiting Worcester Road today is a stark reminder of that September night in 1940. The houses were rebuilt as necessary. All except for number 63 where there is an empty space.

CHAPTER 5

Pilot Officer Jindřich Bartoš

Jindřich Bartoš was born in Lugansk, a large industrial city in south-eastern Ukraine (then in the Russian Empire) on 16 November 1911. The naming of Lugansk follows the ebb and flow of military power in the region, something that Bartoš would play a part in himself. In 1938, it was renamed Voroshilovgrad in honour of the Soviet military commander Kliment Voroshilov, but the original name was reinstated in 1958. It was changed back again following Voroshilov's death in 1970 and finally returned to Lugansk as the Soviet Union collapsed in 1990.

No records exist to explain when, why or indeed how Bartoš left Ukraine and arrived in Czechoslovakia. Given that he attended the Army Academy in Hranice and Prostějov, it is possible that his family fought in the Polish-Ukrainian War of 1918-19. Victorious Polish forces took over most of south eastern Ukraine, including Lugansk, forcing many parts of the defeated Ukrainian Galician Army to seek in neighbouring Czechoslovakia.

In 1934-35, Bartos graduated from the Army Academy as a pilot. He served in that capacity with the 2nd Air Regiment. After Germany invaded Czechoslovakia in 1938, he escaped to Poland in the summer of 1939 and then sailed to France. France was not yet at war with Germany so Bartoš was given a passport and was expected to join the French Foreign Legion. Refusal to have done so would have led to repatriation to Czechoslovakia. Once war was declared he was transferred to the Armee de l'Air.

There as a pilot in fighter squadron Groupe de Chasse I/3, he fought in the Battle of France. At the outbreak of the Second World War, Groupe de Chasse I/3 had been equipped with the comparatively weak Morane-Saulnier MS.406. After seeing combat during the Phoney War, the squadron relocated to southern France. While at Cannes-Mandelieu on the Mediterranean coast, the unit converted to the new Dewoitine D.520 fighter, which was much more of a match for the Bf 109.

When the Battle of France began in May 1940, his was the only unit to be operationally ready with the D.520, which it first took to battle on 12 May after hastily relocating to Wez-Thuisy in north eastern France, east of Paris, near the borders with Germany and Luxembourg. Groupe de Chasse I/3 was then based at Esbley, nearer Paris, between 17 May and 18 June 1940. Flying a D.520, Bartoš was engaged in a dogfight over Paris on 3 June 1940 and was shot down. He crash-landed having sustained light wounds but was credited with damaging his opponent's aircraft, a Heinkel He III.

In late June 1940, as the fall of France became inevitable, Groupe de Chasse I/3 crossed the Mediterranean to Oran in Algeria to escape capture. From there, Bartoš sailed via Casablanca on the *Royal Scotsman* and Gibraltar where he transferred to the *David Livingstone*, and sailed for Great Britain. He docked in Cardiff on 5 August 1940.

After retraining on Hawker Hurricanes, Pilot Officer Bartoš, RAF Service Number 83220, was posted to the newly formed 312 (Czechoslovak) Squadron at RAF Duxford in Cambridgeshire on 5 September 1940. 312 Squadron was the second Czechoslovakian fighter unit that had been formed a week earlier on 29 August 1940 at the Czechoslovakian aircrew depot at RAF Cosford in Shropshire. The shortage of fighter pilots was a grave concern for Sir Hugh Dowding who understood the essential need for foreign pilots to man the controls of Hurricanes and Spitfires during the Battle. Although Dowding understood the need to form foreign units, he was hesitant of the Czech and Polish pilots to begin with as he later confessed:

> I had been a little doubtful of the effect which their experience in their own countries and in France might have had upon the Polish and Czech pilots, but my doubts were soon laid to rest, because all three squadrons swung in the fight with a dash and enthusiasm which is beyond praise. They were inspired by a burning hatred for the Germans which made them very deadly opponents. The first Polish Squadron. (No. 303) in No. II Group, during the course of a month, shot down more Germans than any British unit in the same period. Other Poles and Czechs were used in small numbers in British squadrons, and fought very gallantly, but the language was a difficulty, and they were probably most efficiently employed in their own National units.

312 Squadron's motto was 'Non multi sed multa' meaning 'not many but much'. The squadron badge was a stork volant, a reference to the French 'Escadrille des Cygelines' with whom the original pilots of the squadron had flown prior to coming to Great Britain.

Two days later on 31 August, the first nine used Hawker Hurricanes Mk.Is were flown into Duxford and on 4 September 1940, a Miles Master Mk.I arrived. Bartoš was among the Czechoslovakian airmen, flying personnel and ground staff who arrived at RAF Duxford during the afternoon of 5 September 1940.

P/O Jindřich Bartoš
j12.yaf

Jindřich Bartoš by David Pritchard.

The squadron was based around a core of experienced pilots who had already seen combat during the Battle of France.

On 6 September 1940, the pilots began with theoretical preparation for flying Hurricanes and with training flights on the Master. Training was very slow because the unit had just the one trainer aircraft. For faster retraining of the pilots another Master was loaned from 310 (Czechoslovak) Squadron.

After nearly a month the level of training was very high and on 26 September, the squadron moved to its new home, the RAF station at Speke Airport, Liverpool. There the unit completed its retraining and in the last days of September, the squadron obtained further Hurricanes.

On 2 October 1940, 312 Squadron was declared operational and given the task of protecting the Liverpool area from enemy raids.

In October 1940, Bartoš became an operational pilot. At first he served as a section leader and after promotion to Flying Officer he was appointed deputy flight leader of B flight. The squadron's first taste of combat occurred on 8 October when 312's Yellow Section engaged a lone reconnaissance Ju 88 of 3.(F)121 over Merseyside at 1615 hours. After receiving an order to patrol Hoylake, Flight Lieutenant Denys Gillam, AFC, took-off from the aerodrome with Pilot Officer Alois Vasatko and Sergeant Josef Stehlik following his lead. Once the section had reached 1,000 feet, anti-aircraft bursts up river attracted the attention of Stehlik who then sighted the Junkers flying westwards at 1,200 feet. Suddenly, the enemy aircraft began to climb sharply towards cloud cover and the chase was now on. Stehlik was the first to snatch a burst at the Ju 88, but the engagement was followed by continual astern attacks from Gillam. Both Stehlik and Vasatko followed Gillam's lead as they weaved in and out attacking the Junker's from below and above. The enemy continued to climb through cloud but the Hurricane pilots continued their determined attacks until finally the Ju 88 lost height with both of its engines on fire. Vasatko and a large number of ground observers saw the Ju 88 fall flat down on a meadow on the left bank of the Mersey. According to the report made by 312's Intelligence Officer, Gillam had spent 2,400 rounds in the attack, Vasato 144 and Stehlik 504. In spite of the unfavourable position the German crew found themselves in, they did not go down without a struggle. An extract from the squadron's intelligence report explains:

> During the combat heavy and accurate return fire was experienced from the E/A up to the last moment before the crash. Slight damage was sustained by all our aircraft, a bullet hitting the windscreen of Yellow 1 [Gillam] another the exhaust manifolds of Yellow 2 [Vasatko] while Yellow 3 [Stehlik] sustained damage to petrol tank and the gun pipe line (He states in his individual report he returned thinking all his ammunition was gone).

It had been a successful day for the new Czech squadron, but also a tragic one for the RAF who earlier in the day lost its most reputed Czech fighter pilot, Sergeant Josef František of 303 Squadron. In just two months, František became Fighter Command's top scoring ace in the Battle of Britain with seventeen confirmed victories to his credit. František was known as a maverick in the air that lacked discipline and order, but in combat he was a true warrior of the skies. On an early morning patrol, František suddenly broke away from his squadron and for unknown reasons crashed to his death at Ewell near Sutton, Surrey. Some theorists believe he crashed after 'beating-up' his girlfriend's house and possibly rolled his aircraft too low to the ground, while others believe mental and physical fatigue finally finished him off.

Two days later, tragedy continued to ride its ugly course when Bartoš' squadron comrade and compatriot Otto Hanzlíček was killed after engine failure forced him to bail out into the River Mersey.

Bartoš was part of a detachment sent to RAF Penrhos in North Wales on 22 December 1940 to fend off attacks on the airfield by German bombers. Taking-off out of RAF Penrhos on 13 February 1941, Bartoš was flying Hawker Hurricane V6885 (DU-V) participating in mock dogfighting with Sergeant Votruba. At 1430 hours, Bartoš' aircraft was seen to go into a spin/dive from

5,000 feet by Votruba. It crashed at Talacre near Prestatyn on the mouth of the River Dee opposite the end of the Wirral peninsula. The reason for the crash is unknown but it is thought that it was caused by failure of his oxygen equipment.

The accident was witnessed by Mr Frank Parsons and his friends who were at school at the time. They saw the Hurricanes swooping around in the sky over the nearby range when suddenly one of the fighters fell away and fluttered down like a leaf until it disappeared out of sight behind some trees. Mr Parsons was one of the boys that the headmaster sent across to the crash to see what had happened. Upon arriving at the scene of the crash, they saw the pilot's body being removed from the cockpit by a number of locals including the district nurse and then being wrapped up in his parachute and placed alongside the wreck.

When a salvage crew arrived all non-essential persons were removed from the site and placed behind a wall. During the salvage operation the crew threw pieces of the Hurricane to the local children behind the wall. A bell tent was placed in the garden of an adjacent holiday cottage to act as a guard post. Mr Parsons and his friends recalled that the aircraft was buried up to its wings and sticking out of the ground at about forty-five degrees with its tail in the air and was the correct way up.

Bartoš was buried with full military honours on 18 February 1941 in Liverpool West Derby Cemetery, section RC, row II, grave no. 392. He shares this with Sergeant Otto Hanzlíček. Representatives of the Czechoslovakian depot at RAF Wilmslow attended his funeral. Bartoš had approximately 863 flying hours to his credit with twenty-seven of those on Hurricanes. Bartoš was one of eighty-nine Czechoslovakian airmen who fought in the Battle of Britain.

When the war ended, relatives of some of the 513 Czechoslovak airmen who died whilst serving in the RAF requested the remains of their loved ones returned to Czechoslovakia for reburial. When the practicalities of doing this were investigated, Brigadier General Karel Janoušek, Head of the Czechoslovak Air Force in Great Britain, said it would be too expensive to exhume each body so suggested it would be better to have a symbolic exhumation instead. A sample of soil from each of the graves was taken and transported to Czechoslovakia to be placed into new urns before being formally interred. Graves left in the original cemeteries in the United Kingdom would have a standard type of British military headstone.

The urns from the British graves of Czechoslovak RAF airmen were moved to Prague. They were then stored in boxes whilst plans for an appropriate memorial were considered. In February 1948, communists took control of Czechoslovakia and those who had fought in the West for the freedom of their homeland now found themselves to be victims of persecution. Under this new regime the urns were simply forgotten.

On 15 January 1990, during the reconstruction of a National Monument at Vítkov, Prague, workmen discovered boxes which contained the 302 wooden urns. Unfortunately, due to poor storage conditions, sixty-three of the urns had rotted and their contents had mixed together. The mixed soil was placed in one communal urn. The contents of the remaining 239 urns were placed in new urns.

Jindřich Bartoš urn is at the memorial at the Olšanský cemetery in Prague.

CHAPTER 6

Sergeant Otto Hanzlíček, G de C, MC (Czech)

Otto Hanzlíček was born on 18 June 1911 at 21 Straße Sandhöhe/Ktinigshtihe in Ústí nad Labem, an ethnically German and Czech city in Austria-Hungary. He was the eldest of two children, his sister Jirana being three years younger than him.

Ústí nad Labem is in the region of Bohemia, about eighty km north of Prague close to the border with Germany (also known as the Sudetenland, its majority population being ethnic Germans). After the Second World War, Bohemia became the core of the newly formed country of Czechoslovakia. Under its first president, Tomas Masaryk, Czechoslovakia was an island of calm in a turbulent Eastern Europe. It was a safe haven, progressive, prosperous and multi-cultural with more than a fifth of the population German speaking.

Serious issues though were emerging around the Czechoslovakian people's relationship with the native Germans. These issues would come to a head in the most brutal fashion in 1938.

Hanzlíček trained as a mechanic but always maintained an interest in aviation. This led to him volunteering for the Czechoslovak Air Force in 1930. Hanzlíček attended the Military Aviation School in Prostejov where he trained with 15th Squadron 4th Aviation Regiment. His graduation was confirmed on 7 January 1932. In 1934, he was transferred to Aviation Regiment No. 3 in Vajnory, near Bratislava. After completion of fighter pilot training and promotion to Sergeant in August 1935, he flew fighters for 37th Fighter Squadron at Piestany.

The gathering storm clouds of war cast a shadow over Czechoslovakia and on 10 October 1938, it was incorporated directly into the Reich when the country was forced by Nazi Germany to accept the terms of the Munich Agreement. The remnants of Bohemia and Moravia were annexed by Germany in 1939. From 1939 to 1945, Bohemia and Moravia formed the German Reichsprotektorat Bohmen und Mahren (Protectorate of Bohemia and Moravia). Any open opposition to German occupation was brutally suppressed by the Nazi authorities and many Czechoslovakian patriots were executed as a result.

Clearly this was no place for Hanzlíček so he flew to Prague where, because of the amount of flying time he had accrued, he had been included in the National Research Institute of Aviation in the Letňany district. He stayed with his sister Jirana who had fled occupied Ústí nad Labem with the rest of his family after the Nazis had begun searching out families of Czechoslovak airmen for deportation.

Anticipating German actions, Hanzlíček had clearly made plans to escape the Nazi occupation of his homeland. With two friends he headed for Ostrava, which was close to the Polish border, and on 8 June 1939, managed to cross into Poland. From Kraków, he made his way to Gdynia on the south coast of the Baltic Sea. On 25 July, just eight weeks before the Germans occupied the city, he caught a ship to France where he landed at Calais on 31 July 1939. From here he was transferred to Paris. As France was not yet at war with Germany, Hanzlíček was given a passport and, with other immigrants, expected to join the French Foreign Legion. Refusal to do this would have led to repatriation to Czechoslovakia. Once war was declared he was transferred to the Armee de l'Air.

After retraining on French aircraft at the fighter school at Chartres, south-west of Paris, he was posted to Groupe de Chasse II/5 at Toul Croix-de-Metz near the German border in December 1939. Initially flying Curtiss Hawk 75, an American-built fighter, contemporaneous with the Hawker Hurricane and Messerschmitt Bf 109, he started off on fighter escort missions for bombers. His first recorded kill was a Dornier Do 17P on 24 April 1940.

On 10 May 1940, Hitler commenced Operation Fall Gelb, his anticipated assault on Western Europe.

The very next day, Hanzlíček shared a Heinkel He 111H of 2/Kampfgeschwader 53 (the infamous Condor Legion) bringing it down at Bois de Chene, 100 km east of Toul on the German border. Then, on 18 May 1940, he shared a Bf 109 with French pilot Lt G. Ruchouxem. Immediately, Hanzlíček was attacked by another Bf 109. The pilot of this particular Messerschmitt was Luftwaffe ace Günther Rall of 8/JG 52 who would end the war with an impressive 275 confirmed victories. Rall blasted Hanzlíček's plane causing it to burst into flames. Hanzlíček was forced to bail out and was fortunate to parachute to safety. The loss of his plane is reported to be Günther Rall's first recorded kill. Rall described the action in his own words:

I see the purposeful grey-green fuselages adorned with roundels and recognise them as French Curtiss fighters that are intent on nailing our recce machine. I see Lothar Ehrlich dive on the French leader and wrench my own Messerschmitt into a steep curve down towards the enemy formation. Within seconds I am sitting on the tail of one of the leader's two wingmen. He immediately reefs his machine into a sharp turn. But too late! A quick judge

Otto Hanzlíček by David Pritchard.

of distance, a light pull on the stick, and the Curtiss disappears beneath the cowling of the Me 109, now! - a burst of fire, I relax my grip on the stick, see that my opponent is burning – and at this instant a hail of bullets smash into my own machine.[15]

Rall returned safely to his base at Ippesheim but doubted that he had destroyed Hanzlíček's machine because he lost sight of him after being fired upon himself. The action was witnessed by Lieutenant Lossnitz who filed a written report stating he saw Rall fire at a Curtiss P-36 at around 1840 hours and then watched it go down in a spin, on fire and trailing black smoke. The pilot took to his parachute. Kapitan Ehrlich congratulated Rall on his first victory.

In all, Hanzlíček made 113 flights, totalling over 100 hours, for the Armee l'Air and was awarded the Croix de Guerre with Silver Star and Bar and the Czechoslovak War Cross.

On 18 June 1940, Winston Churchill told the British Parliament, 'What General Weygard called The Battle of France is over. The Battle of Britain is about to begin.' Hanzlíček having fought in the first battle was about to join the second. Having escaped from Czechoslovakia, Hanzlíček now had to escape from France and find his way to Great Britain. Along with other Czechoslovak pilots he managed to get to North Africa. On 9 July 1940, he sailed from

Casablanca on the *Royal Scotsman* to Gibraltar where he transferred to the *David Livingstone*, and on 21 July, sailed for Cardiff where he arrived on 5 August 1940.

Hanzlíček joined the RAF Volunteer Reserve and was given the service number 787697. On 19 September 1940, he was posted to 312 (Czechoslovak) Squadron. The home base of the Squadron was RAF Duxford in Cambridgeshire, the same airfield where 310 (Czechoslovak) Squadron was based. Czechoslovak airmen arrived at RAF Duxford with other Czechoslovak flying personnel and ground staff during the afternoon of 5 September 1940. Based around battle-hardened pilots who already had combat experience in the Battle of France, many of whom with more than one victory, the squadron was ready for action.

So it was on 26 September it moved to its new home, the RAF station at Speke, Liverpool. Here the unit completed its retraining and the squadron was allocated a number of older aircraft, which resulted in many servicing difficulties for the ground crew. On 2 October 1940, 312 (Czechoslovak) Squadron was declared operational and its task was to protect the Liverpool area from enemy raids.

The squadron was most heavily involved in night patrols defending the Liverpool docks. At 2350 hours on 7 October, Speke aerodrome was attacked, an Audax aircraft being destroyed and a Douglas DF7 damaged. Although windows in the hangars were hit the aerodrome remained serviceable, although only half the squadron was operational.

On 8 October 1940, pilots of 312 Squadron's Yellow Section shot down their first enemy aircraft, a Ju 88 that had tried to attack the Rootes aircraft factory on the perimeter of the airfield. The factory manufactured Halifax bombers. The Ju 88 crashed on the opposite bank of the River Mersey at Brombrough. This victory was recorded as probably the fastest kill of the war taking around eleven minutes from take-off to landing and was watched by squadron personnel and local residents.

On 10 October 1940, Hanzlíček took-off from Speke in the oldest Hawker Hurricane in service, L1547, along with Pilot Officer Dvořák on practice enemy aircraft attacks over the River Mersey. As he banked round the opposite bank of the Mersey, less than three miles from Speke, the engine of his aircraft caught fire and he was forced to bail out near Oglet. The wind blew him out over the river and, after problems with his parachute caused by bailing out too low, he fell into the water some 300-400 yards from the river bank and drowned.

Mr Alan Davie was a British member of 312 Squadron serving at Speke and had vivid memories of the moment the aircraft crashed into the river:

> I had just returned from lunch when I heard the sound of engines approaching.
> I thought it was the Germans as they had flown in a few days earlier and
> tried to bomb the airport, but our lads had shot them down. When I realised

what was happening, I just put my hands together and said a prayer. I saw the Hurricane and pilot falling from the sky. If the wind had been kind to him, he could have landed in Ellesmere Port and survived. He fell into the river and his parachute was falling from the sky behind him. As he went into the water he went under but then came back to the surface. As he did, his parachute came down on top of him. I witnessed some horrific sights during my time in the air force, but that particular day is one I will never forget.

Hanzlíček was seen to fall into the water on the north side of the river by a farmer near Oglet, but when he arrived at the scene ten minutes later there was nothing to be seen. His aircraft came down into the river off the end of runway 8 and had been seen to be emitting smoke over the river just opposite the airfield by personnel at the station. Three weeks later on 1 November 1940, Hanzlíček's body was found five miles to the east of Speke at Widnes. On 4 November, the inquest into the cause of his death was held at Widnes, the finding of which was death due to asphyxia from drowning. At the age of twenty-nine, Hanzlíček was the first pilot to be killed from 312 (Czechoslovak) Squadron. At the time of the accident he was a vastly experienced pilot having amassed in excess of 930 flying hours.

On the morning of 5 November 1940, Hanzlíček's funeral was held at the Roman Catholic Church in Allerton when, after a short service, he was taken to West Derby Cemetery. His coffin was draped with the Union Jack and Czechoslovak flags on which rested his Croix De Guerre. He was buried in Section RC11, grave No. 392. The stone gives his name as Otta Hanzlíček that he shares with Jindřich Bartoš. Hanzlíček is remembered on the Battle of Britain Monument in London, the Battle of Britain Memorial in Capel-le-Ferne on the white cliffs of Dover, a plaque at the RAF Museum at Hendon and a plaque at the Czech Club in London. The urn with soil from Hanzlíček's grave was placed at the memorial at Ústí nad Labem. Most recently there has been a street named after him in his home town of Ústí nad Labem, Hanzlíčkova.

Hanzlíček was born in a fledgling nation, a liberal nation that should have allowed him to reach his potential and fulfil his ambitions. Such dreams destroyed, he was forced to flee his country. When the opportunity came to stand up to his oppressors he grasped it, going head to head with them in the skies above northern France. Pushed back again, he stood side by side with the young fighter boys of the RAF in defence of Great Britain. Posted to the North West of England, his job was to repel enemy raiders and help prevent an invasion. It was a job he gave his life for.

Hurricane L1547, which Hanzlíček piloted on his final flight, was the first production aircraft built by Hawker Aircraft Ltd of Kingston and Brooklands to Air Ministry specification F.15/36 under contract No. 527112/36. The first 430 aircraft were manufactured with fabric-covered wings and the remaining 170 with metal-covered wings. However, some aircraft were later refitted with metal wings at maintenance units within the RAF. Deliveries of aircraft for this order commenced on 15 December 1937 and were completed on 6 October 1939.

L1547 first flew on 12 October 1937 at Hawker's Brooklands factory. It was flown by Phillip Lucas, Flight Lieutenant P. W. S. Bulman's assistant test pilot, and subsequently was used for flying performance and engineering trials at various establishments before entering squadron service.

L1547
First flown on 12/10/1937
Taken on charge by Hawkers on 29/03/1938
Taken on charge by A&AEE on 23/06/1938
Taken on charge by Rolls Royce on 28/06/1938
Taken on charge by A&AEE on 21/07/1938
Taken on charge by 15 MU on 29/05/1940
Taken on charge by 10 MU on 10/06/1940
Taken on charge by 312 (Czechoslovak) Squadron on 31/08/1940
Fatal accident on 10/10/1940
Struck off charge on 29/10/1940

Up until the 1970s, aircraft wreckage believed to be from this Hurricane could be seen at low tide, but has now disappeared into the ever-shifting deep mud and it is thought that the remains are now buried under ballast of a light gantry for the airport. A few pieces of the aircraft were recovered in the 1960s when a couple of spars were showing about fifty yards out and these are now at the War Plane Wreck Museum at Fort Perch Rock, New Brighton. The canopy was apparently found on Cartwright's farm and went to 7F Squadron ATC in Liverpool. However, although aware of the story, they do not have possession of the canopy any more.

CHAPTER 7

Flight Lieutenant Wladyslaw Szulkowski, KW

The Poland Wladyslaw Szulkowski was born into on 6 November 1909 was a country on the brink of massive social and political change. In the 1890s, extreme poverty had caused some four million Poles to emigrate to America. The three powers that partitioned Poland in the late 18th century, Austria, Germany and Russia, would soon be on opposite sides in The Great War, Russia siding with the Entente Forces and Germany and Austria with the Central Powers. Poland would be the war's Eastern Front. In the aftermath of the First World War, Poland was restored as an independent state but was still embroiled with regional conflicts and threats from increasing hostile neighbours.

It is little wonder then that a military career appealed to Szulkowski and with flying offering new and exciting opportunities, he applied to join the Polish Air Force. Requirements for applicants to the Szkoly Podchorazych Lotnictwa (Polish Air Force Academy) at Deblin were high. They had to have a secondary education achieving the necessary results in key subjects, to have completed a pilots course with an Aero Club, pass a medical and psychological examination and finally an entrance exam. At the age of twenty-one, Szulkowski was accepted. After two years of intensive study and many hours flying, he graduated from the Academy's seventh class and was commissioned as a First Lieutenant on 15 August 1933.

From 1933 to 1937, he was a pilot in the Polish Air Force during which time he flew the PZL P.7 single-seat fighter plane. Unusually for the time it was an all metal, high-wing monoplane with a radial engine and was armed with two machine guns. It is likely that he also flew the newer, faster single-seat PZL P.11c that could carry under-wing bombs. In 1939, he flew as an instructor at the Advanced Flying School in Grudziadz-Ulez near Deblin, about seventy miles south east of Warsaw, teaching new trainees how to be fighter pilots in the PZL P.24 trainer/fighter.

At the same time as Szulkowski was training fighter pilots, the fate of Poland was being determined in Moscow with the signing of the Treaty of Non-

Aggression between Germany and the Soviet Union, otherwise known as the Molotov-Ribbentrop Pact. Although it was announced as a non-aggressive pact, it included secret protocols in which Germany and the Soviet Union divided northern and Eastern Europe into spheres of influence. And so on the 1st and 17th of September, Germany and the Soviet Union crossed their respective borders and invaded Poland.

Szulkowski fought as a fighter pilot in the defence of his country flying with the 'Deblin Group'. However, most of the Polish Air Force was easily destroyed. There are no surviving records that detail his action during September 1939. What is known is that he escaped certain death at the hands of the Germans and Russians when he evacuated with his trainee pilots to Romania and later went to France to serve with Polish Air Force comrades in the Armée de l'Air. It is unclear if he was among the 7,000 Polish airmen who fought in the Battle of France. From France he came to Britain and joined the RAF as a Pilot Officer, Service Number 76747.

After operational training with 5 OTU at Aston Down in Gloucestershire and conversion training to Spitfires, he was posted to 65 (East India) Squadron at Hornchurch on 5 August 1940 and took part in the Battle of Britain. Documents about Szulkowski's time in the Battle are scant. Even the books that are commonly taken as definitive fail to mention any confirmed victories, yet surviving combat records are unequivocal that he did shoot down at least one enemy aircraft. On 22 August, flying Spitfire R6712 as Blue 3, he destroyed a Bf 109 just off Dover. He described the action in his own words:

> 65 Squadron were detailed to patrol to intercept raiders. I was flying in the position of Blue 3 when we engaged many Me109's over Dover at 20,000 feet. I became separated from my section and attacked one of the stragglers. Before he could attempt evasion I fired several bursts from 350 yards closing to 100 yards and the e/a burst into flames and crashed down into the sea where I saw it before turning back to base.

The Squadron's Intelligence Officer, A. Hardy, filed an Intelligence Patrol Report for 24 August in which he described nine aircraft, including one flown by Paddy Finucane, scrambling from Rochford to intercept raiders approaching from Dover. After being vectored to Manston, they sighted two formations of thirty and forty bombers escorted by forty Bf 110s and a large number of Bf 109s. The squadron climbed to engage the fighters and at 28,000 feet broke into sections to attack. The squadron claimed a Bf 110 destroyed and a Bf 109 as a probable before returning to Rochford. Szulkowski did not make a claim but managed to fire 482 rounds during this action.

On 27 August, the squadron was transferred to Turnhouse, just west of Edinburgh in Scotland. In November 1940, the squadron moved south again and began offensive sweeps over northern France.

Wladyslaw Szulkowski by David Pritchard.

Szulkowski was not the only Pole in 65 Squadron. Also serving were Pilot Officer Boleslaw Drobinski and Flight Officer Franciszek Gruszka. In his memoirs, currently in possession of his family in Poland, Gruszka described his first sortie against a German bomber formation on 14 August 1940.

> Battle of August. I am starting to fight. Many Germans above and just twelve of us (only two Poles are me and Władzio Szulkowski). We attack bombers; German fighters attack us from behind. One of them is closer and closer. I make a sudden turn, get his tail, and send a series (burst of shots). He is going down to the clouds, inertial. I cannot go after him, because in the same moment two other 'Jerries' attack me. Have no chance, I hide in clouds.

Gruszka was killed in action on 18 August 1940. The squadron was scrambled and he took-off in Spitfire R6713 to intercept a German bomber formation. Gruszka was last seen dogfighting over Canterbury and chasing a fleeing Luftwaffe fighter. He was to never return to base. As no news was heard of him again he was listed as missing in action. His story was to have a fitting end when in the spring of 1975, the remains of his aircraft were found in marshes in East Sussex. Gruszka was still in the cockpit. He was buried at the Polish War Memorial on the outskirts of RAF Northolt, London, with full military honours on 17 July 1975.

In December 1940, Szulkowski volunteered to join a soon to be established Polish squadron that would be based at RAF Speke in Liverpool. On 8 January 1941, the Air Ministry approved the formation of 315 (Polish) Squadron at RAF

Acklington in Northumberland and assigned the code letters 'PK' to its aircraft. As a British advisor, Squadron Leader H. D. Cooke became its first commander with Flight Lieutenant Davy and Flight Lieutenant Edy commanding Flights A and B respectively. The Polish Air Force Inspectorate issued an order for Flight Lieutenant Stanislaw Pietraszkiewicz from 307 (Polish) Squadron to take command of this newly formed unit, promoting him to the rank of a Squadron Leader at the same time. Technical Officer, Flight Lieutenant Jurand and Intelligence Officer, Pilot Officer Narkiewicz, assisted him in recruiting the personnel in co-operation with the depots at Kirkham and Weeton that were attached to RAF Blackpool.

On 21 January, Squadron Leader Pietraszkiewicz arrived at Acklington. This date became officially the day the squadron was formed, and in the next few days all of the squadron personnel including Szulkowski arrived at the station. Pietraszkiewicz gave command of A Flight to Flight Lieutenant Wladyslaw Szczesniewski and command of B Flight to Szulkowski. Most of the pilots and ground crew of 315 (Polish) Squadron were from the Szkola Podchorazych Lotnictwa military academy in Deblin, which is why in September 1941, General Sikorski, Head of the Polish Armed Forces, gave the Squadron the name: 'Deblinski' or 'City of Deblin'.

In January 1940, the Polish Commander-in-Chief, Wladyslaw Sikorski, issued an order re-introducing the Krzyż Walecznych, the Cross of Valour. In a clear recognition of his service on 1 February 1941, Szulkowski was awarded the Polish Cross of Valour. 315 (City of Deblin) Polish Fighter Squadron transferred to Speke on 13 March 1941 and became operational with Hurricanes. Its role was to defend Merseyside and to fly patrols over naval convoys in Liverpool Bay. Antoni Mackowski, the squadron's chief armourer, recalled:

> In the beginning of March the Squadron transferred to Speke near Liverpool where it patrolled over convoys. As armourers we did not have much to do, since our aircraft very rarely met the enemy. We weren't idle either. Every two hours we had to change six-cartridge colour flares, which were used to signal friendly in aircraft to convoy escort. Till the middle of the May, Liverpool was regularly heavily bombed at night and the noise made it difficult to sleep. Yet in the morning everybody had to be in good shape to do the hard work.

27 March 1941 was turning into a typically grey and overcast early spring day. At 1000 hours, the two sections of B flight took-off from Speke to participate in formation practice flying and simulated attacks at 25,000 feet. The exercise that was meant to last around an hour and fifteen minutes went disastrously wrong. After just fifteen minutes, Sergeant Piotr Zaniewski returned to Speke because of high oil temperature, landing at 1015 hours. He was to be the lucky one.

First altitude was at 15,000 feet over Preston, but heavy cloud meant the operations room changed this to 20,000 feet. Whilst the squadron was engaged in simulated attacks, the operations room changed the status of their flight from practice, instructing them to an operational patrol. A new course of 270 degrees at 27,000 feet was set to intercept a formation of enemy aircraft. The flight became separated in the cloud but Pilot Officer Tadeusz Hojden and Flying Officer Kazimierz Wolinski sighted the enemy and gave chase but without engaging them.

On the way back to base they were vectored erroneously by the operations room and Pilot Officer Hojden, descending due to lack of fuel, crashed into the sea. Flying Officer Wolinski, flying on a similar course to that given by the operations room, also ran out of fuel and ditched in the sea off Blackpool. Fortunately, he was picked up by a Fleetwood trawler and reported safe at 2100 hours. He reported that Hojden had passed him at high speed in clouds and had presumably dived into the sea. No trace of Hojden or his aircraft were ever found. Pilot Officer Eugeniusz Fiedorczuk had also started to experience problems when his engine stopped and was unable to switch fuel tanks due to a frozen valve. Only when he descended to 10,000 feet was he able to succeed and made his way to RAF Squires Gate in Blackpool where he landed safely at 1145 hours. Further south, Sergeant Edward Paterek's Hurricane (V7187), code-lettered PK-W, was seen to enter the sea with Szulkowski's Hurricane (V7188), code-lettered PK-X, by British ships in the vicinity of the Mersey Bar lightship, *Alarm*, which stood at the entrance to the Queen's Channel shipping lane into Liverpool.

After landing, Pilot Officer Fiedorczuk stated that he saw Sergeant Paterek collide with Szulkowski's aircraft at 25,000 feet. He saw Paterek's propeller cut into Szulkowski's tail and severed it. An officer at RAF Squires Gate asked for the Blackpool lifeboat *Sarah Ann Austin* to be launched. The order was approved by the Coast Guard at Hoylake on the Wirral and so the lifeboat was launched at 1150 hours and reached the crash site some forty minutes later. Wreckage was collected that confirmed the crashed aircraft to be Hurricanes V7187 and V7188 and the lifeboat returned at 1530 hours. A lifeboat from the Isle of Man was also launched to search for survivors. Shipping was requested to keep a look out for aircraft in the sea at 270 degrees, thirty-two nautical miles from Blackpool. One Anson and one Botha of No. 3 School of General Reconnaissance at RAF Squires Gate were sent out to search and drop inner tubes on the sea. There was no trace of Paterek's or Szulkowski's bodies.

This apparently routine formation practice flying exercise had seen four aircraft and three pilots lost. Two of the pilots, Paterek and Szulkowski, were Battle of Britain veterans.

Three and a half weeks later on 20 May 1941, the body of Szulkowski was washed up on the shore at Freshfield, twelve miles north of Liverpool. It was taken to a mortuary at Formby to be formally identified by the Polish Medical Officer. An examination of the body gave no reason for the cause of the accident. No parachute was found and it appeared certain that he entered the sea whilst in the aircraft. His wristwatch had stopped on impact at 1125 hours.

On 24 May 1941, Szulkowski was laid to rest in West Derby Cemetery, Liverpool, by the Reverend Henry Moffat. As befitted a decorated officer who had fought to defend his own country in the Polish Campaign, fought to defend Great Britain in the Battle of Britain and died protecting Liverpool from the threat of German bombers, he was buried with full military honours. Led by his brother Corporal Szulkowski who was chief mourner, all officers from 315 (City of Deblin) Squadron B flight attended together with a sergeant and forty Polish airmen acting as an escort party for his coffin. Wreaths were sent by the Station Commander, the British Officers, 315 Squadron A and B Flights and his previous unit, 65 Squadron, then based at Kirton Lindsey. He was buried in the Roman Catholic section of the cemetery, row 11, grave no. 392. That his funeral was such a grand affair indicates the esteem in which he was held, not just by his fellow Polish pilots but by comrades from his former squadron too.

Szulkowski was one of 145 Polish pilots who flew in the Battle of Britain destroying 130 enemy aircraft. It was a Polish squadron, 303 (Kościuszko) Polish Fighter Squadron, who claimed the highest number of kills of any Allied squadron during the Battle. Without the overall contribution of Polish soldiers and airmen in all theatres of the Second World War, the outcome of the war may have been very different.

CHAPTER 8

Flight Lieutenant Kenneth McLeod Gillies

It was a typically hot and stifling August afternoon in 1890 when Robert Gillies, a clerk with the Liverpool, Midland and Scottish Railway, married Kate Sleeman, a dressmaker, at Emmanuel Church, Everton. The newlyweds settled into their home in West Derby and looked forward to married life together and becoming parents. Their hopefulness though was short lived as just one year after getting married Kate was diagnosed with pulmonary tuberculosis. As the disease began to take hold, she and Robert moved out of Liverpool and settled in West Kirby on the Wirral coast in the hope that the sea air would aid her recovery. Robert spent the next few years nursing her but to no avail. Kate's condition deteriorated as she contracted laryngeal tuberculosis. Tragically she was not to recover and Robert was at her bedside when she died on New Year's Day 1896 aged twenty-nine. The following notice was placed in the Liverpool Mercury on 4 January 1896:

> GILLIES – New Year's morn, at 5, Mercia-terrace, West Kirby, aged 29, Kate Louise, the dear wife of Robert W Gillies of this city. Deeply regretted. Interment at West Derby Cemetery this day (Saturday), Jan 4, at two p.m.

During his time in West Kirby, Robert had met Maude Ring McLeod, the daughter of a well-known Birkenhead-based bread and flour dealer. Their friendship blossomed after Kate's death and it was not long before he asked her to marry him. The ceremony took place on 21 April 1897 at St Peter's Church, Birkenhead. Rather than return to West Derby where he had lived with Kate, Robert moved his new family to Curzon Street, Waterloo, and shortly after Maude gave birth to a daughter, Vera. Robert's career was progressing well and he had been promoted to Head of Department. So the family moved again, this time only a short distance to Queens Road, Great Crosby. In 1903, Maude gave birth to a son, Robert. It was a family tradition from Maude's side that a child should take the mother's maiden name, so when she gave birth to another son on 12 April 1913, he was christened Kenneth McLeod Gillies.

Kenneth, known as Ken in the family, was to enjoy a happy childhood. The Gillies were friends of Robert and Ann Runcie who lived over the road from them. Their respective children would play together and enjoyed many a game of back garden cricket. One of the Runcie children, Robert, went on to serve in the Second World War as a tank commander winning a Military Cross before becoming Archbishop of Canterbury in 1979.

Ken Gillies attended Ballure House School before entering Merchant Taylors' School for Boys in January 1924. He was a capable student who showed an aptitude for music, in particular the piano. After leaving school, he was a pianist in an amateur dance band. He was also a first class marksman and a member of the Liverpool Miniature Rifle Club. He left Merchant Taylors in July 1929 and joined his brother's timber and paper business, Gillies and Co. and Gillies Saw Mills Ltd. This did not suit him and soon left and took up a post with the Scottish Widows Fund and Life Insurance Company. However, this did not satisfy him either and, according to family stories, he saw the direction Europe was taking so decided quit civilian life altogether and join the RAF.

Gillies joined the RAF as a Pupil Pilot on 9 March 1936. He was granted a short service commission as Acting Pilot Officer on probation with General Duties Branch on 4 May before being posted to No. 8 Flight Training School at Montrose on May 16. No. 8 FTS had only been operational since 1 January. On 25 December, he joined 66 Squadron at Duxford. On 9 March 1937, he was confirmed as a Pilot Officer, Service Number 37799. In June, Gillies flew with the rest of the squadron as they took part in that year's Hendon Air Display flying Gloster Gauntlets.

Gillies settled into RAF life and enjoyed the social scene that came with it. Duxford was a Mecca for the young, attracting them from the surrounding areas for dances. The Red Lion became an extension of the Officer's Mess and just the place for the young airmen to meet girls. It was around this time that Gillies met Ethel Mary Holman, known as Mary, an attractive and vivacious girl who worked in the village shop in Great Chesterford, a small village less than five miles from Duxford. His great friend from the squadron, Canadian Jack Graafstra*, was dating Mary's sister Peggy so they would take their girls dancing to The Dorothy Ballroom in Cambridge. Gillies and Mary started spending as much time as they could together, being all too aware of the ever present threat of war and what it would mean.

In August of 1938, the squadron received its first Spitfire (K9790). Gillies had obviously acquitted himself well in the squadron being appointed Armament

---

* John William (Jack) Graafstra was a Canadian pilot who went on to join 242 Squadron and flew in the Battle of France. On 21 May, whilst escorting Blenheims to Cambrai in Hurricane P2809, he was shot down and killed by a Bf 109 of Jagdgeschwader 1, possibly flown by Luftwaffe ace Major Ludwig 'Zirkus' Franzisket , over Douai and crashed near Wancourt. He is buried in Wancourt Communal Cemetery.

Ken Gillies by David Pritchard.

Officer and on 9 September 1938, he was promoted to the rank of Flying Officer. In November, 66 Squadron became only the second unit in Fighter Command to be fully equipped with Spitfires.

Gillies' romance with Mary had continued to flourish so it was with some pride that he took her up to Great Crosby to spend Christmas 1938 with his parents. They were not to know this would be her only visit. Gillies' parents clearly approved of his girlfriend, so they began to make wedding plans. They settled on 9 September 1939 as the date for their wedding day and agreed that it would be easier for Gillies to get leave if the wedding were to be held in Mary's village. They commissioned a Court dressmaker to make Mary's dress and three bridesmaid dresses. Mary booked the church, organised the flowers, cake and refreshments for the guests. Everything was in place for the happiest day of their lives.

On 30 August, with Germany's invasion of Poland imminent, Gillies was granted a forty-eight hours leave to get married that weekend as all leave was to be cancelled indefinitely thereafter. They were married on 1 September in the Parish Church in Great Chesterford. Far from being the grand affair they had envisaged, the ceremony was witnessed by Mary's father and a family friend. They spent their wedding night at The George Hotel in Huntingdon. Gillies was back at Duxford on 3 September, the day Britain declared war on Germany. On 4 September, Mary's wedding dress was delivered to her home.

Gillies began flying interception patrols over Duxford and the surrounding area. He took to circling Mary's house on his way back to base and dipping his

Left and right: Ken Gillies, 66 Squadron.

wings to let her know he was safe. Mary knew this as a signal to hop into their newly acquired Austin Seven and drive over to Grange Road, Duxford. Gillies, having landed, would cross the fields, still in his flying kit, to meet her.

Gillies was sent on to RAF Northolt to attend his Air Fighting Development Establishment course on 22 October. On 13 November, Gillies was promoted to Acting Flight Lieutenant and posted to 254 Squadron at RAF Stradishall where he was made O.C. 'A' Flight. His role was to bring the squadron up to an operational state of readiness for convoy duties. Fortunately, Mary was able to join him on this posting. One of his responsibilities was to complete a monthly summary of events from the Operations Record Book. The first one he submitted was for December 1939.

As winter turned to spring he began to fly patrols, protecting fishing fleets and convoys in the squadron's Blenheims. Offensive patrols were still very much a part of his duties and he regularly flew over Haisborough Sands on the Norfolk coast in search of enemy aircraft. He also flew escort flights, most notably when he escorted two Ansons of 206 Squadron, again flying a Blenheim Mk.I.

From 9 April, 254 Squadron carried out reconnaissance and offensive patrols over Norway in support of the Allied Campaign following the German invasion. They saw action over Stavanger and Bergen. Although Gillies flew in these patrols, he did not engage the enemy. On 7 May, he was transferred back to 66 Squadron. On his return to 66 Squadron, his extensive fighter training and natural flying ability ensured he was the obvious choice to take over command of A Flight. A week of local flying ensued before offensive patrols commenced over Holland. During this time, he offered sound tactical advice to the squadron's sprogs such as Bobby 'Oxo' Oxspring. Before Oxo's first scramble, he said 'Whatever circus you get tangled up in Bobby, for Christ's sake watch your tail!' Oxo was to remember these words. On 13 May, Gillies led A Flight in an early morning sortie over Rotterdam. They observed several Ju 87s and engaged them. Gillies singled out a Junkers and opened fire. He described the action in his combat report as follows:

> Tracer was observed apparently from the rear guns but ceased after several seconds of fire. Therefore the Junkers 87 went into a steep dive with smoke issuing from it and disappeared down to the ground.

Gillies brought his flight home safely and claimed this as a confirmed kill and a Bf 109 as damaged.

On 16 May 1940, 66 Squadron moved from Duxford to Horsham St Faith. Once again it carried out local flying but was ordered up on interception patrols. Gillies' A Flight also investigated 'X' raids and carried out some night flying.

On 31 May, all aircraft of the squadron were ordered to Kenley and Gravesend to take part in operations covering the British Expeditionary Force's evacuation from Dunkirk. Gillies flew two sorties from 1550 to 1810 hours and again from 1840 to 2100 hours. The squadron continued to fly operations over Dunkirk on 1 June and 2 June when Gillies was sent out at 0700 hours and again at 2130 hours. On 3 June, they moved to Duxford and then to Martlesham Heath for operations over the North Sea and Dunkirk. The remainder of June was spent carrying out interception, convoy and night convoy patrols from RAF Coltishall.

66 Squadron's first action of the Battle of Britain occurred on 10 July 1940 when Sgt Fred Robertson intercepted a Do 17 off Winterton-on-Sea and attacked it with Pilot Officers Charlie Cooke and John Studd. Their combined firepower sent it crashing into the North Sea. By now the squadron was on constant standby and continued to be scrambled. Gillies would to take A Flight out on patrols, usually two a day, but frustratingly without engaging any enemy aircraft.

At just after 1030 hours on 20 August, Gillies and his flight were scrambled yet again. Flying south of Lowestoft at 7,000 feet, they spotted enemy aircraft 4,000 feet above them. After passing under them they started a climbing turn to port in order to attack from the rear and below. Gillies positioned Red Section in line astern. However, the enemy aircraft, three Bf 110s, spotted them and attempted a steep diving turn to starboard to try and shake them. Singling out the rear enemy aircraft, Gillies led his section into a diving number one attack. He got in two bursts of three seconds each causing its starboard engine to slow. The enemy broke formation and headed for cloud cover. Sergeant Mathew Cameron managed to attack the third aircraft setting its starboard engine on fire. As it began to lose height, Gillies got a final burst in on the Bf 110 and watched it crash into the sea in a ball of flames. It had been an intense dogfight and when Gillies landed he saw his Spitfire (N3225) had sustained damage to its oil tank and port wing. He was credited with half of the destroyed Bf 110.

Gillies next engaged the enemy on 31 August. He led A Flight on an interception patrol, this time over Comer. He spotted a Do 215 at 20,000 feet so began to climb in pursuit of the enemy aircraft. Being a light bomber, the Dornier managed to out-climb Gillies' Spitfire. However, the pilot made what was to be a fatal error when he began a shallow dive. Gillies knew he had the bomber in his clutches, so positioned his fighter so that the sun was behind him and prepared to carry out a quarter attack. Red 2, Pilot Officer Crelin 'Bogle' Bodie, fired first hitting the Dornier's starboard engine. Gillies moved in and fired two four-second bursts also hitting the starboard engine. By now black smoke was pouring out of the damaged engine and the Dornier was losing height. Bodie pressed home the attack before Gillies moved in for the kill, firing two more bursts and in doing so ran out of ammunition. He turned and headed back to base as Bodie watched the Dornier crash into the sea near Felixstowe. Gillies was credited with half the destroyed Do 215.

On 3 September, the squadron relocated to RAF Kenley, one of the key fighter stations responsible for the defence of London. By now, Mary was expecting their first child so she and Gillies decided it would be safer if she returned to Great Chesterford. On 4 September, the squadron found themselves in the thick of the action when they were scrambled to intercept a raid of sixty-plus enemy aircraft. Gillies was forced to return to base after twenty-five minutes flying with a mechanical fault. The squadron lost one pilot and four aircraft on this patrol.

On the afternoon of 10 September, the squadron moved again, this time to RAF Gravesend, a satellite airfield of Biggin Hill, where they were the only operational squadron. Gravesend had a club house belonging to Essex Aero that doubled as a pilot room and bar. There was a piano that Gillies commandeered as his own and between patrols would lighten the mood by playing Jerome Kern's 'All the Things You Are', Hoagy Carmichael's 'Stardust' and the entire songbooks of Cole Porter and Irving Berlin.

Poor weather meant there was little flying over the next few days. The respite was only brief, however, as on 15 September, the Germans sent over two formations of aircraft so large that every fighter in the sector was scrambled to repel them. Gillies was flying as Green 1 at 1142 hours to intercept an incoming raid that had been sighted heading north over London. He led the squadron round to head them off but were engaged by a number of Bf 109s. The squadron took evasive action and broke formation in the process. Gillies cruised around looking to rejoin the squadron when he saw Bodie diving through a formation of Do 17s. He had singled out an enemy aircraft on which he made repeated attacks. Gillies came up alongside him and took up the charge blasting the cowling and cabin, and causing the enemy's starboard engine to stop. The Dornier was seen to crash ten miles east of Canterbury. Gillies returned to base and was credited with a third of a confirmed kill.

There was to be no rest on this day of days. At 1410 hours, the squadron was scrambled again and Gillies was flying one of eleven Spitfires that were ordered to patrol Biggin Hill. En route to their patrol line, they were vectored on to a bomber formation that was travelling North West over Gravesend. They engaged the enemy and Gillies described the action in his combat report:

> I was following the leading section of 66 Squadron when they attacked a formation of HE.111's flying west over London. Attack was from lower forward beam. On breaking off after the first attack I saw one HE.111 fall out of its formation so I immediately attacked him with a long burst from 300-100 yards dead astern. I observed pieces of fuselage fly off and bullets struck both engines (which were smoking). Just prior to ceasing my fire the E.A.'s oil system burst and showered oil over my aircraft, covering my windscreen. Other friendly fighters were in the vicinity so I broke off, landed at Biggin Hill and cleaned wind-screen. I also refuelled and took off to rejoin the action.

Gillies was credited with half a Heinkel He 111 as a probable.

After returning to base and having less than two hours rest, the squadron was scrambled for a third time, but without incident. If they had hoped that they had flown their last sortie of the day they were mistaken. At 1910 hours, the telephone in the dispersal hut rang and the order to scramble was given. For the fourth time, Gillies leapt into the cockpit of his Spitfire (X4320) and prepared to lead his section into battle. They had only reached 8,000 feet when they sighted a He 111. Using the cloud as cover, Gillies was able to close within 300 yards before firing a four-second burst. The enemy aircraft dived for cloud cover, but was unable to remain hidden for long. Gillies attacked the bomber again, killing the rear gunner and damaging the port engine so much so that it stopped dead. The enemy aircraft was losing height so Gillies, now out of ammunition, followed it down reporting its position to control. He lost sight of it in cloud ten miles east of Dungeness. Gillies was credited with a third of a He 111 damaged.

On 18 September, 66 Squadron was scrambled to support 92 Squadron over Biggin Hill**. Gillies led Red Section in the rear of 92 Squadron and spotted several bombers descending from a thin layer of cloud. He alerted the leader of 92 Squadron over the R/T who then turned to attack them. Gillies then sighted the escorting Bf 109s and led his flight to engage the fighters. Gillies fired a quick burst, damaging one but the Bf 109s dived away and made off. During the melee, Gillies lost touch with his squadron so went searching for the enemy on his own. He observed a formation of He 111s, but before he could attack two squadrons of friendly fighters arrived on the scene and proceeded to engage the bombers. Gillies selected a Heinkel that had detached from the protection of its

---

** The respective Squadron Operations Record Books confirm that on these two occasions Gillies was flying on the same patrol as another of the Merseyside Few, John Drummond. These two men lived less than a mile away from each other and were laid to rest in the same cemetery, their graves being a matter of feet apart. Yet they never knew each other in life.

formation and carried out a stern attack shattering the rudder and damaging its engines. Before he could finish it off, another Spitfire joined in and both pilots watched as the He 111 half-rolled, dived and crashed in flames at the mouth of the River Thames. Gillies was credited with half a confirmed kill for the He 111 and with damaging a Bf 109.

On 23 September, Gillies led 66 Squadron to join 92 Squadron over Biggin Hill. On reaching 25,000 feet, they were bounced by Bf 109s and forced to take defensive action. Gillies made a diving turn to shake a Bf 109 off his tail. Having done so, he spotted further Bf 109s circling above, so climbed towards the sun while keeping them on his beam. On reaching 29,000 feet, he turned flying out of the sun to face them head on. The Bf 109s broke up and climbed away but Gillies latched onto one that suddenly began to dive. He followed the fighter down, giving two long bursts of ammunition but he could not get any closer than 350 yards. Some metal flew off the enemy aircraft and it started to waver. The German pilot was now clearly heading for home. As the chase had taken them over the channel, Gillies decided to let him go and return to base. He claimed the Bf 109 as damaged.

There was simply no respite for 66 Squadron or Gillies as they continued to be on standby from first light until dusk. On 27 September, they were scrambled four times to meet the enemy, but it was only on the first and third patrols that they engaged them. At 1005 hours, Gillies was leading Green Section when he sighted two formations of Bf 110s approximately ten miles south of Biggin Hill. He gave the order to attack and as they did so the enemy aircraft made off towards the south coast. Gillies came up behind one of the twin-engine heavy fighters as he was turning and gave it a five-second burst. The Bf 110 went into a stalled turn with smoke pouring from an engine and went into a vertical dive from which it would never recover. Gillies claimed this as a probable. In the afternoon, the squadron was again needed to defend Biggin Hill against a raid from Do 17s. Gillies was credited with one third of three confirmed kills.

Gillies' final victories of the Battle of Britain were claimed on 30 September, a probable Bf 109 over Biggin Hill and a confirmed Bf 109 over Horsham in his final patrol of the month. September had been a remarkable period for the squadron and Gillies in particular. He had flown more than forty patrols and shared in the destruction of twelve enemy aircraft. The seemingly endless summer of glorious blue skies and blazing sunshine that had lasted into September at last begin to break. Clouds, bringing with them mist, rain and moderate visibility were a sure sign autumn had arrived so operational flying was kept to a minimum.

Gillies was at readiness but not expecting any action as the weather was so poor. Around 1500 hours, however, the telephone rang and Operations advised that a German bomber had been spotted lurking around the area and gave the order for it to be intercepted. As Flight Commander, Gillies knew that he had to go and volunteered Pilot Officers Hugh Heron and Arthur Watkinson to make

Ken Gillies in the cockpit of a Spitfire.

up his Flight. Taking off in Spitfire X4320, he led the flight up with Heron as his number 2. They hit cloud almost immediately and it was continuous during the climb. On breaking through the cloud they were given a course and headed off in the direction of the bomber, a He III. It was soon spotted, so they went towards it. Just as they were closing in on the bomber, the crew must have observed the incoming British fighters as the He III changed course and dodged in and out of cloud. An experienced pilot would have remained hidden in the cloud, but as he kept coming out of it Gillies was able to get nearer to the intruder and ordered an attack. Gillies went in first followed by Heron and Watkinson. It is not clear what happened next, but Heron described it as follows:

> ...then Gillies said over the radio "I am obliged to break off combat." That was all. I don't know what happened to him, whether he was wounded or there was some damage done to his plane. People's voices in combat situation were usually excited or strained. I couldn't tell whether he was in pain from the way he sounded. I never saw him again.

Heron and Watkinson returned to base at 1550 hours. Pilot Officer Hugh 'Dizzy' Allen recalled:

> Ken should have been an intelligence officer as he had that sort of mind. One of his tricks was to get so close to a German aircraft that he could read the squadron letters, even the number. Poor old Ken; he did this once too often. It was of course valuable intelligence in that the general deployment of the units of the Luftwaffe was thus interpreted by British eyes and this was useful information. But one turbulent day Ken took off with his number two into a sky filled with cumulo-nimbus clouds, veritable thunderstorms were beating

against the earth, and we never saw him again. He lost his number two on the climb in the thick clouds and we heard later that he had relayed by R/ T the squadron letters and number of a Heinkel III to the controller. Then there was silence. Clearly he must have been flying in close formation on the German bomber to gain this information; in which case, machine-guns apart, the gunners could have killed him with their Mausers.

Allen's observation is borne out by the great details in Gillies' combat reports. As one of the original members of 66 Squadron, Gillies' loss was keenly felt by all. Pilot Officer John 'Durex' Kendal said of him:

...a very fine chap he was too and one of the best shots in the R.A.F. also. If he had lived, he would most probably be a D.S.O., D.F.C. "type" by now.

Gillies' body was washed up on Covehithe Beach, Norfolk, on 20 October 1940. The cause of death was recorded as being 'due to war operations'.

Although his life with Mary was very much in Great Chesterford, Gillies' mother wanted his funeral to take place in their local church, St Luke's Great Crosby, and for him to be buried locally. So it was. Gillies' funeral was held on 30 October 1940. In attendance were the Mayor of Crosby and many friends from his Merchant Taylor's days, his time with Scottish Widows and working in his brother's paper business. Absent though was Mary. For her, by now six months pregnant, the journey north would have been too much. She did not want to mourn her husband in strange surroundings and in the company of strangers, so stayed in Great Chesterford. At the same time as the funeral, a service of remembrance was held for Gillies in the Parish Church but she could not bring herself to attend that either. Instead, she decided that she preferred to be alone and went for a walk in the hills above the village. Twenty-six days later, Mary gave birth to a son, Kenneth John Richard Gillies.

The loss of a son was too much to bear for Robert and he passed away three weeks after his grandson was born. He was laid to rest in the same grave as Ken Gillies on 1 January 1941, exactly forty-five years to the day after his first wife had died. Eighteen months later, tragedy was to strike the Gillies family again. Ken Gillies' sister Vera's son, Robert Emmett, a Second Lieutenant with the Royal Artillery 25th Field Regiment, was killed at Tobruk on 20 June 1942 during Rommel's second offensive. Although he is buried in Knightsbridge War Cemetery in Acroma, he is commemorated on Ken Gillies' headstone.

Mary died in December 1992 and her son, now a qualified pilot, arranged for a service of remembrance to be held in the Parish Church before her ashes were interred in the family grave. In an echo of that momentous summer and autumn of 1940, he circled the churchyard in a Spitfire as his father used to circle the house and dipped his wings in tribute to his mother, just as his father used to do.

SECTION THREE
FANTASTIC FOUR

CHAPTER 9

Conny: Flight Lieutenant Stanley Dudley Pierce Connors, DFC and Bar

Stanley Connors was born 8 April 1912 in Calcutta, India. He was educated at St Pauls School, Darjeeling, before returning to the family home in England. Connors joined 500 Squadron, Auxiliary Air Force, in early 1936, and the following year was granted a short service commission in the RAF. After completing his training, Connors was posted to 111 Squadron at Northolt on 27 June 1938. In November 1937, 111 Squadron was privileged to be the first unit to receive the Hawker Hurricane, aircraft L1547 being the first to arrive at Northolt. Not only was it the squadron's responsibility to convert to Sydney Camm's marvellous creation, but also to report any faults it may have and to recommend modifications to get the aircraft operationally up to scratch.

It was in the cockpit of a Hurricane fighter that Connors would go to war when in May 1940 he joined the squadron on operations in France where he would be challenged by the redoubtable Luftwaffe. On 18 May, 111 Squadron Hurricanes were airborne on a late afternoon patrol when they encountered enemy aircraft for the first time. Sergeant John Craig's engine was badly damaged in combat with Bf 110s near Douai and he crash-landed north of Vimy at 1550 hours. Craig was unhurt but was forced to abandon his Hurricane. Not long after leaving his aircraft, Craig made his way into an adjacent field where he saw a downed Heinkel He 111, its crew alleged to have been murdered by French troops.

During this time, Flight Lieutenant C. S. Darwood was shot down by Bf 109s and killed south of Mons. Connors, known as 'Conny' among his friends, succeeded in destroying a Ju 88A that crash-landed near Amiens at 1645 hours. The aircraft was a write-off but the bomber crew were unhurt and rescued. When Connors returned from the patrol he also claimed a Bf 109. At 1630 hours, the squadron lost an additional two Hurricanes at dispersal during a low-level bombing attack by Do 17s.

On 19 May, activity over France was proving lethal when the squadron attacked a formation of He 111s. Flying Officer David Bury was shot down and killed by

Flight Lieutenant Stanley
Connors. (*Chris Goss*)

Bf 109s south-west of Douai and Pilot Officer Iain Moorwood was also killed
after being shot down by Bf 109s. Squadron Leader Thompson's glycol tank was
damaged in the melee and his undercarriage collapsed when landing. Connors
claimed the destruction of three He 111s and a Ju 88, but his aircraft, Hurricane
L1564, was damaged by return fire west of Cambrai at 1530 hours. Connors was
unhurt and his aircraft was soon repaired.

On 31 May 1940, Flying Officer Connors was awarded the DFC. His citation
in the *London Gazette* reads as follows:

> This officer showed outstanding fighting ability and gallantry when, during
> two consecutive days in May, 1940, whilst greatly outnumbered, he shot down
> three Heinkel 111s, two Junkers 88 and one Messerschmitt 109.

By the evening of that same day, Connors was leading 111 Squadron's B Flight on
an evening patrol. At 1850 hours, they rendezvoused with a squadron of Boulton
Paul Defiants over Deal and then proceeded on to Dunkirk. Enemy formations
were spotted flying east to west about 1,000 feet above their positions so the
squadron readied itself for action. Connors, flying Hurricane P3548, climbed from
his current position and tucked in behind his squadron leader as a formation of
Bf 109s attacked the Hurricanes from head on. Connors took immediate action

by turning his aircraft away from the attack. The evasive manoeuvre worked as he ended up behind the enemy fighters which began to split in all directions. The sky became a scene of disarray as machines from both sides attempted to outfox each other. During the scuffle, Connors fired two quick bursts at various aircraft and then at a height of 19,000 feet, he saw five He IIIs fifteen miles out to sea heading south-east of his position. Connors gave chase and performed a stern attack from 250 yards range, firing a three-second burst from his guns. Connors was forced to break off from the attack when two Bf 109s latched on to his tail, but he climbed to port and rejoined the safety of his section that was circling in the vicinity. Connors returned to base and reported that one of the He IIIs he attacked issued black smoke and was seen by Green 2 to drop out of the formation. During the fight, Connors had fired 200 rounds. The squadron also took its licks from the action when Sergeant J. Robinson's Hurricane was hit by return fire over Dunkirk and was forced to land at Manston with a wounded ankle. Sergeant William Dymond's aircraft was also struck by return fire causing damage to his oil system, port wing and tail, but he managed to touch down at Manston unhurt.

Despite the gloomy backdrop of an Allied retreat in early June, the fighter squadrons continued to fly patrols over France and brawl with the Luftwaffe. On 2 June, 111 Squadron's Pilot Officer R. R. Wilson was forced to bail out of his Hurricane after it was attacked by Bf 109s of JG 51. Wilson evacuated his aircraft over the Channel and landed near Manston without injury. Connors claimed a 'possible' aerial victory as his combat report accounts:

Combat Report
2/5/40
I was leading Green Section when we met 20 M.E. 109s at 20000' E/a climbed for height and so did we – At 23000' as M.E. 109s did not look like starting a fight I went down with my section and joined in a fight that was going on at 18000' with M.E. 110s. I attacked one M.E. 110 which was firing at a Hurricane and drove him off. A little later I attacked another M.E. 110 and gave him a burst of 2 sec. which killed the rear gunner and also did some damage to the aircraft. It is possible that I put the second M.E. 110 out of action.

During an evening patrol on 7 June, Connors, leading Green Section, sighted a Bf 109 and attacked it as it dived towards enemy lines. After a hearty chase and diving at 370 mph, Connors got within range and thumbed his gun button for three to four seconds that forced the enemy aircraft to plunge into the ground four miles west of Abbeville. This was to be Connors' final victory of the Battle of France, but his combat prowess continued into the summer of 1940 when Britain was isolated against the threat of German invasion. By the beginning of July, the Luftwaffe's front line units were composed of 1,464 fighters and 1,808 bombers. Dowding's Fighter Command had only 903 fighters of which 754 were single-seat fighters. The odds did not look favourable for the RAF fighter pilots, but the possibility of defeat did not seem plausible for many if not all of Churchill's marvellous 'Few'.

The squadron's first action of the Battle of Britain took place during the afternoon of 10 July after radar detected enemy aircraft forming up over Calais. The Luftwaffe's primary target was the large shipping convoy 'Bread', which Do 17s were detailed to attack under the protection of Bf 110s and Bf 109s. Initially, 32 Squadron Hurricanes were scrambled to protect the convoy but reinforcements were evidently needed, so nine Hurricanes of 111 Squadron scrambled from Croydon. Air Vice Marshal Keith Park also ordered 74 and 56 Squadrons into the air to meet the oncoming raid. On arrival, flying in line abreast, 111 Squadron charged into the swarm of bombers head-on, passed through the formation as it began to scatter and then turned to attack the rearmost aircraft. The bold head-on attack succeeded in diverting the Do 17s from attacking the convoy, but it also claimed the life of twenty-three-year-old Flying Officer Thomas Higgs. Flight Lieutenant 'Tinky' Measures leading 74 Squadron's Blue Section saw Higgs' demise from the cockpit of his Spitfire after he had attacked a Bf 110. An extract from Measures' combat report describes what he witnessed over the Channel:

> I also saw an Me.109 collide with either a Do.17 or an Me.110. The Me.109 was completely destroyed, but the twin-engined machine went down in a slow spiral.

The aircraft that Measures mistakenly took for a Bf 109 was Hurricane (P3671) of 111 Squadron piloted by Higgs. During the head-on attack, Higgs was attacked from above by a Bf 109 of JG 51 and his Hurricane's wing collided with a Dornier 17Z of 3/KG2 at 6,000 feet. Higgs bailed out of his doomed Hurricane but did not survive. The squadron's diary states that Higgs rammed the enemy aircraft, but a deliberate ramming in this instance is unlikely. Asides from the Dornier that was brought down by Higgs' Hurricane, another Do 17 was claimed as destroyed after sustaining general attacks from 111's Hurricanes off Folkestone. 111 Squadron's Commanding Officer, John Thompson, also observed the Hurricane and Dornier collision and reported that he saw both aircraft diving out of control towards the sea. Thompson then spotted a German crew 100 yards to his left taking to their parachutes. He then pressed on to attack another Dornier that had been shot at by other pilots in his squadron. Thompson exhausted the remainder of his .303 ammunition from 250 yards range but observed no results. In his combat report, Thompson considered the Dorniers to be heavily armoured and noted '...that astern attacks with the armament at present in use are quite ineffective'.

Another claim was made by Flying Officer Henry Michael Ferriss, who after attacking a Dornier out to sea, saw a Bf 109 ahead of him diving south of his position. Ferriss followed the fighter down in a dive accumulating a speed of 400 mph and then settled snugly behind the Bf 109, lined it up in his gunsight and opened fire. The Bf 109 bled a trail of white smoke, dropped its left wing and nosedived into the sea. Suddenly, Ferriss felt a splinter in his right leg and whipped his head around to find three Bf 109s attacking from astern. Ferriss soon discovered that his aircraft's left aileron control had been shot away. He turned for the English coast. The Messerschmitts followed his damaged aircraft to within five miles of the coast, but using the Hurricane's superior turning circle Ferriss evaded their attacks and gained vital distance before the enemy aircraft broke off. Ferriss returned to Croydon and despite his exhaustion, climbed into a fresh Hurricane and took-off once again to rejoin his squadron over the Channel. Such was the devotion of Connors' colleagues.

On 16 July, Hitler issued Directive No. 16, which began as follows:

> As England, despite the hopelessness of her military situation, has so far shown herself unwilling to come to any compromise, I have therefore decided to begin preparations for, and if necessary to carry out, an invasion of England. The aim of this operation is to eliminate Great Britain as a base from which the war against Germany can be fought, and, if necessary, the island will be completely occupied.

Nine days after the first official day of the Battle of Britain, Connors led 111 Squadron's B Flight on a patrol off the coast between Folkestone and Dover. At 1240 hours, Green 2 spotted enemy aircraft off the coast and informed Connors over the R/T. Connors then echoed the message to Squadron Leader John Thompson and 111's section leaders and the order to intercept was issued. Connors led Green Section towards the enemy invaders and engaged Bf 109s which were attacking a squadron of Defiants. Connors carried out a beam attack from close range and watched his bullets enter a Bf 109's cockpit and fuselage. The enemy fighter erupted in flames and plunged into the sea. Connors then attacked another enemy fighter that was followed up by Green 2, but he broke off when several Bf 109s engaged him. Using evasive turns, Connors was able to shake off the bandits and return to base. Connors landed his Hurricane at 1330 hours no doubt exhausted by mortal combat. From the engagement, Connors reported seeing ten enemy aircraft dive into the sea, four of them in flames.

Another pilot from B Flight, Acting Pilot Officer Jack Copeman, engaged a Bf 109 once his section leader had broken away. Copeman opened fire from astern and fired 800 rounds into the enemy fighter from a range of 250 yards closing to 150. The Bf 109's wings were smoking from the attack but Copeman sensibly broke away from the engagement as he was approaching the French coast and had lost contact with his section.

The timely arrival of Connors and his comrades was a saving grace for four Defiants of 141 Squadron which had almost been annihilated by German fighters of JG 51. Before the Hurricanes interrupted the free for all attack, five Defiants had been shot down by Bf 109s in swift succession and two others had been hit.

During the afternoon of 25 July, Connors was amongst the heat of the day's conflict near Dover as his combat report details:

Combat Report
25/7/40
I was leading Green section on mid-channel patrol when I sighted M.E. 109's, 2000' above. On approaching they climbed into a layer of cloud 200' above. I led my section down to attack 2 M.E. 109 on the tail of a Spitfire, and forced them to break off, I attacked head on giving a half second burst. He broke away violently to avoid collision, and I noticed his port leg was half way down. I fired three further burst of one second each from astern and noticed pieces falling from the e/a. I broke away as I suspected another M.E. 109 on my tail. The attack was then confirmed by Sgt. Carnall Green 3, who gave him a further burst of one and a half seconds. Black smoke was seen to issue from e/a by Green 2, who considered it unnecessary to attack further as it was obvious e/a was going to crash.

On 31 July, Connors was scrambled on an early morning patrol from Hawkinge to Dungeness where two enemy aircraft were plotted. On arrival, Connors saw Blue Section patrolling at 3,000 feet. He was vectored fifteen miles out to sea where he came across a Ju 88 flying 300 feet above his aircraft. Connors climbed to attack the bomber, which also climbed towards cloud cover 500 feet above. The Ju 88 succeeded in reaching the cloud before Connors could attack and it disappeared from view. Connors continued to chase the bomber for over a minute and finally got within a 300 yard range. Connors lined the Ju 88 up in his gunsight and opened fire, closing in to 100 yards. Connors reported that the '...enemy employed considerable evasive tactics, turning to left and right, and alternatively diving and climbing. I got into point blank range and gave him a one second burst. As no result was apparent, I did two quarter attacks and ended up with a further stern attack and finished my ammunition. Just prior to this I saw large quantities of dense black smoke pouring from both engines.'[16]

Connors broke away from the robust Luftwaffe bomber to watch Green 3 perform a series of stern attacks. When Green 3 had fired everything he had at the enemy aircraft, Green 2 put in a shift until his guns also fell silent. The latter of the three Hurricane pilots followed the Ju 88 down to about 1,000 feet as it dived vertically towards the sea. Due to thick mist, Green 2 lost sight of the bomber but a Group Controller confirmed the enemy aircraft was brought down as RDF plots suddenly ceased.

111 Squadron continued to fly and fight in the defence of British airspace and on 11 August against overwhelming numbers, Connors continued to make his

mark. Whilst on patrol with the squadron at 17,000 feet in the region of Margate, Connors spotted fifteen Bf 109s pass overhead and disappear into the sun. A few moments later he noticed a single Bf 109 climbing up behind Green 3. Connors turned his Hurricane towards the enemy fighter that immediately dived for cloud cover. Connors followed it down through an opening in the clouds and found a destroyer under attack by a Ju 87. Then searching his surroundings, Connors saw a number of Bf 109s below the cloud base and attacked the nearest one. A two second-burst was fired from dead astern and the Bf 109 was hit whereby it crashed into the Channel on fire. Connors then observed a Hurricane spin slowly into the sea. It was Green 3. Connors then attacked a Bf 109 with a short burst and then a Ju 87, but was forced to turn for base as his windscreen was covered in oil from the first Bf 109 he had brought down. The day had proved unkind to 111 Squadron. Pilot Officer Jack Copeman was killed off Margate at 1420 hours, Pilot Officers J. W. McKenzie and R. R. Wilson were missing, and Sergeant H. S. Newton crash-landed on marshes at Boyton near Martlesham Heath after running out of fuel. Sergeant Robert Sim was another young man from 111 Squadron to lose his life when his Hurricane P3942 was shot down into the sea.

15 August 1940 was a fine, warm day with some cloud over the Channel. The pleasant weather was an ideal day for flying which regrettably meant that it was also an opportune day for fighting. The day's battle would rage like never before over Britain and 111 Squadron was in the thick of it. Connors' first claim of the day occurred in the afternoon when he was leading Green Section towards hordes of enemy aircraft. Flying as Green 1, Connors climbed to 12,000 feet where he found a lone Bf 110 3,000 feet above the squadron. Connors climbed to attack the Bf 110, but it turned south-east of his position and in doing so he observed six Bf 109s, 2,000 feet above the Bf 110. Connors altered his course and followed the enemy fighters towards London where he came across a large formation of Dorniers proceeding north. Connors attacked one of the Dorniers south of Kenley, first from the quarter and again from astern, causing damage to its port rudder and tail plane. The Dornier began to lose height but Connors broke away once his ammunition was exhausted.

Later that evening, the squadron was scrambled to Shoreham to intercept a raid heading towards Thorney Island. At 15,000 feet, the squadron intercepted the bombers and Connors let off a short burst at a Ju 88. He was instantly attacked by escorting Bf 109s, so broke off from the engagement. Once clear of the Bf 109s, Connors encountered another Ju 88 of 4/LG 1 that he damaged by shooting pieces off its port engine. Connors also observed smoke emitting from its starboard engine as the bomber began to glide towards the deck. Before Connors fled the scene, he watched the Ju 88 make a forced landing in a cornfield where its crew, Uffz Fritz Dieter and Uffz Otto Rezeppa, waited to surrender to British soldiers. The latter was taken away by stretcher to a hospital

Stanley Connors by David Pritchard.

in Chichester having sustained a bullet wound in his right leg. Uffz Willi Rimek was killed having been shot in the back of the head during the Hurricane attack. Connors later reported that the bomber had been shot down near Earnley, five miles north of Selsey Bill. He claimed one Ju 88 damaged and one Ju 88 shot down.

After 1900 hours, Connors returned to the action, this time over Croydon where he encountered formations of He 111s, Bf 110s and thirty Bf 109s as fighter escort. The following combat report illustrates his part of the fight:

Combat Report
15/8/40
I was leading Green Section when attack started on Croydon aerodrome from a height of 10,000 feet. I fired short bursts at three M.E. 110s but was not able to stay behind enemy for long as others attacked me. I was able to give the third M.E. 110 a very long burst and a great deal of smoke started to come from his starboard motor. Green 2 went in and fired at aircraft which dived straight into the ground, bits falling off it on the way down – enemy aircraft crashed South of Redhill.

By the end of the day, 111 Squadron had lost twenty-three-year-old Flying Officer Basil Fisher – who bailed out of his aircraft when it was shot down in flames over Selsey – but was killed as a result and his Hurricane crashed at Greenwoods Farm. New Zealander Athol McIntyre was wounded and forced to land at Hawkinge after his aircraft was damaged in combat over Thorney Island. Flying Officer Ferriss' aircraft was damaged over the Thames Estuary in combat. Despite a dead engine, he impressively landed safely at Hawkinge. Sergeant William Dymond was also affected in the erratic skies, landing at West Malling after his Hurricane was damaged by Do 17 defensive fire over the Thames Estuary. On this day, Flying Officer Thomas Higgs' body washed ashore at Noordwijk on the Dutch coast following his collision with a Do 17 on 10 July.

The squadron's base, Croydon, had also been attacked when Erprobungsgruppe 210's bombs fell, hitting some of the airfield's buildings and factories outside the perimeter. A Hurricane repair plant was hit as well as an aircraft hangar and armoury. Charles Cooper, one of 111's armourers, was in the building when the alarm sounded out across Croydon. Cooper remembered:

> I went to a gun position, with our Flight Sergeant Clements, which consisted of one Browning .303 machine-gun which we had mounted on a home-made steel tripod. On hearing the sound of the bombs coming down, we dived into a nearby shelter, fortunately in time to miss the bomb which hit the armoury. I think we lost four of our armourers off the squadron, including two friends of mine, Bernard Mills and Alf Couland. The same bomb killed Gangster, Flight Lieutenant Connors's dog.[17]

At 1245 hours the next day, twenty-two-year-old Ferriss, flying Hurricane R4193, was killed in a head-on attack over Marden when his aircraft collided with a Do 17. On the same patrol, Sergeant Ralph Carnall was shot down during combat over Kent. He crashed at Palmers Green Farm, Brenchley, and was badly burned. Carnall would spend a year in hospital under the care of the pioneering plastic surgeon Archie McIndoe. Connors was leading Green Section in Hurricane V7222 during this patrol when he briefly attacked a Do 17 before being repelled by seven Bf 109s. After returning to base with a damaged aircraft, Connors reported shooting at one of the enemy fighters during the melee but was unable to witness results due to being attacked by a Bf 109. Sergeant Thomas Wallace also sustained damage to his Hurricane after duelling with Bf 109s over the Channel.

At lunchtime on 18 August 1940, twelve Hurricanes of 111 Squadron were scrambled to intercept an enemy raid destined for Kenley aerodrome. Connors, flying as 'Waggon' Green 1, led his section towards nine Do 17s of the 9th Staffel of Bomber Geschwader 76. The Dorniers were sighted flying at low-level between forty and fifty feet through a chorus of anti-aircraft guns thudding into the air in rapid succession. Connors, with great boldness and daring, flew his Hurricane through the maelstrom of flak and machine gun fire to reach the bombers. Despite the immediate dangers, Connors opened fire at the bombers but his aircraft, Hurricane R4187, was thumped either by the anti-aircraft fire, the Do 17s return fire or possibly both. Connors broke away from the firestorm and turned northwards for Croydon. Pilot Officer Peter Simpson, flying as Green 2, had followed Connors down towards the Dorniers which he estimated were flying at treetop level. Simpson attacked one of the Do 17s from astern, firing three long bursts until his ammunition boxes were empty. He reported that the enemy's starboard engine was badly hit as smoke and flames poured out into the air. As Simpson broke away from his target, he became exposed to the return fire of another Dornier that clobbered the belly of his Hurricane. Simpson's foot received a splinter causing intense pain and his aileron control runs were severed. He then desperately searched for somewhere to land until he spotted a golf course at Woodcote Park where he made a wheels-up landing. Sergeant Thomas Wallace, flying as Green 3, also followed his section into the inferno and attacked a Do 17 from astern, which he claimed was destroyed. He also fired at a further two Do 17s on their return and observed tracers to enter the German machines, which he judged to be in a spot of bother before he broke away. The intense action between the Hurricanes and Dorniers over Kenley was over in a matter of minutes, but for Connors the engagement would prove final. Almost immediately after Connors had broken away from the action, his Hurricane crashed into the ground at 'The Oaks', Wallington, at 1318 hours. The twenty-eight-year-old fighter pilot, husband and father was killed.

Two privates of the Keston Home Guard witnessed the engagement taking place over Kenley from Layhams Farm. One of the privates, 'Chip' Manchip, recalled his own eyewitness account to author and historian Stephen Bungay:

> I looked south along the valley which runs through below the level of the airfield and saw a twin engine aircraft flying towards us, very, very low, with the wing burning and trailing smoke. Behind it was the unmistakable shape of a Hawker Hurricane and that too appeared to be on fire, but I'm sure he was firing at the bomber in front. I don't know if the Hurricane pilot knew it but behind him was another twin engined aircraft which could have been firing at him.

In light of Manchip's account, it seems that despite a burning Hurricane, Connors exemplified true grit by continuing to fire at the bomber despite his own immediate safety. Down below, Manchip and his colleague Private Walters took cover from the Dorniers until the sky fell silent. When they emerged into the open they could see Connors' burning Hurricane from across the valley but their section leader forbade them from rushing off towards it. The order most likely saved both of them from harm's way as the Hurricane's ammunition began to explode. Almost quarter of an hour later, when the explosions had finally ceased, the two men were ordered to guard the wreckage until further notice, so Manchip and Walters set off towards the crash site. Manchip's account continues:

We made our way down the valley and climbed the high fence surrounding the orchard where the Hurricane had crashed. Making our way up to it we could see that the engine had torn free from the rest of the wreckage, the tail and tail wheel were stuck up in the air at a crazy angle and the aircraft was still burning. The pilot had been thrown clear of the main wreckage. His body had been badly burned but was still recognisable. Some of his uniform was missing but much of his harness was left in place.

There was nothing we could do for him; we didn't even have a coat to drape over his body. We stood guard on the wreck until an RAF corporal in an ambulance was able to drive up through the orchard. He took care of the pilot and we helped to wrap his body in a blanket and lift it on to a stretcher. As we were doing this the corporal asked if I had a knife and on my offering him my small jack knife he worked for a moment close to the pilot's body then asking me to take the knife and to hold something, he then dropped two identity discs into my open hand. They fell face up and I will always remember reading the name of P O Connors SDP.[18]

With twelve confirmed victories to his credit, Connors had demonstrated his superb abilities as an exemplary fighter pilot and his last engagement over Kenley bore further testimony of his resolute determination and fighting spirit in bringing down enemy aircraft in the defence of his homeland. His body was later taken back to his native town of North Berwick in East Lothian.

After his death, Connors was awarded a Bar to the DFC. It was gazetted on 3 September 1940 as follows:

ACTING FLIGHT LIEUTENANT STANLEY DUDLEY PEARCE CONNORS, D.F.C. (since killed in action). This officer has led his flight in all its operations against the enemy with great skill and courage. In a week of almost continuous action he shot down at least four enemy aircraft, bringing his total successes to twelve.

James 'Sandy' Sanders, who joined 111 Squadron in 1936, said that '...'Conny' was a 'very, very nice, gentle sort of person.'[19] He was also an excellent fighter pilot and evidently a formidable adversary of the Luftwaffe.

CHAPTER 10

Henry the Pole: Squadron Leader Henryk Szczesny, VM, DFC, KW

On 5 August 1940, two Polish fighter pilots arrived at Elm Park Station. It was a foggy day and the foreigners found locating Hornchurch aerodrome a difficult task, until finally they found someone to direct them to their new station. Soon enough, Flying Officer Henryk Szczesny and Flight Lieutenant Stanislaw Brzezina arrived at Hornchurch where they were introduced to their new unit: 74 Tiger Squadron. After introductions were made, the two Poles were shown their rooms in the Officers Mess and were given a batman to attend to them. Szczesny was informed that he would be serving with B Flight, commanded by a slender and charming Liverpudlian called John Mungo-Park. The two Poles were quickly welcomed into the squadron but the pronunciation of their surnames 'Brzezina' and 'Szczesny' soon became a bind for the other pilots, so to make things easier the two Poles were nicknamed 'Breezy' and 'Sneezy'. Szczesny would also become known as 'Henry the Pole'.

At thirty-one years of age, Szczesny was much older than most of his colleagues, being born on 27 March 1910 at Ruszkowo, Warsaw. In 1931, Szczesny joined the PAF and attended the Air Force Cadet Officers' School at Deblin. He was commissioned in 1933 and was posted to the 5th Air Regiment before moving to the 3rd Air Force Regiment as a fighter pilot. In 1937, Szczesny's flying capabilities were noticed and was transferred to SPL in Deblin as an instructor.

In September 1939, Szczesny fought against the Luftwaffe in the defence of Poland flying the outdated Polish PZL P.7 and P.11 fighter aircraft. On 14 and 15 September, Szczesny, while defending his airfield, shot down a He III on each day and possibly damaged additional others, but was wounded in the leg by metal fragments and evacuated to Romania. After being treated in a hospital in Bucharest, Szczesny escaped on a Greek ship that carried him to Malta. The fleeing Pole finally made it to France and then to Britain where he would get a second chance to fight against a hated enemy.

In February 1940, Szczesny was stationed at RAF Eastchurch. The following month he was sent to Manston to take charge of a platoon of Polish cadets. In

Henryk Szczesny by David Pritchard.

July, Szczesny was posted to 5 OTU, Aston Down, for a conversion training course and on completion was posted to Hornchurch to join the Tigers. So far, 74 Squadron had been actively involved in the fighting over Dunkirk and now in the defence of Britain. They were a crack fighter unit with a compilation of fine flyers and combatants that included Sailor Malan, Johnny Freeborn and Harbourne Mackay Stephen. Szczesny, although a thoughtful and good humoured man, relished the aggression that stirred within the Tiger squadron as he later recalled:

> After my escape from Military Hospital in Bucharest – leg operation – I arrived by sea via Turkey and Malta to France. A few months later I came to England to join the Royal Air Force and to be trained in OTU – on Hurricanes and Spitfires. In August 1940 I was posted to 74 Squadron 'Tiger' – CO Sailor Malan. My knowledge of England was – nil – but flying spirit and bloodthirsty killing in revenge for Poland – very high indeed – so I could not care about R/T – always being off – only looking in the sky – when airborne for Hitler's Swastikas.[20]

Sailor Malan was given command of the Tigers on 8 August, a popular choice amongst the majority of the squadron who had been under his leadership in the air since May. Malan was an intelligent, natural born leader, a proficient marksman and experienced flyer. In the cockpit of a Spitfire, Sailor was self-assured and devoted to bringing down enemy aircraft which gave the Tigers confidence when following him into battle.

On 11 August, the Germans made the most of the bright morning weather by launching Erprobungsgruppe 210 on a strafing run over and around the Dover area. Several balloons were shot down and some light bombs were dropped, but the main purpose of the attack was to draw British fighters up into the air where they could be shot down. This attack was not intercepted as Keith Park anticipated that the small fighter-bomber raid was a prelude to a heavier attack by bombers. As a precaution, Park ordered fighters from his sector stations into the air as a means of support to the squadrons that were nearing the end of their dawn patrols. Twelve Spitfires of 74 Squadron had already landed and refuelled at Manston, but they were again scrambled to intercept Bf 110s at 0745 hours. By the time the Tigers arrived at their patrol line, the Bf 110s had fled back across the Channel. Malan then led the squadron up towards the sun and once they reached 20,000 feet, he turned the squadron down sun and towards Dover where Bf 109s had been sighted. The Tigers approached the Bf 109s at high speed and watched the Messerschmitts half-roll and dive to evade their attacks. Several Bf 109s were damaged and others claimed as destroyed. 74 Squadron's only loss was Spitfire P9393 flown by Pilot Officer Peter Stevenson who managed to bail out of his damaged aircraft after falling victim to one of the enemy machines. Stevenson spent ninety minutes in the sea in his Mae West life jacket before being fished out by a friendly rescue launch. The squadron would fly another three hard fought patrols throughout the day suffering the losses of Pilot Officers Denis Smith and Don Cobden in the process. Both men were killed on the same engagement when the squadron engaged Bf 110s over convoy 'Booty'.

13 August 1940 was the German's 'Adler Tag' or 'Eagle Day'. It was the day on which the Luftwaffe began its all-out assault against the RAF, attempting to rid British aircraft from the sky and to destroy their bases on the ground in preparation for Hitler's invasion. But by the end of the day, the Luftwaffe lost thirty-nine aircraft to Fighter Command's fifteen.

Early in the morning, Szczesny would score his first victory as a Tiger flying a Spitfire Mk.I. After first light, 74 Squadron received orders to patrol Manston and from there they were vectored towards the first incoming raid of approximately forty enemy aircraft. The squadron sighted the raid off Whitstable flying at 3,000 feet below cloud base in four sections line astern. Malan led the Tigers towards the unescorted bombers which turned out to be Do 17s of KG2 and gave the order to attack. Szczesny found three Do 17s in front of him and readied himself to attack the third of the formation, but the Dornier broke away to the right. Szczesny turned his aircraft to the left and ended up on the tails of the Dorniers. He saw one of them out of formation as it jettisoned several bombs into the sea. Szczesny attacked it from astern, getting in a good burst at close range. The Dornier dived towards the sea, but as it flattened out the bomber burst into

'Henry the Pole'. Note the 'Tiger' Squadron insignia on his Mae West. (*Wojciech Zmyślony*)

flames and crashed into the water. Szczesny reported that it must have crashed in the Thames Estuary, East of the Isle of Sheppey, but he became disorientated and elected to force-land at West Malling with his undercarriage up as it had failed to engage. Szczesny was unharmed and his aircraft, Spitfire K9871, was damaged but repairable. His countryman, Brzezina, was shot down by Do 17 return fire over the Thames Estuary. An explosion in his cockpit forced him to bail out. His Spitfire was lost but he later returned to Hornchurch unhurt.

Szczesny's next claim occurred on 11 September 1940 when 74 Squadron was operating from Duxford with the Big Wing. At this point, the Luftwaffe had turned its attention away from RAF airfields and directed its attacks on British towns and cities, London being the prime target. At 1630 hours, the Big Wing was airborne with orders to intercept a London raid. The Tigers had been instructed to engage the bombers while 19 and 611 squadrons engaged enemy fighters. As expected, a mass of Ju 88s were spotted at 20,000 feet, but as Malan led the squadron towards them they were engaged by Bf 109s which dived down and attacked:

Szczesny's combat report details his part of the fight:

Combat Report

11.9.40

I was Red 3 of No. 74 Squadron which took off at 1534 hrs to intercept hostile raid 44 at 20,000ft over London. I sighted two E/A bombers and delivered astern attack at 100 yds giving 3 – 1 sec bursts, but observed no apparent damage. I then saw two M.E.109's attacking two Spitfires and chased to attack one E/A giving 4 – 1 sec bursts at 200 yds range from astern. E/A dived steeply apparently out of control. I then sighted one lone M.E.110 and chased it, attacked from astern giving 5 – 1 sec bursts from 300 to 150 yds range. E/A dived and crashed to ground in flame. Owing to shortage of ammunition I returned toward base but was unable to obtain homing so returned to home base at 1740 hrs.

By the evening, the Tigers had safely returned to Coltishal with ten probable to their credit and one confirmed Do 17 destroyed that was shot down by Johnny Freeborn and seen to crash-land in a field near Dungeness before bursting into flames. Szczesny and Freeborn became good friends during the Battle of Britain and their parents began to correspond with each other by secret letters until contact from Poland ceased. It was later learned that Szczesny's parents had been gassed by the Nazis.

While at Coltishal in September, the squadron was re-equipped with Spitfire Mk.IIs and Szczesny's comrade, Stanislaw Brzezina, proudly moved on to command the recently formed Polish Squadron, No. 308.

On 5 October, during an afternoon patrol with 74's Green Section, Szczesny encountered a Dornier some thirty miles east of Harwich. As Green 3, Szczesny followed Green Leader and Green 2 in to attack and was the last to make a pass at the bomber. As the bomber dived towards the sea, Szczesny followed it down and opened fire at 250 yards range. Ever determined to seal the enemy's demise, the Pole continued to sink his ammunition into the Dornier's engines and fuselage until all of his bullets had been used up. Szczesny pulled up and away from the pursuit at 1,000 feet and lost sight of the flaming Dornier in the haze.

Ten days later the squadron left Coltishal behind and moved to Biggin Hill. When 74's Spitfires landed at Biggin for the first time the aerodrome was peppered with bomb craters. It was plain to see that the Tigers had arrived at the heart of the front line. Being stationed at 'Biggin on the bump' as it was known at the time was a testing period for the pilots and ground crews. Szczesny's friend and colleague Freeborn later remarked:

I never liked Biggin Hill, even to this day. I remember one awful day in particular. We just had a runway built and we were sitting in the dispersal hut talking and suddenly there's a whoosh! An 88 came right over at low level and

(L to R): Roger Boulding, Henryk Szczesny, Johnny Freeborn and H. M. Stephen during the Battle of Britain. (*74 Squadron Association*)

dropped bombs all the way down the new runway and disappeared. There was no way we could catch it. I thought he was a brave guy for doing that, but it was a loathsome time.

With the Battle of Britain being decisively over on 31 October 1940, the RAF had emerged victorious in stopping German boots and machine tracks imprinting the King's green pastures. But the air war with the Luftwaffe would undoubtedly continue. Despite the hardships Szczesny had endured, he continued to channel his aggression in the air with thoughts of Poland ever present in his mind. As well as being a battle-hardened fighter pilot, Szczesny was also a husband and father to two sons. Thoughts of his family unquestionably kept his morale high and spurred his deep desire to see Allied victory over the Nazi regime.

At around midday on 1 December, the squadron received orders to patrol Canterbury at 27,000 feet. Once in the vicinity of Dover, Szczesny, flying as Red 3, sighted nine Bf 109s circling at 32,000 feet. As the Spitfires climbed, a Bf 109 dived towards them like an eagle to its prey. Malan, flying as Red 1, turned to attack the enemy fighter and Szczesny followed suit. Due to his position, Szczesny was first to close in on the Bf 109. He began his attack from a range of 250 yards closing to 150 yards, squeezing the gun button for four seconds. He scored direct hits which were confirmed by white smoke that omitted from the Bf 109's starboard side. The enemy aircraft was seen to plunge into the sea ten miles north east of Dover. Szczesny then made way for home.

The following day, 74 Squadron joined 66 Squadron on a patrol over Maidstone at 15,000 feet. Enemy aircraft were soon reported so the squadrons climbed towards the Dover/Dungeness area. Malan led the Tigers up to 26,000 feet and turned south where they spotted Bf 109s flying to the north. The burly South African led the Tigers into action and Malan swiftly latched on to one of the Messerschmitt's, catching it turning south-east into the sun. From behind, Malan fired a succession of deadly bursts which contributed to its destruction. A long final burst from close range put the enemy aircraft into a gentle dive, bleeding oil into the air and all over Malan's windscreen. Sailor saw the German's canopy break free to the right before the Bf 109 submissively turned onto its back and went down into the sea upside down.

Szczesny, flying as Red 3 to Malan, also attacked a Bf 109 as his combat report explains:

Combat Report
2nd. December, 1940.
I was No. 3 of Red Section flying about 26,000 feet over Dungeness – Dover area. I saw to my right and below about 7 Me.109's returning home. Squadron Leader dived on to them and I followed him and saw behind the formation one Me.109. I dived on to him and opened fire at a range of 400 yards closing to 50 yards, head on. The enemy aircraft dived steeply and I saw black smoke coming from his fuselage after three bursts. I broke off to another attack and lost sight of the first enemy aircraft.

When Szczesny returned to base he claimed one Bf 109 as damaged.

Szczesny was always proud to have been a Tiger and to have fought on the wingtips of the skilled leader, Sailor Malan. The Pole believed that Malan was the greatest pilot and fighter ace of the Second World War. Reflecting upon his great friend and leader in later years, Szczesny remarked:

I am very proud I was his Number Two on many, many occasions and defending his tail, because he told me to do and to follow blindly his orders. He was shooting down Jerries and I was very close to him – defending his tail. Order is the Order.

Once he told me by radio to put Pipsqueak (Identification signal) on. Of course, I could not hear him; my radio was always (switched) off – my English was practically nil, so why bother to listen to it? So, poor Operation Room at Biggin Hill, intercepted our 74 Squadron as bandits 12 plus, with Hurricane squadron over Kent. Then Sailor show me two fingers up, so I did also show him my two fingers up. He laughed and laughed – after pancake. (Order to land, and having landed)

He also introduced me to Winston Churchill, when he was passing to Chartwell, near Westerham, Kent. At Biggin Hill, at dispersal of B Flight, when we came to readiness. He smiled and shook hands with me and asked in his usual deep voice, "Henry the Pole, how many today?" I replied shyly, "Only one Me109, Sir." He said, "Good, many more to come."[21]

On 5 December, Szczesny would claim his final victory with 74 Squadron while over the Channel on a late afternoon patrol. Flying as Red 3, Szczesny engaged a Bf 109 by climbing and delivering an attack from astern, closing to a range of 300 yards. The Pole snapped off a two-second burst at the enemy fighter and then watched it turn steeply to the right issuing white smoke. Szczesny continued to engage, this time firing for five seconds. The Bf 109 did a half-roll as Szczesny closed in to a 150 yards range. The enemy aircraft was puffing black smoke when Szczesny delivered a final blow: the Bf 109 dived and spun into the sea. Szczesny reported that the German pilot did not bail out of his aircraft that crashed eight to ten miles south-east of Dover. In total, Szczesny had fired 600 rounds, claiming the Messerschmitt as destroyed.

On 12 December, the Tigers reluctantly said farewell to Szczesny when he was posted to Bob Stanford-Tuck's 257 Squadron at North Weald. A week later, Szczesny was again posted, this time to 302 (Polish) Squadron's Operations Room.

On 1 February 1941, Szczesny was awarded a Krzyż Walecznych (Cross of Valour) and Bar. Before the end of the month, Szczesny returned to operations when he joined 317 (Polish) Squadron at its formation at Acklington. It was here that Szczesny acquired his third wartime nickname: Hesio. On 1 April, Szczesny was awarded two more Bars to the KW. At its formation, 317 Squadron was initially equipped with Hurricane Mk.I's, but these were later replaced by Mk.IIs in July. On 10 February, Szczesny, now a Flight Lieutenant, would clash with the enemy just after lunchtime when the squadron was flying a Blenheim escort mission.

Flying as Black 1 somewhere between 500-2,000 feet near Port Le Havre, Szczesny heard Brzeski, flying as Black 2, yell 'Bandit above on your port!' over the R/T. Szczesny looked up and saw a Bf 109 in front attacking one of their Hurricanes from out of the sun. Szczesny went after the Bf 109 using full throttle from astern and slightly to starboard. He opened fire from 200 yards giving the enemy three short bursts. Brzeski then overtook Szczesny and positioned himself to the right. Both Hurricanes fired at the Bf 109, Szczesny giving it three more bursts at close range. The enemy aircraft was crippled by the attack. It emitted white smoke and rose steeply before stalling and diving down into the sea at 1248 hours. A second Bf 109 dived towards Szczesny but for some reason it broke away and disappeared towards the sun. An extract from Szczesny's combat report adds further details to this encounter:

No deflection used. Range 40-250 yards. No. Of rounds 130 from each gun. Then I saw 2 E/A above and on beam which circled between ourselves and the sun. The weather was very hazy and foggy. Visibility at sea level was at 1-2 miles. Higher up visibility was good. Camouflage dark yellow noses Green and brown top, pale blue under sides of wings and fuselage, small black cross clearly visible.

On 14 July, 317 Squadron took-off from base at 1555 hours to patrol a convoy ten miles south of Worms Head. The convoy was comprised of twenty-three ships and two destroyers. At 1600 hours, Szczesny reported to the Operations Room that he was now in position to patrol. Szczesny sighted friendly aircraft on two occasions before reaching the convoy. Once over the convoy, the squadron flew at a height between 600-1,000 feet. Then at 1629 hours, while banking left, Szczesny caught sight of a single aircraft flying southwards towards the centre of the convoy about 500 yards away. Szczesny radioed his number 2. 'Goody Blue Two, Bogey in sight, give full boost and follow me.' Szczesny and his number 2, Brzeski, raced towards the enemy aircraft that turned out to be a Ju 88. When the Junkers was approximately 200 yards away from the first line of ships, bombs began to fall into the sea. By this time, Szczesny was positioned on the beam of the enemy aircraft and opened fire. A couple of two-second bursts and he then saw bombs exploding about 100 yards from one of the ships below. Using full boost, Szczesny latched on to the tail of the enemy that hopped over one of the ships. Szczesny held his fire for fear of damaging the ship, but when the bomber rose over the next ship in line, he unleashed his guns. From a range of 150 to 50 yards, Szczesny fired a series of short and long bursts, directing his sights on both engines and cockpit. The Ju 88 reduced its speed and Szczesny saw sporadic trails of white smoke issuing from its engines. Brzeski was next to attack the bomber, firing all of his ammunition into the German machine that lost both height and speed. Szczesny flew above and on the port side of the enemy aircraft and reported it to the Operations Room. The Ju 88 eventually descended towards the sea and its tail touched the water. The bomber then stalled and crashed into the sea. Szczesny reported that the aircraft sank quickly seventeen miles south of Tenby and amid the wreckage and patches of oil there was at least one survivor. Szczesny reported the engagement and circled the wreckage for ten minutes before returning to base.

On 18 August 1941, Szczesny took command of the squadron and the following month was awarded a Srebrny Krzyż Virtuti Militari (Silver Cross of Virtuti Militari) on 15 September. On 30 October, Szczesny was awarded a DFC, which like all non-Commonwealth pilots was not gazetted. The predominant reason for this was as a means of protection for a pilot's family should they be living in an enemy occupied country. In early March 1942, Szczesny was posted to HQ 10 Group as a Polish Liaison Officer, moving to HQ 12 Group in May and on 28 December 1942, was appointed Squadron Leader Flying of the Polish Wing at Northolt.

(L to R): Tadeusz Baranowski, Henryk Szczesny, Unknown. (*Wojciech Zmyślony*)

On 4 April 1943, Szczesny was leading the wing when it was escorting seventy B-17 Flying Fortresses which had been detailed to attack the Renault factory near Paris. On their return, they were attacked by Focke-Wulf Fw 190 fighters and Szczesny shot one down. But the skirmish would prove unfavourable for the Pole. Flying a 315 Squadron Spitfire Mk.IX, Szczesny was forced to evacuate his aircraft when his wing collided with a Fw 190. Szczesny was captured by a German patrol that was awaiting his landing. The fighting was over for 'Henry the Pole' who ended up as a POW in Stalag Luft III.

In late April 1945, Szczesny was freed and returned to Britain. He performed various duties in the RAF until 27 March 1965 when he retired as a Flight Lieutenant, retaining the rank of Squadron Leader.

During the late 1970s, Szczesny was to be found living in Ireland with his family, running a sweet shop that he had set up in Monasterevin, then called Drodheda Street. It was around this time that a young man called Martin Doheney met Szczesny and struck up a lasting friendship, as Doheney recalls:

When I got to know Mr Szczesny I was working in the town in Willoughbys Hardware, which is still running today. Mr Szczesny had an account there and on many occasions I had served him and got him to sign for his goods. He was an absolute perfect gentleman in every way and always impeccably turned out and always had time for everybody. He was very well liked by all the locals and the teenagers who used to frequent his shop, opposite the school, St Paul's Secondary School, Monasterevin. Nobody in the town of Monasterevin had any idea who this quiet war hero was. I had the fortune of meeting Mr Szczesny in my teenage years and becoming a very close friend. He was, I have to say, one of the main people who influenced me in my life in a very positive way. I joined the Orange Free State Army and when I signed up, I told Mr Szczesny. He shook my hand and said "I have got something for you." He went into a room and came out again and he handed me a luminous set of rosary beads which are quite rare. He said the idea was that if you dropped them in the dark they would shine up. I believe that's what they were designed to do. He also said that these rosary beads were carried in battle while he was flying Spitfires and Hurricanes. He having said this meant a lot to me. I still have these rosary beads in my possession and cherish them as a gift that someone would only get once in a lifetime.

Szczesny, the good humoured, gallant Pole, who had fought so bravely against the Luftwaffe during the Second World War died on 25 July 1996 in London. The passion that Szczesny and his Polish countrymen possessed during the Battle of Britain was later praised by Dowding who wrote that, '...had it not been for the magnificent material contributed by the Polish squadrons and their unsurpassed gallantry I hesitate to say that the outcome of the battle would have been the same.'

Additional notes
74 Squadron
'I Fear No Man'

Squadron Leader Stanislaw Brzezina, VM, KM, was born on 5 March 1904 at Lodz in Poland. In 1925, he joined the Air Force Officers' School at Grudziadz and was commissioned as an observer in 1927. After completing his flying training, Brzezina developed into a chief instructor and in 1939, flew in the defence of Deblin. When Poland was defeated, Brzezina reached France via Romania and from there went to Britain in early 1940. He was commissioned in the RAFVR in February and posted to No. 5 OTU at Aston Down. He then joined 74 Squadron at Hornchurch where he fought in the Battle of Britain. On 25 September 1940, he was posted to take joint command of 308 (Polish) Squadron at its formation at Baginton. In June 1941, he took command of 317 Squadron at Colerne and destroyed a Bf 109 on 9 June. In August 1941, he was appointed Wing Leader of No. 2 Polish Wing at Exeter. Sadly, Brzezina was killed in a flying accident on 13 February 1946 en route to England from Germany in a Douglas Dakota. He is buried in St Mary Cray Cemetery, Orpington, Kent.

Group Captain Adolph Gysbert Malan, DSO and Bar, DFC and Bar, was born in Wellington, South Africa, on 3 October 1910. He served as a cadet on the training ship *General Botha* and joined the Union Castle Steamship Line in 1927. His seafaring background earned him the name 'Sailor' among his pilot colleagues when Malan joined the RAF after applying for a short service commission in 1935. On 20 December 1936, Malan joined 74 Squadron at Hornchurch. During the evacuation of Dunkirk, Malan led 74 Squadron on many occasions and continued to do so throughout the Battle of Britain. He took command of the squadron on 8 August 1940. Throughout his career, Malan was reputed as an excellent leader, fighter tactician and marksman. By the end of the war, Malan was credited with an impressive twenty-seven and seven shared enemy aircraft destroyed, two and one shared unconfirmed destroyed, three probable and sixteen damaged. After a successful career in the RAF serving in many different appointments, Malan decided to retire from the RAF in 1946. He returned to South Africa with his family where he died on 17 September 1963. Besides his British awards, Malan also received the Belgium Croix de Guerre, the French Legion d'Honneur and the Czech Military Cross.

Wing Commander John Connell Freeborn, DFC and Bar, was born on 1 December 1919 in Middleton, near Leeds. He joined the RAF on a short service commission in January 1938 and began flying solo after just four hours and twenty minutes flying training. In October 1938, Freeborn joined 74 Squadron at Hornchurch and fought with this unit over Dunkirk. Throughout the Battle of Britain, Freeborn flew more operations hours than any other RAF pilot. In December 1942, he served as a flight commander with 602 Squadron and the following year took command of 118 Squadron where he remained until June 1944 when he was appointed Wing Commander Flying of 286 Wing in Italy. Freeborn retired from the RAF in 1946 with eleven and two shared enemy aircraft destroyed to his credit, but with additional others that were unconfirmed, probable and damaged to his tally. Freeborn died on 28 August 2010 at the age of ninety.

Budge: Flight Lieutenant Alan Stuart Harker, DFM

Alan Stuart Harker was born on 16 July 1916 in Bolton, Lancashire. In October 1937, he joined the RAFVR to begin his flying training and on 12 March 1938, Harker went solo for the first time in a Tiger Moth. After war was declared, Harker was posted to No. 10 Flying Training School at Turnhill, Shropshire, on 12 September 1939. At Turnhill, Harker flew twin-engine Avro Ansons until 5 November when he was posted to Leconfield to join the newly reformed 234 Squadron. Fellow Squadron colleague Flight Lieutenant Keith Lawrence remembers the following of Harker and those early days with 234:

> Alan Harker was known to us all as 'Budge'. He was a founder member of No. 234 Squadron in November 1939, and until July 1940 we trained as a Squadron on first, Bristol Blenheims and then on Spitfires. Budge was good company and well liked, but it was not until August and September, when the German attacks intensified that he proved himself to be a really good fighter pilot and, unusually, was awarded a Distinguished Flying Medal during the Battle.

Harker would indeed prove to be a prolific fighter pilot during the summer of 1940, his first claim occurring on 8 August 1940. On this day in the south, the Luftwaffe had concentrated an intense attack on a convoy codenamed 'Peewit', which was subsequently left devastated by persistent dive-bombing attacks. This heavy onslaught marked the first day of sustained clashes between the RAF and the Luftwaffe over home waters, which resulted in frenzied engagements over the Channel. 234 Squadron was not involved in the heat of the battle, but the day would not pass without incident. On a morning routine patrol, Sergeant Jozef Szlagowski flying Spitfire N3278 force-landed at Pensilva after running out of fuel. Szlagowski was unhurt but his aircraft was written off.

Then later at 1410 hours, the squadron's Red Section was ordered to intercept a bandit at 'Angels 10' over Falmouth. On this patrol, Harker was flying as

Above: Alan Harker sitting in Spitfire 'AZ-N' in 1940. (*Randell family*)

Left: Sergeant Alan Harker. (*Randell family*)

'Cressy' Red 2 in Spitfire N3242. Once in the correct location, Harker and his section noticed anti-aircraft fire 3,000 feet below and approximately 500 yards behind the bandit, which indicated the enemy's position to the three Spitfire pilots. Harker heard 'Morty' Mortimer-Rose, flying as Red 3, inform Red 1 of the bandit's position. Harker and Mortimer-Rose then climbed to intercept the enemy aircraft, losing sight of Red Leader in the process. The bandit was a Ju 88 and it appeared to be unaware of the danger creeping towards it from above. Harker watched the Ju 88 turn about 190 degrees and then dive steeply into the cloud cover below. Harker, positioned 800 yards to the Ju 88's port, followed the enemy down but soon lost sight of it. In a great hurry, Harker climbed above the cloud and then re-entered it after finding a clear space that allowed him to get a good view of the enemy aircraft that was just 400 yards ahead of him. Harker observed the Ju 88 making way for another cloud bank, so seizing the moment he opened fire, giving the enemy a three-second burst from astern. Harker experienced return fire from the Ju 88's rear gunner, but he continued to fire short bursts from the port quarter as the bomber ducked in and out of cloud. Mortimer-Rose also attacked the Ju 88 from astern, but because of the cloud cover Harker eventually lost sight of it and rejoined Red 1. After searching the sky for a further thirty minutes without any luck, Red Section was ordered back to base. Harker had fired a total of 240 rounds from each gun.

On 10 August, Harker was so exhausted that he landed Spitfire P9468 at St Eval with its undercarriage retracted. Two Poles from the squadron, Sergeants Josef Szlagowski and Zygmunt Klein, nicknamed 'Slug' and 'Zig' by their colleagues, found Harker unhurt and promptly took him to the pub. As a consequence, Harker got alcoholic poisoning and for the next two days slept on a stretcher in dispersal to recover. For his troubles, Harker was confined to camp by Squadron Leader Dickie Barnett and reprimanded for his carelessness in causing damage to his aircraft. But such incidents were not unheard of during 1940. The constant state of readiness mixed with combat fatigue and sleep deprivation all played their part in the loss of aircraft and pilots.

On the Luftwaffe's 'Eagle Day', Barnett relinquished his command of 234 Squadron, much to the delight of Harker as he frankly remarked:

> He was a hopeless CO. He did all his flying in the hanger. I was delighted to see the back of him.[22]

It was around this time that the boys began to turn to an Australian in the squadron for leadership, Pat Hughes. With a natural quality to boost morale, Hughes won instant respect from the airmen for his willingness to guide the squadron into battle.

On 14 August, the squadron moved from St Eval to Middle Wallop in Hampshire. On arrival, the pilots landed on a grass airfield away from the hangers, which proved to be very fortunate as the hangers were hit by bombs thirty minutes later. It was a rude introduction to life in the thick of the battle as Wing Commander Bob Doe explained:

> We were a very green bunch of pilots, still believing in the laid down fighter tactics and without a C.O. or one Flight- Commander, who seemed to have disappeared when we were ordered to Middle Wallop. My feelings at the time were very mixed. I had no idea what to expect in combat and I knew that I was not a good aerobatic pilot... The following day, the whole squadron was scrambled south of Swanage, against some two hundred plus bandits, and in retrospect, we did everything wrong that we could possibly do wrong. We formed into four sections of three, in tight formation, with sections astern, so that the only person not concentrating on formatting was the C.O. We flew to the same height that we had been told the enemy were flying and proceeded to patrol up and down the sun. After one such turn, we found there were only nine of us left. The rear section had disappeared. Subsequently, one pilot was found dead and the other two turned up in France under unusual circumstances. The remaining nine of us ploughed on until, to our astonishment, we were in the middle of the German raid without quite knowing how we had got there.[23]

The patrol that Doe refers to took place on the evening of the 15 August when at 1700 hours British radar detected a large build-up of aircraft across the Channel. Five minutes later, all available Spitfires of 234 Squadron were scrambled from their new station at Middle Wallop with orders to patrol the Swanage area at 15,000 feet.

It was during this patrol that New Zealander Cecil Hight was shot down in Spitfire R6988. Hight was seen to bail out of his aircraft, but his parachute failed to open. It is possible that Hight was already dead as he fell to earth due to the bullet wounds he had sustained. His body fell into the grounds of 'Hambleton' on Leven Avenue in Bournemouth where a local vicar found him and offered a prayer where the dead pilot lay. Pilot Officer Vincent Parker, an Australian from Durham, was also shot down by enemy fighters near the Isle of Wight and bailed out at only 900 feet. Parker fell into 'the drink' but was rescued four hours later by the Germans and taken to Cherbourg. Pilot Officer Richard Hardy was also bounced by the enemy and was forced to land his damaged Spitfire (N3277) at Cherbourg East, home to JG53. Both Hardy and his Spitfire were captured by the Germans.

After a shambolic engagement with the enemy, the boys of 234 Squadron began to amend their tactics as Bob Doe described:

> A week or so after that there was a sergeant pilot called Budge Harker; he and I had been talking about the war and we worked out that if he and I flew

234 Squadron at Leconfield, 1940. (*L to R*) Cecil Hight, Hugh Sharpley, Alan Harker, Morty Mortimer-Rose, Pat Gordon and Dick Hardy. (*Randell family*)

abreast of each other a couple of hundred yards apart, well, between 100 and 200 yards, I would see and try to protect him from behind and he would see and try to protect me from behind. One time he saved my life because of it he called me up and said "Look out; there's someone on your tail." So I just went into a tight turn and Budge came across and shot him. It worked.[24]

On 18 August, 234 Squadron took part in the 'Hardest Day' of the Battle of Britain when its Spitfires engaged enemy fighters that were shooting up barrage balloons over Portsmouth and the surrounding area. Doe opened fire on a Bf 109 that immediately nosed down and bolted in the direction of France. Doe followed the Bf 109 down to 100 feet and let off a few snap shots of ammunition. The Bf 109's speed decreased and its canopy suddenly flew off. Doe took his Spitfire to the right of the Bf 109 and flew alongside it and for the first time saw a German looking back at him. The chase had left Doe's Spitfire low on fuel, so broke away from the Bf 109 and wished the German 'bonne chance' as there was a lot of water to cross between him and France.

Alan Harker in the cockpit of Spitfire 'Nellore', a city in south-east India that had raised a financial contribution towards the cost of this aircraft. Note the eight swastikas representing Harker's victories. (*Randell family*)

It was a strange but chivalrous encounter for Doe who felt that he could not shoot the German pilot down in cold blood, despite the fact that the German pilot could well be back tomorrow to shoot him down. Perhaps it would not matter, for on his return to the coast, Doe looked back and saw the crippled German fighter splash into the sea. Later, Doe learned that the pilot was Hauptmann Rolf Pingel, Commander of 1/JG26. Pingel, an experienced fighter who had served in the Condor Legion, managed to land his aircraft in the water and was later rescued by a German rescue service. Pingel would return to the Battle shooting Zulu Lewis down the following month.

Harker also staked his claim during this engagement with the Bf 109s whilst flying as Red 3 in A Flight. Harker spotted three Bf 109s in line astern formation and decided to attack the rearmost fighter. The enemy aircraft broke away and dived to sea level as Harker closed in firing two bursts. Fuel streamed out from the Bf 109's wings and covered Harker's screen, forcing him to break away. But it was too late for the Bf 109 that burst into flames before hitting the sea. Harker then saw another Bf 109 circling the wreck, so he turned his Spitfire and chased the Bf 109 twelve to fifteen miles south of the Isle of Wight where he shot it down in flames.

Harker was undoubtedly developing into a fine fighter pilot and his successes continued into September 1940 when the Battle for Britain continued to flourish. 4 September was a fine, warm day with some haze in the Channel and the Straits. Shortly after 1300 hours, 234 Squadron received the order to patrol Tangmere at 15,000 feet. When the Spitfires neared their destination, fifty Bf 110s were sighted approaching the coast with a further fifteen Bf 110s circling south of Haslemere in a loose formation. The latter formation of Bf 110s was thought to be a decoy and the main formation also comprised of two vics of Do 17s. 234's Blue Section was slightly ahead of the squadron, so Flight Lieutenant Pat Hughes (Blue 1) led a head-on attack on the fifteen Bf 110s which formed into a defensive circle. Hughes fired two short bursts at the leading aircraft and then pulled up and fired one short burst into the enemy's fuselage. His target caught fire and crashed just north of Brighton. Hughes then attacked another Bf 110 from dead astern and after two quick bursts it rolled on its back and dived to the ground and blew up ten miles north-east of Tangmere. Hughes then came under attack by three Bf 110s whilst another circled around behind him. He fired a succession of three short bursts to break up the defensive circle and one of the twin-engine heavy fighters dived away. Hughes pursued the fleeing aircraft and emptied the remainder of his ammunition into its engines which appeared to catch fire. Hughes saw a Hurricane fire a short burst at the same aircraft before the enemy eventually hit the water.

Meanwhile, Red, Green and Yellow sections were heavily engaged with the main formation including Harker who was flying as Yellow 3 in Spitfire R6957. Harker attacked a formation of twenty Bf 110s and after a short burst one of the heavy fighters dropped out of the formation and crashed. Doe also claimed a Bf 110 that he attacked with a full deflection burst of two seconds. The stricken aircraft crashed into the sea. Doe engaged another Bf 110 from the circle using the same tactics and achieved the same result. Then before returning home he saw a Bf 110 chased by a Hurricane, and so fired a full deflection shot from 200 yards and watched it crash into the sea. Other members of the squadron also made claims making it a very successful patrol for 234 Squadron. The only cause for concern was for Pilot Officer Zbigniew Olenski whose engine was hit during the attack. Despite having his windscreen covered in oil, he returned to Middle Wallop unhurt and his Spitfire was repaired.

The following day, the squadron was to patrol Kenley at 20,000 feet. Anti-aircraft fire bursting into the sky in the direction of Gravesend caused the squadron to investigate. On approach, Blue Section was suddenly attacked out of the sun by three Bf 109s. Flight Lieutenant Pat Hughes turned to attack and saw a dozen Bf 109s in two vics of five and seven approaching from the Thames Estuary. Hughes turned and dived and was soon joined by two Hurricanes. A dogfight ensued over Eastchurch with Hughes firing a deflection shot at a Bf 109 that blew up and spun towards the earth. Pilot Officers Janusz Zurakowski and Michael Boddington, flying in Hughes' section, also claimed a Bf 109 each. Doe was another member of the squadron to claim a Bf 109 that he saw attempting to attack a formation of Hurricanes. He was then attacked by six Bf 109s which he evaded by half-rolling his Spitfire down and around the edges of barrage balloons at high speed. He then went through a pall of smoke above burning oil tanks at low level and at full boost. Finally, weaving up a river he made it back to Kenley where he landed.

During a morning patrol on 6 September, Harker was back in the thick of it. Flying as Red 3, he dived on a formation of six Bf 109s and opened fire at 100 yards range with a three-second burst that struck one of the Messerschmitt's wing roots and sent it downwards. To regain height, Harker pulled back on the stick and took his Spitfire up to 25,000 feet before levelling out. Continuing to search his surroundings, Harker noticed a formation of fifteen Bf 109s underneath his position, so again Harker pounced on his prey from above with blazing guns. After two bursts, one of the enemy fighters turned onto its back streaming fuel. Harker estimated that the Bf 109 stayed inverted for ten seconds flying straight before bursting into flames. This early patrol had been a lively one for Harker, but the action was to continue when he spotted a Spitfire being pursued by a Bf 109. Harker intervened with a short burst and watched the enemy aircraft half-roll and duck out of the fight. He then attacked another Bf 109 and managed to blow a large piece of its tail off before his ammunition ran dry. With nothing else left to do, Harker returned to base claiming two Bf 109s destroyed and two damaged. Squadron Leader O'Brien confirmed Harker's destroyed Bf 109s and also claimed two for himself.

Doe, flying as Red 2, was also involved in the scrap when he sighted two Bf 109s on Red 1's tail. He fired at the rearmost fighter and shot it down north of Dover where it crashed on land. Doe then took his aircraft up to 5,000 feet and sighted a formation of Do 17s in sections of three, five, three and three astern. Doe attacked each enemy aircraft of the rear section from above and behind and observed his tracer bullets penetrate the bombers and put a stop to the return fire. Out of ammunition, Doe broke away from the formation by diving and returning back to base using full boost. He later wrote in his log book:

...the 109 never saw what hit him, neither did the three Dornier rear gunners. Things got a bit hot after that & I had to land quickly.

The next day, Harker would continue to add to his tally during an evening patrol with the squadron over London. One of the requirements asked of pilots when completing a combat report was to include the number of enemy aircraft they were up against. In respect of this particular patrol Harker simply wrote 'Too many to count'.

Below is the combat report Harker wrote after returning from this patrol:

Combat Patrol

7.9.40

As Red 3 I attacked a ME.109 over South London, I gave him a 3 second burst and his port wing caught fire. He then went into a vertical dive. I saw what I thought was a ME.109 attack a Spitfire, as I was about to attack, I recognised it as a Hurricane. He was definitely firing. He broke away and disappeared before I could see his markings. I proceeded to Dover and attacked the outside starboard 109 of a formation of seven. Red 2 joined me and also attacked. I gave the 109 a 3 second burst and he dived into the sea. This was seen by Red 2. The remaining 6 ME.109's turned to attack and I broke away. I circled round over the Coast and saw a 109 about to attack Red 2. I attacked from beam and the 109 turned and did a head on attack on me. I dived and his fire went over my head. I lost him for a few minutes and then saw him again on Red 2's tail. I again attacked from the beam and my bullets hit him behind the cockpit. He broke away and I lost him again.

For this date, Harker wrote in his logbook that he attacked a '...German-flown Hurricane on P/O Doe's tail.' It is tempting to assume that the Hurricane probably mistook Doe's Spitfire for a Bf 109, but it is impossible to clarify. Such misidentification was often a by-product of high-speed aerial dogfighting.

Red 2 as mentioned in Harker's combat report was Doe flying Spitfire X4036 whose combat report for this action also tells of the scrap:

Combat Report

7.9.40

I was Red 2. When the attack started I climbed up to 30,000 ft. and saw in front about 150 bombers well below me. I dived onto the rear one and gave the port engine a 1 sec. burst. It burst into flames. 3 ME.109's attacked me so I dived past the bomber and pulled up underneath it and gave the starboard engine 1 sec. burst. This also caught fire. 1 person baled out of the rear cockpit. The same 3 Me.109's were still firing at me so I went down over Dover and there met Red 3 and with him attacked 7 109's in line abreast. I hit the right hand one but did not have time to notice results as 1 ME.109 with white spinner and engine was on my tail. N.B. I saw Red 3 shoot one down.

Alan Harker, fifth from the left. (*Randell family*)

Alongside its victories, the squadron also suffered two great losses during this patrol when Flight Lieutenant Pat Hughes, DFC, and Squadron Leader Joseph O'Brien, DFC, were killed in action. As usual, Hughes was leading from the front with Blue Section in Spitfire X4009 when he dived towards the bombers. He went after a straggler with Blue 2 following and carried out a quarter attack on the enemy aircraft that blew up with such force that it wrecked his Spitfire. Hughes had no time to bail out of his aircraft and was seen by Blue 2 spinning wildly towards the deck. It was a tremendous loss for the squadron who had relied upon Hughes' terrific morale and leadership qualities during the Battle of Britain, but especially for Kathleen, his wife of only five weeks. At twenty-eight years of age, O'Brien was shot down over St Mary Cray and his Spitfire P9466 crashed near Biggin Hill.

Fours day later, the squadron returned to St Eval to recuperate. Harker recalled the squadron's plight:

Only about three pilots and five aircraft from our original squadron had survived to return to St Eval. I was quite twitchy myself by then.[25]

On 22 September, the Luftwaffe sent a Ju 88 from 4.(F)/121 on a weather reconnaissance flight but was interrupted from its course after Harker, flying as Red 1, sighted the aircraft at 25,000 feet heading west of his position. He climbed into the sun and chased the Junkers that used evasive tactics to no avail. Harker opened fire from approximately 150-100 yards. Before turning for home, Harker saw the Ju 88 crash in flames twenty-five miles south-east of Lands End. Flying Officer Terence Kane, flying as Red 2, also reported attacking the Ju 88 after Harker had broken away. On 2 March 2011, Wing Commander Kane recalled the following about the engagement:

> I am afraid I hardly knew Sergeant Harker although if I remember correctly he was quite well thought of in the Squadron. As a recent arrival on the Squadron I was appointed to fly No. 2 to Harker and I wasn't given the best aircraft in the Squadron! So he outpaced me in pursuit of the Ju 88, got close enough to fire at him and damaged it – smoke was coming from it when Harker, either because he was out of ammunition or short of fuel, turned for home. I continued on, got close enough and fired and hit the 88 which immediately steepened its dive and went into the sea. I then returned to base. We were each awarded a half share in the victory.

Although Harker believed the German crew did not survive the attack, they were picked up by a trawler after spending several hours in a dinghy.

Harker would find another Ju 88 in his sights on 15 October. When on patrol as Red 1, he sighted anti-aircraft fire over Falmouth at 15,000 feet. He then noticed a smoke trail heading north so followed it and found a Ju 88 ten miles away. While Harker prepared to attack the bomber, it dived and continued to evade the stalking Spitfire. Just before his target entered cloud cover, Harker pressed his gun button for two seconds but observed no results. He then caught the bomber in a gentle dive and made a full beam attack from the sun firing a long burst. Pieces of glass blew out from the shattered Junkers cockpit and the bomber turned on its side. Harker followed up the attack but his ammunition gave out so climbed towards the sun. At 18,000 feet, Harker last saw the Junkers diving towards cloud. Although claiming the Ju 88 as damaged, Harker mentioned in his combat report that Red 2, who was below his position at the time, saw the enemy crash into the sea with a burning engine.

On 22 October 1940, Harker was awarded the DFM. The following was written about him for this achievement:

Alan Harker in dress uniform.
(*Randell family*)

This airman displays great courage and determination in facing the enemy and
has personally destroyed not less than 5 enemy aircraft. His cool determination
is an example to his colleagues.

During the Battle of Britain, Harker had proven himself to be a proficient
fighter pilot and a tremendous asset to 234 Squadron. In March 1941, he was
commissioned. Although 'Budge' Harker undoubtedly had many more
experiences as a Spitfire pilot than is recorded, the latest report available details
a patrol that occurred on 3 March 1941 when Harker was leading 234 Squadron's
Yellow Section on an afternoon patrol.

At 1330 hours, Harker took-off with Sergeant Martin flying as Yellow 2. When
the section neared Lyme Regis at 25,000 feet, Martin caught sight of a smoke
trail ten miles south-west of their position going north. Harker led the section
to intercept a Bf 110 that began to dive to the east as the Spitfires approached.
Harker led the attack by diving after it and at 12,000 feet, he unleashed his guns,
firing a short deflection burst from above at a distance of 150 yards. Harker then
broke off to reposition himself for a second attack. On approach, he observed the
heavy fighter diving, so he went after it in a screaming dive, his Spitfire almost

bunting and buckling under the tremendous speed. Harker managed to let off another burst at the Bf 110 before it escaped into cloud at 9,000 feet. At this point Harker blacked out but recovered. He had fired 422 rounds from his guns. Martin, who had followed Harker down closely, was next in line to attack the enemy aircraft. He fired a short burst from astern but lost the Bf 110 to cloud. Yellow 3 did not open fire during the attack. Yellow Section landed at Warmwell at 1425 hours. The Intelligence combat report from Warmwell concluded:

> Because of the quickness of the engagement and the violent evasive action of the e/a it was impossible to observe any result of the fire and the engagement must therefore be regarded as inconclusive.
>
> The camouflage was earth brown and green. The r/t was good except for the fact that Yellow 1's r/t went u/s immediately after he had fired.

On 1 April 1941, Warmwell came under a low-level attack by Luftwaffe fighters and Harker was wounded in the arm. Laurie Hooper-Smith recalled the incident:

> The only time I came close to death was on 1 April 1941. No flying in the morning, early lunch in the Sergeants' mess; we were having soup. I bent down to pick up my napkin and there was a rattle of machine gun fire. I got up, the pilot on my right had a hole in his head. 'Budge' Harker (another Battle of Britain veteran) on my left had a bullet in his forearm, the bullet had come through his shoulder. In front of me was a bullet hole; I never found the bullet. I took Harker to hospital.[26]

On 19 May 1941, Harker experienced another close shave with his wingman in Green Section, Sergeant Parker, when they were jumped by two Bf 109s on investigating a ship that was on fire during a convoy patrol south-west of Portland. After Harker's aircraft was hit by the fighters, he weaved his way towards Portland with a cockpit full of smoke. Riding his luck, Harker turned in on one of the Messerschmitt's as it passed him but his guns failed to work, so the Bf 109 was spared. Suffocated by smoke and with the glycol temperature rising, Harker decided to switch off his engine and glide towards the coast evading further attacks. With a sigh of relief, he landed in a field near Tatton House, Langton Herring. As for Parker, he destroyed a fighter before being forced to bail out into the sea where he was rescued.

A few months later, Harker was posted to No. 53 Operation Training Unit, Llandow, to instruct. On 4 August 1941, he was made a Flight Lieutenant. In June 1942, Harker's marksmanship abilities were utilised when he was sent to CGS at Sutton Bridge as a gunnery instructor. In December 1943, Harker moved to Llanbedr to form a Rocket Projectile School and on 5 July 1944, was posted to Italy where he served as an MT Officer with a mobile radar unit.

Harker continued his service as an Operations Officer with the US Liberator and Polish supply-dropping squadrons. In November 1945, Harker was released from the RAF and returned to civilian life as a heating engineer. He died on 6 August 1996.

Additional Notes
234 Squadron
'Ignem mortemque despuimus'

Flight Lieutenant Paterson Clarence Hughes, DFC, was born in Cooma, New South Wales, on 19 September 1917. He joined the RAAF as a Cadet at Point Cook in 1936 and sailed for the UK on 9 January 1937. He was commissioned in the RAF and joined 64 Squadron at Martlesham Heath before joining 234 Squadron at Leconfield on 30 October 1939. On 7 September 1940, Hughes was killed when attacking a Do 17. His Spitfire was seen spinning out of control with part of its wing missing. Some accounts of the incident suggest that it was a collision that caused his death, but the official report states that after attacking the Do 17 from close range, a large section of the bomber broke off and hit Hughes' aircraft. His Spitfire X4009 crashed at Darks Farm, Bessels Green. Hughes' body was found with an unopened parachute in the garden of a house in the nearby village of Sundridge. With fourteen confirmed victories, Hughes was the highest scoring Australian pilot of the Battle of Britain. He is buried in St James' churchyard, Sutton, Hull.

Squadron Leader Joseph Somerton O'Brien, DFC, was the son of a major killed in France in 1917. After spending several years at sea in the Merchant Navy, O'Brien joined the RAF on a short service commission in March 1934. On the night of 18/19 June 1940, when serving with 23 Squadron, O'Brien was the captain of a Blenheim that shared in the destruction of a He 111 near Cambridge. His aircraft was shot down by return fire that killed his observer, Pilot Officer King-Clark, and his gunner, Corporal Little. O'Brien managed to bail out. In July 1940, O'Brien was posted to 92 Squadron and the following month given command of 234 Squadron at St Eval. On 3 September, O'Brien was presented with his DFC by the King at Buckingham Palace. On 6 September, he destroyed two Bf 109s and was shot down and killed on 7 September. O'Brien is buried in St Mary Cray Cemetery, Orpington, Kent.

Wing Commander Robert Francis Thomas Doe, DSO, DFC and Bar, was born in Reigate, Surrey, on 10 March 1920. In March 1938, he joined the RAFVR and was commissioned in January 1939. After completing his training, Doe was posted to 234 Squadron on 6 November 1939 until 27 September 1940 when he joined 238 Squadron at Middle Wallop. Throughout the Battle of Britain, Doe proved to be an exceptional fighter pilot claiming fourteen enemy aircraft destroyed with several others shared and damaged. During a night patrol on 3 January 1941, Doe's Hurricane's engine stopped, forcing him to land on a snow-covered airfield. Upon a difficult landing, his harness broke and he was thrown forwards. The impact broke his arm and his face smashed into the reflector sight. He was treated at Park Prewitt Hospital where he was cared for by a distinguished plastic surgeon called Harold Gillies. Doe retired from the RAF on 1 April 1966 as a Wing Commander. Doe settled in Tunbridge Wells where he died on 21 February 2010, aged eighty-nine.

Beaky: Squadron Leader Pecival Harold Beake, DFC, AE

Percival Harold Beake was born of Bristolian parents in Montreal, Canada, on 17 March 1917. In 1925, the Beake family returned to Bristol where Percy was educated at Victoria Park School and Bristol Grammar School. In April 1939, Percy Beake joined the RAF Volunteer Reserve flying Tiger Moths from Whitchurch airfield at evenings and weekends. By the time war was declared on 3 September 1939, Beake had chalked up almost fifty hours flying Tiger Moths. He was then posted to Hastings where an Initial Training Wing was being formed to support fitness and ground studies. It was not until the end of March 1940 that flying training became available at Redhill Elementary Flying Training School where Beake received instruction on Miles Magisters. Training continued through intermediate and advanced stages and culminated at Hawarden where Beake flew a Spitfire for the first time in September 1940. With the Battle of Britain already underway and with nineteen hours of Spitfire flying under his belt, Beake was posted to 64 Squadron at Leconfield on 22 September. Beake recalls the circumstances of his new squadron at that time:

> The Squadron was being rested from combat activity in the south and there was only a skeleton of experienced pilots there, the numbers being made up of newly trained pilots like myself. The main activities there were Squadron exercises interspersed with convoy protection patrols and the odd scramble to intercept and identify aircraft which normally turned out to be friendly.

On 15 October, Beake moved to Coltishall, near Norwich, where activities were much the same but with more frequent scrambles. At the end of the month, the Battle for Britain had been decided and on 10 November, 64 Squadron was posted to Hornchurch to commence operations across the Channel. For good measure, Beake carried his black leather bound New Testament Bible in his breast pocket on every operational trip.

Percy Beake keeping fit at No. 3
ITW, 1939. (*Percy Beake*)

We were returning from an operational patrol and a sweep of the French coast
when, having crossed the English coastline, our Flight Commander called us
in to tight formation. We were heading for our temporary base at Rochford
and seemed to be making very slow progress – maybe a strong headwind was
responsible. We had been airborne for longer than usual and I was getting
concerned about my fuel usage especially since I was flying a brand new Spitfire
Mk.II which had been allocated to me on the previous day. The Spitfire's fuel
gauge is not a continuously registering one – a button had to be pressed to
activate it. To take your eyes off an aircraft on which you are closely formatting
to do this is not to be recommended! However my concern was such that I
pulled away from my leader to allow me safely to do this and was horrified
to see that my tank was almost empty. I radioed my Flight Commander and
said I was breaking away because of fuel shortage and immediately started
looking for an aerodrome on which I could land. I couldn't see one so I turned
my attention to finding a large, level field on which I could try a wheels down
landing. However, all such fields had obstructions placed across them to
prevent enemy gliders from landing. My engine cut and I had to make a quick
decision. My concern for my new Spitfire transcended that of my own safety. I

spotted a reasonably sized field and decided to try a wheels down landing even though it was surrounded by trees. On my gliding approach I could see that these trees were much taller than I had expected so as I crossed them I put my aircraft into a sideslip to get down quickly but was just a little late in levelling out with the result that my port wheel hit the ground first and buckled under the aircraft. This made the port wing dig into the ground; it was torn off and caused the plane to roll over so that I was now skidding along on my head and thought that I would surely collide with something that would end my life. However, the plane eventually stopped and I was surprised to be still alive. I was of course virtually helpless – just able to release my safety straps and free myself from my seat. The cockpit of a Spitfire is quite small and there was little room to move. My great fear was that a fire might break out and I would be completely trapped. However, as time went by and there was no sound or smell of a fire (no doubt because I had run out of petrol) I began to relax. I had landed in Shepherdswell in Kent and an army camp was not far away so it was not long before I heard voices and the sound of running feet. When the runners were at the aircraft I shouted out to tell them that I was still alive and not badly injured. I persuaded someone to put their hand into the cockpit and feel around for the lever on the flap cover which we climbed into and got out of the airplane. Seeing the position, some soldiers went around to the tip of the inverted starboard wing and weighed down on it to roll the fuselage over to give more room for me to be pulled out by my extended arm. Apart from my skinned forehead, I felt reasonably well but I was concussed and was sent to the RAF Officer's Hospital in Torquay. I returned to the Squadron on 27 March – an absence of over seven weeks. Two other members of the Squadron had to force land because of fuel shortage but they were much more sensible than me in that they both landed with their wheels retracted, were unhurt and their aircraft were repairable. Whereas I had landed with my wheels down, thus risking my life in the hope of saving my new Spitfire, but which ended in my plane being a complete write-off and hospitalisation for myself.

In May 1941, 64 Squadron was posted to Turnhouse in Scotland. On 26 June, Beake found himself sitting next to his Commanding Officer at a squadron dinner in Edinburgh. During their conversation, Beake remarked that he was disappointed at the lack of combat opportunity and asked when the squadron would be returning to the south. The CO was unable to say but the following morning Beake was summoned to his office. Beake picks up the story:

No doubt mindful of the fact that alcohol had been flowing liberally the night before, he said "Beaky, do you remember what you said to me last night?" I replied "Yes, sir I do." "Well then..." he said, "...where would you like to go – Biggin Hill or Manston?" "Where would I be likely to see most action?" I asked.

Percy and Evelyn Beake on their wedding day at Victoria Park Baptist Church, 1 October 1941. (*Percy Beake*)

He said "Biggin Hill I would think." And with that I was unceremoniously dispatched to No. 92 Squadron at Biggin Hill. I had made it known to the CO that I was planning to get married on 1 October and I would like to know if I could be sure of getting some leave at that time. It was the end of June and the CO said "October is a long way off and a lot can happen between now and then. You had better ask nearer the time." That reply was almost prophetic for on 8 July, while returning from a Circus operation covering 4 Stirlings bombing Lens we were attacked by ME 109F's just off the French coast at Gravelines. My radiator was hit and glycol came streaming out. I knew that my engine would soon overheat and I had to make quick decisions. Should I turn back and force land in France risking becoming a POW or should I try and get as far away from the French coast as possible, bale out hoping that my parachute would open, that I would land safely in the water, that my dinghy would work and that I would be picked up by a rescue launch or friendly ship. I opted for the latter of course. We had been flying at 15,000 feet so I knew that I would have some gliding distance after my engine had seized. I headed north, switched my R/T to the Mayday channel and radioed every now and then to give our rescue services good chances to get an accurate fix on my position. My first CO had said the best way of baling out of a Spitfire was to put the side flap down, sit in the opening and somersault backwards out of the plane. When my engine seized I knew that my time in the plane was limited so I radioed 'MAYDAY' very frequently. When I decided it was time to get out I opened my hood, removed my helmet to save R/T cords, oxygen tubes etc., becoming entangled around my neck, lowered my flap, released seat belts and tried to stand on my seat and then sit in the opening. Whether or not my legs were a bit rubbery, I don't know, but try as I may I just could not get to stand on my seat. Becoming apprehensive because of the altitude I was losing I decided to invert the plane and fall out. I rolled the plane over but still I didn't fall out of the small cockpit which seemed to hang on to my parachute and dinghy pack strapped to my backside. I kicked wildly with my rubbery legs and eventually I fell out. Almost immediately I felt a jerk and feared that my chute may have got caught on the plane but looking up there was the comforting sight of my parachute billowing out. Because of my rapid loss of altitude I think I must have taken hold of my rip cord handle when I turned my plane upside down and the jerk when I finally kicked myself free made me pull it without any memory of so doing. Even so I just had time to blow up my Mae West before I was about to enter the water. I released my parachute straps at about the right time and the chute itself floated away from me just leaving my dingy pack tethered to my waist by a material strap. Supported by my Mae West I pulled the dinghy pack towards me, opened it and carefully unfolded the dingy before slowly opening the compressed air bottle to inflate it. Once in the dinghy I fitted the hand pump and used it to make the dingy even

Rescued from 'the drink' by the Launch HSL 146 on 8 July 1941. (*Percy Beake*)

more buoyant. I had shipped quite a lot of water whilst initially inflating it and then climbing in so I set about scooping this water out with my hands. The first dinghies were very basic the only equipment being the hand pump and some wooden pegs for plugging any leaks. Anyway I decided to keep active to avoid hypothermia. Our operation had been an early morning show on a lovely July day and the sun was rising east. I therefore turned the dingy away from the sun and, heading westward, I started paddling with my hands. There was, of course, water all around with no markers to enable one to estimate progress or otherwise. Anyway before too long I heard the sound of Merlin engines and saw two Spitfires searching the area. There was quite a mist over the water and I knew it would be very difficult for the pilots to see me. If only I had some flares to reveal myself! The Spitfires soon withdrew without having spotted me so I paddled on and soon I became aware of two white dots in the western distance. Watching these dots closely I eventually saw there were two white trails advancing eastwards whilst tracking south to north and then north to south. I concluded that these were two high speed rescue launches carrying out a search of the area mapped by my Mayday calls. One launch was searching an area well south of my position, probably pinpointed during my early calls, but it was clear that there was no chance of rescue by that one. The other one looked far more promising and my hopes rose as it was getting closer. I waved frantically as it tacked its way towards me and my relief can be imagined when my waves were acknowledged and the launch headed straight towards me. I was hauled up on to the launch HSL 146 and taken below where my sodden clothes were removed and replaced with some blue overalls and a grey blanket to wrap around me and, most welcome, a hot drink. In the meantime the Captain was racing towards Dover some eighteen miles away where an ambulance was waiting which on my arrival took me to Hawkinge. There I had a meal in the Officer's Mess and was then driven to Biggin Hill. I was given a week's leave before returning to operational flying.

On 27 September 1941, the Biggin Hill Wing, led by Wing Commander Jamie Rankin, DFC and Bar, took-off at 1332 hours with orders to act as high cover for twelve Blenheims on a raid to Mazingarbe, France. Thirty-five Spitfire Mk.Vs, one being flown by Beake, rendezvoused with the Blenheims over Manston at around 1416 hours and made way for France through the haze. When the formation was over Mardyck, it was stalked by a large formation of Bf 109s, which appeared to approach the Wing in a wide turn, attempting to get behind it to attack. Owing to this predicament, the Wing split up and various dogfights ensued. 92 Squadron's Yellow Section had already turned back for Biggin Hill before crossing the French coast due to radio trouble, but the remaining sections pressed on, positioned on the port side of the Wing. After the Bf 109s were sighted, 609 Squadron Spitfires dived towards some Bf 109s and 92 Squadron followed them except for Red Section who stayed with the Blenheims as escort cover as they continued on to the target area. A few miles short of the target, 92 Squadron's Red Section engaged with Bf 109s right down to 1,500 feet and out to the coast between Calais and Gris Nez. Heavy anti-aircraft fire was endured, even as far as five miles out to sea. Beake, flying as Red 3, damaged a Bf 109 as his combat report explains:

Combat Report
27-9-41
I was flying No3 in Red Section returning from a Circus Operation directed against Mazingarbe. Shortly before reaching the target area our section had gone down on some Huns and, chasing them to a low altitude, had lost contact with the main gaggle. We turned and headed in the appropriate direction of Calais being menaced by odd pairs and sections of 109s most of the way. Soon after leaving St. Omer on our starboard side, Red A (Sgt Johnston) warned the section of Huns coming down behind. I turned sharply to port and missed all but a couple of bullets fired by a 109(F) which broke away upwards and to port. Pulling the nose of my aircraft up I managed to get him in my sights and opened fire with cannons. The enemy aircraft, obviously hit, staggered and lost height. Again I got him in my sights and, although he was now about 350 yards away and turning gently. Dropping away, he headed inland for St. Omer and lost further interest in us. Red 4 confirms that hits were registered.

In total, Beake had fired eight rounds from his cannons and twenty bullets from his machine guns claiming the Bf 109 as damaged.

Towards the end of the year, a change was on the horizon for Beake, as he explains:

> Whilst at Biggin Hill with No. 92 Squadron I damaged two ME 109s. The Squadron moved to Digby in Lincolnshire in October and at the year end I was declared "tour expired" having done 200 hours operational flying. This usually meant six months "rest" instructing at an Operational Training Unit. I asked the CO if some non operational job other than instructing could be found for me and in January 1942 I was posted to No. 601 Squadron which was equipped with Airacobras which never flew on operations. However, in March the Squadron was re-equipped with Spitfires and posted to Malta. The CO said to me "Beaky, you are still tour expired and I can't take you to Malta so you will have to go to an OTU as an instructor." So on 1 April I was posted to No. 58 OTU at Grangemouth. I carried on instructing there until mid July when I was put in charge of advanced training at their base at Balado Bridge where I stayed until the end of 1942 when I was posted to Harrowbeer in Devon to command "A" Flight of a new Squadron (No. 193) being formed to fly Typhoons. With No. 193 we did a lot of defensive patrols and a lot of dive bombing especially of V1 sites under construction.

On 8 February 1944, four Typhoons of 193 Squadron and four Typhoons of 266 Squadron took-off from Harrowbeer at 1140 hours and flew in two sections of fours line abreast with Wing Commander Baker in the lead. Once the eight Typhoons had crossed the French coast, they began a low-level sweep in the vicinity of Rennes but saw no activity. Baker continued to lead the Typhoons at low-level in the direction of Gael. On approach, two Fw 190s were seen, one was preparing to land and the other was going around the circuit again after apparently overshooting on its initial approach to land. Baker ordered one section to cover the other section of Typhoons that were ordered to attack the enemy aircraft. As one of the Fw 190s was touching down, Baker opened fire from 600 yards and continued his attack until passing over his target having observed many hits. The Wing Commander's number two then followed up the attack by firing two bursts at the aircraft. The Fw 190 was left burning fiercely on the ground with its pilot slumped in the cockpit. Meanwhile, Beake attacked the remaining Fw 190 from dead astern, opening fire at 400 yards and closing to 200 yards. After an accurate burst when strikes were observed all over the enemy aircraft, it caught fire, rolled on to its back and dived to the ground where it exploded just off the perimeter track. With both enemy aircraft out of action, the Typhoon formation continued its sweep in the direction of St Brieuc, but were deterred by a heavy rainstorm. The Typhoons climbed above the storm and passed over Lannion before finally returning to base at 1341 hours.

On 29 May 1944, when returning from a visit to Thorney Island in a Typhoon, Beake's engine failed, but fortunately managed to make a successful wheels down landing at Chilbolton Airfield that earned him a green endorsement in his pilot's log book.

The following day, Beake was posted to command 164 Squadron that was equipped with rocket-firing Typhoons at Thorney Island. It was here that Beake began to prepare for a most momentous day.

> During preparations for D-Day our job was to knock out the German Radar Stations which were heavily defended and fatalities were expected to be high. On D-Day itself my Squadron was attacked over France by FW 190s and I shot one down. Being equipped with rockets our main tasks were ground attacks on all kinds of targets.

On 17 July 1944, the squadron operated from newly constructed airfields in Normandy.

On 25 July, Beake was awarded a DFC. The citation reads as follows:

> This officer has commanded the squadron for several months and during the period has led his formation on many sorties against heavily defended targets with good results. He is a first class leader whose great skill, thoroughness and untiring efforts have contributed materially to the successes obtained. Squadron Leader Beake has destroyed two enemy aircraft.

On 27 June 1944, 164 Squadron received orders to attack a German Army HQ in a chateau at St Sauveur Endelin. Beake recalls this memorable operation that he feared would be his last:

> At the time I was OC 164 Squadron stationed at Hurn and living under canvas. We had been released at midday but, not withstanding that, a signal was brought to me in the Mess tent where we were having lunch requiring four aircraft to be sent to Needs Oar Point to take part in an evening operation.
>
> I was disappointed and annoyed for, having released the Squadron, I now had to countermand that for some. I summoned up my two Flight Commanders, told them the situation and said that I wanted two pilots from each flight – volunteers preferably but, if necessary, they would have to detail participants.
>
> Although only a section of four was required, I made it a practice to take a 'spare' with me part way so that if anyone had to drop out with engine trouble, or for any other reason, in the early stages of the mission I had an airborne

replacement I could call on. If I considered everything was going well I would waggle my wings and the 'spare' would return to base.

Having eaten I gathered the four nominated pilots together and went to dispersal where we donned our flying kits and took off for the 15 minute flight to Needs Oar Point. On the way there my airscrew developed an oil leak. On landing I was warmly greeted by members of No. 193 Squadron with whom I had been a Flight Commander from its formation to three months previously. One pilot climbed up to me in the cockpit and, seeing the oil on the windscreen, said "I certainly wouldn't take this kite if I were you, boss."

We were eventually called in to the briefing where we were told what the target was and shown a map of its location. The general plan was for eight 'Bombphoons' (Typhoon Bombers) in two sections of four to go in first at low level, I had to follow with my rocket firing section and the last sixteen would dive bomb from high level to finish off the attack. The low level bombs would be fitted with 11 second delay fuses. Coming from the briefing all of my thoughts were negative and for some reason my confidence was at an all time low.

I was still suffering annoyance at having been called on when already released, my aircraft had developed an oil leak and could be termed unserviceable, our target would undoubtedly be very heavily defended, I had neither the surprise element of the low level bombers to protect me nor the partial protection of height afforded to the dive bombers. In fact I was beginning to think this may well be my last 'op'.

We took off as planned and these thoughts were running through my mind as I watched the specks of oil gathering on my windscreen. How much oil was I losing and how much could I afford to lose – thinking of the 90 of miles of water we had to cross before reaching France and of the fading daylight that would not leave a lot of time for rescue if I had to bale out. These thoughts nagged at me and I was sorely tempted to call in my 'spare' and turn back to safety. But no! If I did that and any of my four failed to return I would find it very hard to live with myself, so I waggled my wings and my 'spare' broke away to return to base.

We arrived in the target area at 9.30 pm. The first section of four low level bombers was led by W/Co Baldwin and the second section in had to allow at least an 11 second gap before going in to avoid being blown up by the bombs of the first section. Similarly I had to allow a like interval after the second section had gone in before diving down and releasing my rockets. When the first bombs were dropped flak erupted from all around with tracer shells showing up starkly in the gathering dusk. By the time it was safe for me to lead my section down into that inferno without getting hit - but we did and there were no casualties. The chateau and all that was within it was completely destroyed. We withdrew over the Cherbourg Peninsula and made our way across the Channel to our respective bases.

After this worrying ordeal, Beake was relieved that the operation had been hugely successful without sustaining any casualties. He had also demonstrated admirable courage in staying with his faulty Typhoon code-lettered 'FJ- L' when it could have been totally understandable to have used his 'spare' instead.

In August, Beake was removed from operations and returned to the UK to command the Typhoon Squadron at the Fighter Leader's School where courses were run for leaders and potential leaders in the latest tactics from the front line.

> Between courses we tested all kinds of new equipment and gave demonstrations of things such as the Napalm bomb.

The napalm bomb project caused some apprehension among those selected to test it as the bomb was a tank filled with highly inflammable petroleum jelly fitted with a detonator that caused the tank to explode on impact with the ground. This gave a pilot real cause for concern as if his engine was to cut-out upon take-off, the bombs – one fitted under each wing – would explode when the aircraft hit the deck. To test this deadly weapon, the Typhoons would come in at about fifty feet and the bombs dropped 100 yards short of their target. The Typhoons would then turn away sharply to avoid the curtain of fire that would engulf dug-in positions and bunkers with horrifying effect. When the Central Fighter Establishment was set up, the Fighter Leader's School became part of it. Beake remained with the school until the end of 1945 when he was demobilised. His pre-war service in the RAFVR coupled with his wartime service entitled him to the Air Efficiency Medal, which he was deservedly awarded.

SECTION FOUR
'BENNY', ONE OF 'THE MANY'

CHAPTER 13

Squadron Leader Laurence 'Benny' Goodman

Laurence 'Benny' Goodman was born on 24 September 1920 in London. As a young man, he was educated at boarding school that in those days had an Officers Training Corps. At the age of seven, Benny held a rifle for the first time that he remembers being extremely heavy for a young boy to wield. Nevertheless, military service was in his blood. In the First World War, Goodman's father had fought on the Eastern Front against the Bulgars and Turks – a most determined enemy that Goodman recalls his father speaking of with utmost respect due to their fighting spirit.

The Second World War broke out when Benny Goodman was eighteen years of age and decided that he ought '... to do something. It didn't hit me until I was walking along the street one day and I saw army lorry loads of chaps in uniform being taken and I thought "Yes, it's about time I did something." Plus, a great friend of mine was in the Territorial Army and he got snapped up immediately and I thought "What am I doing here?" I decided that I wanted to volunteer for aircrew.' After passing an aircrew medical in Euston, Goodman now faced with much trepidation additional tests which could either send him on his way towards RAF service or ruin his dreams of flying.

On completion of one such test, Goodman remembers confidently walking up to a sergeant and saying 'Oh Serg, that was good! When am I going to get in?' To which the sergeant, slightly bemused, retorted 'Are you talking to me, lad?' A little surprised, Goodman sheepishly replied that he was. 'You're an AC2 now. You will stand to attention when you talk to me and call me Sergeant.' The sergeant then informed Goodman that he would go home and perhaps receive a letter within the next week or two. Six long weeks passed before Goodman was called up for basic training. Goodman's life was soon engrossed with boot polishing, 'square-bashing', rifle drills and parades until he was posted to RAF Abingdon. Abingdon was an Operational Training Unit equipped with Armstrong Whitworth Whitleys. It seemed an exciting place to be for Goodman until a few days later when he and his fellow pupils were told that the RAF had scrapped all 'straight through courses' and that they now had to wait for a posting to an Initial Training Wing before flying. Utterly hacked off by this revelation it seemed that things could not get much worse for the young, green hopefuls, but it did. Goodman was soon told that during the interim period he was to serve as a ground gunner at Abingdon. The appointment would prove rather depressing as Benny recalls:

> Ground Gunners lived in a Nissan hut and we had a Fairey Battle packing case as our sort of recreation and instruction room. We had no blankets, no sheets, no pillows and we dug our own latrines because we lived out on the airfield in a gun emplacement. We didn't go in for meals we used hayboxes, which was "supposed" to keep our meals warm.

As part of the airfield's defence, Goodman and his colleagues were instructed to march around the perimeter at night and dawn to challenge those they came into contact with to make sure they were friend or foe. A new password was issued each day at the airfield, but when the ground gunners challenged most people they were given a four letter word followed by 'off'. Goodman remembers that in general they were challenging aircraft engineers and such like who were busy serving the bombers. It was their duty to do so and if they failed to challenge and were caught by an officer, they would be in serious trouble. With many cold nights out on the airfield, Goodman felt absolutely fed up by his plight. However, after six months, he was finally posted to ITW and '...there they almost treated us like human beings. We spent six very good and informative weeks. We learned about navigation, meteorology, airmanship, and all the things we needed to know for a chance of survival.'

The course ended with examinations which caused a great deal of anxiety for Goodman and the other chaps desperately trying to pass out for aircrew. Fortunately, Goodman passed with flying colours and was soon posted.

> I was bursting, totally overjoyed and I was sent to No. 7 Elementary Flying Training School at Peterborough and from there I was regrettably sent on an instructors course. Now, in the air force during the war, if you were a flying instructor that had done no operations, people didn't think very much of you. I wasn't very happy on the course and I said so. I just didn't feel part of it.

Despite feeling out of place as a flying instructor, Goodman was pleased about the new living conditions at Woodley, Reading. There were better sleeping arrangements, food and someone to clean his boots for a change. But this was not enough to keep Goodman's spirits up. After explaining his feelings once again he was posted to Clyffe, Pyparde, that was a holding unit. After a brief spell at Clyffe, Goodman then found himself at Gourock Docks near Glasgow where he boarded a Norwegian cattle boat bound for Canada.

'Black sections' after an early morning sortie. *(L to R)* Alan Edwards, Benny Goodman, Tommy Turnball and Ian Pondsford. (*Benny Goodman*)

We slept anywhere we could. We got bread but when you opened it there were creepy crawlies everywhere. I'm sure the crew were not any happier than we were, because overcrowding wasn't the word. It was really bad.

When the cattle boat finally made it across the Atlantic without being torpedoed, Goodman thought they had had their luck for the year. Although aware of the likely dangers, Goodman and many of his comrades did not take it as seriously as one might suppose. 'We were too young to be really scared. The thought of death didn't really enter our minds, if you can understand that now living in normal life.' After reaching Canada, Goodman then travelled to RAF Carberry, Manitoba, where he trained on Avro Ansons. Previously, Goodman had flown in an Anson while he was stationed at Abingdon. Benny recalls the flight:

This is how lax it was back in those days: I stood up between the two pilots! Nobody said you should be strapped in for takeoff and landing. There were seats at the back but I didn't want to go and sit back there. Can you imagine these days with all the health and safety? So I stood up, we took off and landed, I loved it and couldn't wait! So at Carberry, I thought because I had been in one once I could fly it, but I soon learnt better I assure you.

After completing the course at Carberry, Goodman was then posted to Kingston, Ontario, to instruct Acting Leading Naval Airmen. The appointment came as quite a surprise for Goodman because naval tactics were totally different from those used by the RAF.

> I was showing and teaching the naval airmen things that I would be court-martialled for in the RAF! Jinking after takeoff, dive bombing and suchlike, but they enjoyed it and I did too. I learnt a lot about flying and instructing.

When his time came to an end at Kingston, a good and trusted friend advised Goodman of a leaving ritual, saying 'When you leave, everybody does it, we expect you after take-off to beat the hell out of the control tower.'

> And like an idiot I believed him! I'd known him for six months or whatever it was when training on Ansons. He was a good mate of mine and I didn't think he'd really drop me in it. So I believed every word and I said "Okay". By that time I was pretty experienced in a Harvard and so I did beat the hell out of the tower. When I got back and landed the Wing Commander was out on the tarmac with two Pilot Officers and I thought "That's funny."

As Goodman climbed out of his aircraft, he heard the Wing Commander shout 'Goodman! You're under close arrest.' I thought 'What have I done?' and he said 'The air traffic controller said he could see the time by your watch.' I said 'Well, I don't think that is quite true sir!' 'Anyhow,' he said, 'you're under arrest and you're going before the Station Commander.' I thought, 'Oh, what a way to end life.' Goodman was confined to his room where a friend of his was supposed to be on guard outside. Benny continues the story:

> I asked if I could see the medical officer because I had very bad hay fever and it occurred to me, with very slender hope, that I might say that I had very bad hay fever after I took off and I was sneezing and sneezing and couldn't control the aircraft. The senior medical officer, who happened to be a Canadian, said "Well, I'll go this far Goodman, I will attest to the fact that you do get very bad hay fever and I treat you for it, but I certainly won't attest to the fact that you lost complete control of the aircraft because of it. The danger you risk is that you could be taken of flying permanently because of hay fever."

Seemingly stuck between a rock and a hard place, Goodman decided it was a risk he had to take. In the presence of the Station Commander and Wing Commander, the medical officer stuck to his word and said that Goodman's hay fever could be controlled with medication, which he apparently had not taken before flying. The Station Commander dismissed the case as a medical issue and thanks to the medical officer Goodman lived to fly another day.

The return journey back to the UK from Canada did not go as smoothly as Goodman had hoped. For a start, he was on a New Zealand passenger boat full of women and children, which seemed most strange given the circumstances in Britain. During the trip home, a US destroyer that was sailing nearby was torpedoed by a U-boat. The attack also affected the passenger boat, flooding part of it. Goodman's trunk, which contained his flying logbook, was lost. Fortunately, it was returned to him six months later with water damage, but Goodman was utterly relieved to get it back.

Soon after, Goodman was posted to an Operational Training Unit at Silverstone. It was there that he flew Wellingtons. After this, Goodman went to a Heavy Conversion Bomber Unit at Swinderby to fly Stirlings. Goodman was then posted to a Lancaster bomber conversion unit and once completed found himself on the brink of operations. An interview followed that caused Goodman's crew a great deal of curiosity as they wondered what trouble he had got himself into this time. However, when Goodman returned from the interview he announced that they were being posted to 617 Squadron. A few laughs and comments of disbelief ensued until the crew realised that their captain was being serious. It was a time of great excitement for Goodman and his crew for 617 Squadron was infamous for its exploits during the Second World War, the Dambusters raid being one of them. Goodman's great friend, Tony Iveson, who was a Battle of Britain pilot was also awed being a part of 617 Squadron. Iveson recalls:

> Being in 617 I did feel part of an elite force. There was that extraordinary reputation, and the fact that we had this big bomb, 12,000lbs, when the original specification for the Lancaster laid down a limit of 8,000lbs... We were the only squadron with the SABS bomb sight, and the only squadron doing these special ops on our own. We knew very well that much was expected of us, and we had to live up to the Squadron's reputation.[27]

Goodman's first operational flight did not go as planned. They had been detailed to bomb the shipping pens at Brest, but after take-off Goodman was interrupted from carrying out his course due to an unforeseen occurrence. Goodman explains:

> The aircraft caught fire! The whole cabin filled with smoke and I couldn't see the instruments. The Wireless Operator said "Skip, my set's on fire! I'll try and get it out." The Navigator wasn't best pleased but I couldn't see anything, so I did my best to keep us on a reasonable course. He got it out fairly quickly, but that wasn't a very good baptism of fire for us as a crew. My fourth trip, believe it or not, was to the *Tirpitz*!

Spitfire and Lancaster of the Battle of Britain Memorial Flight, Headcorn Combined Operations show, August 2011. (*Ady Shaw, Warbirdsphotos.net*)

Just before 0200 hours on 29 October 1944, Goodman climbed into Lancaster NF992 (code-lettered 'KC-B') with his crew. The squadron had left RAF Woodhall Spa on 28 October and flew to Milltown, Scotland, in preparation for an attack on *Tirpitz*, Hitler's infamous battleship that Churchill referred to as the 'Beast'. Goodman's faithful crew consisted of Flying Officers Watkinson and Hayward and Sergeants Burnett, Booth and Hulbert. It was a miserable night with low cloud base and heavy rain. While waiting on the perimeter track, Goodman set about to doing all of the necessary cockpit checks when suddenly his flight engineer nudged him in the ribs and said, 'Look!' Goodman looked up and saw a massive undercarriage wheel flying right over his cockpit. Goodman instinctively ducked as Iveson's Lancaster roared overhead into the night. It was a nervous moment, but Goodman soon settled down and got back to the task at hand. It was also a time of anxiety for Iveson who also had to calm his nerves as he climbed his aircraft into the dark sky, destined for his second attack on the *Tirpitz*.

The German battleship *Tirpitz* was the sister ship to the *Bismarck*. *Tirpitz* was launched in 1941 and with its heavy armament had proven a great threat to Allied shipping. The battleship was armed to the teeth with eight fifteen-inch guns, twelve six-inch guns and eighty flak guns. A number of attempts had been made by the Allies to sink the *Tirpitz*, but the battleship's resilience had kept it afloat. Under the command of Wing Commander Willie Tait and in conjunction with 9 Squadron, 617 had previously attacked the battleship on 15 September 1944 with Tallboy bombs. The Lancasters operated from Yagodnik near Archangel in Russia, but accurate bombing runs were foiled by a smokescreen that covered the ship. However, one of the thirteen Tallboy bombs dropped scored a hit and put the *Tirpitz* out of action. It was Tait's bombardier, Danny Daniels, who had damaged the vessel. As a result, *Tirpitz* was towed to an anchorage near Tromso where it was reasonably sheltered off the coast of Norway. For the squadron's second attack, which Goodman was involved in, each Lancaster carried a 12,000 lbs Tallboy bomb and extra fuel to carry out the twelve hours and twenty minute round trip. The Lancasters flew north to Tromso to arrive just after dawn, but the *Tirpitz* was blanketed by a low cloud base. Goodman and his colleagues carried out their bombing runs and dropped the Tallboys despite the poor visibility. As a result of this operation some damage was sustained, but the *Tirpitz* continued to live up to its reputation.

On 12 November, 9 and 617 squadrons, led by Squadron Leader A. G. Williams, DFC, and Wing Commander James Tait, DSO, DFC, took-off from Lossiemouth at 0300 hours to attack the *Tirpitz* once again. This time visibility was good and in the space of four minutes 617's Lancasters dropped their bombs from 15,000 feet. 9 Squadron also made its run but one of its aircraft was damaged by flak and forced to land in Sweden. The initial attacks saw near misses but the battleship soon received two direct hits and the infamous *Tirpitz* capsized and was finally beaten.

Another memorable operation that Goodman recalls with clarity took place on 12 January 1945. The squadron, along with 9 Squadron, were ordered to Bergen to drop Tallboy bombs on submarine pens. Mustangs of 315 (Polish) Squadron were instructed as escort and the bombers were also complemented by two Mosquitoes from 100 Group. In total, thirty-one aircraft would be involved in the Bergen attack.

> Sometimes what made ops a little more stressful perhaps is when waiting by your aircraft for a red Very or green Very. Red meant "scrub", green meant "go!", so you were left to think for a bit, but I can truly say once I got into the aircraft any nerves I may have had were gone once I had something to do. I had the responsibility of flying the aircraft and doing it properly, so I got on with it.

Once Goodman had taken-off, he flew on to Peterhead in Scotland with the squadron to rendezvous with thirteen Mustangs that had been equipped with long-range fuel tanks in order to make the long trip to Bergen. Owing to a brake fault on his usual aircraft, Iveson took-off in Lancaster NG181 after the squadron had left for Scotland. Despite the frustrating delay, Iveson managed to catch up with the squadron that were flying in loose formation on route to the target. One of the first Lancasters over Bergen successfully dropped its Tallboy, but the explosion threw up a large cloud of smoke and dust that remained over the target as there was no wind to clear it. An order was given for the remaining Lancasters to orbit the target area in the hope that the cloud would disperse, but hanging around over enemy territory was the last thing a bomber crew wanted to do. The order would prove costly as Iveson recalls:

> After a while my rear gunner, Ted Wass said, "Okay, skipper, we've now got the fighters." He thought they were the Polish Mustangs and so did I. They were not. We learned very quickly that we had attracted a collection of some 20 Focke-Wulf 190's and Me109's. The next thing we knew there was lots of noise... I remember there were sheets of white stuff going over the top of the canopy and the port inner engine suddenly burst into flames. At the same time, M-Mike (Iveson's aircraft) tried to stand on its tail! A Focke-Wulf 190 had come in behind us and fired at us.[28]

The pilot of the Fw 190 was Heinz Orlowski of 9 Staffel. As well as setting the Lancaster's port inner engine ablaze, his attack had struck the aircraft's port fin, rudder, port elevator and tail-plane. The Luftwaffe fighter pilot was convinced that he had destroyed the bomber as its engine was on fire, trailing smoke and three of its crew bailed out. Under this impression, Orlowski broke off from the engagement and went after a Lancaster of 9 Squadron. By the end of the operation, three Lancasters had been lost. Contrary to Orlowski's claim, Iveson's 'M-Mike' was not one of them. Amid the enemy fighters and heavy flak, Iveson, in a marvellous feat that earned him the DFC, expertly flew the crippled bomber back to Britain with the assistance of his flight engineer, Taffy Phillips, navigator Jack Harrison and bombardier Frank Chance. On 16 March 1945, the *London Gazette* printed the following:

> This officer has completed numerous sorties on his second tour of operational duty, including three attacks against the battleship Tirpitz. In January, 1945, he was detailed to attack the U-boat pens at Bergen. Whilst over the target his aircraft was attacked by two fighters. The first burst of machine-gun fire from the enemy aircraft struck the tailplane, rudder and elevator. The port inner engine was set on fire and the rear turret was put out of action. After the fighters broke off their attack Squadron Leader Iveson's aircraft came under heavy fire from the antiaircraft batteries. It was almost impossible to maintain level flight. Squadron Leader Iveson instructed another member of the crew to lash the control column in such a way as to ease the strain. Under these most trying conditions, Squadron Leader Iveson flew clear of the fire zone

and afterwards reached a home based airfield where he landed his seriously damaged aircraft safely. By his great skill, courage and determination, this officer was undoubtedly responsible for the safe return of the aircraft.

Like Iveson, Goodman does not remember observing Mustangs over the target during this hair-raising operation, but unlike some was able to get out of the hot zone and safely return home. There were, of course, other times that Goodman's aircraft was struck by enemy fire as he recalls:

On one night trip I really did smell the flak it was that close! My bomb-aimer was lying flat and a piece of flak came through the aircraft and lodged in his boot. The wireless op had an even luckier escape on one occasion when something came through just as he bent forward, just for a second, and it came through one side of the fuselage and went out the other. It was quite a large hole and we reckoned that it certainly would have gone through his head. We also had an engine shot up, but I suppose everybody did really. Once or twice we came back on three engines but it was a no brainer; there was nothing in it with three engines and no load, as we had dropped our bombs. I was fully confident in our Merlin engines. Oh, the noise those beautiful engines made when you throttled back, there is no other sound in the world like it.

On 19 March 1945, 617 Squadron bombed a railway viaduct at Arnsberg with six Grand Slam bombs which blew a forty-foot gap in the target. Goodman was one of those who dropped a 22,000 lbs Grand Slam. He remembers:

I never had any concern, carrying a Grand Slam bomb on take-off, that it wasn't going to get off the ground. It was a little but sluggish, but anything they put on, a Lancaster was capable of handling. It was slow in climbing, but we got to bombing height and joined the others and got over the target. My recollection was that we didn't have to say 'bomb gone' because the aircraft went up like a rocket. But my flight engineer Jock said, not only did the aeroplane climb quickly, but he heard a hell of a bang; it may have been the release mechanism. It never got to the point where the whole squadron had Grand Slams, we always had a mixture with Tallboys. There were no complaints about the flying characteristics, despite the huge load.[29]

On 9 April 1945, Goodman flew one of seventeen Lancasters of 617 Squadron that bombed U-boat shelters in Hamburg. But unavoidably, Goodman's bomb did not release immediately over the target and fell into workers houses around the port area. On the return to base, Goodman experienced an eerie encounter with an unexpected foe. Goodman's flight engineer, Jock, nudged him to get his attention and cast his eyes to their right. Goodman continues:

Battle of Britain Memorial Flight
Lancaster at Farnborough 2012
(*C. Yeoman*)

> I looked out of the window and there was a Messerschmitt Me262 in close
> formation with us, which to say the least was a bit disconcerting!

Time seemed to stand still for Goodman and his crew as the Luftwaffe jet stuck
menacingly to the Lancaster's starboard. Goodman entertained the idea of
performing a corkscrew manoeuvre to evade the jet, but with other Lancasters
in the vicinity it was too risky. There was no mid-upper turret, so in their current
position there was nothing the Lancaster's defences could do. Goodman
decided that it was best not to provoke the Me 262. Then suddenly, to the relief
of Goodman and his crew, the jet broke away into the dark sky.

> We decided he had probably run out of ammunition and couldn't shoot us down,
> so he had decided to give us a bloody good fright, which he did! Jets in those
> days were in their infancy but to have one watching you like that wasn't a terribly
> comfortable feeling. About two years ago, I was talking to John Langston, who
> was a navigator at the same time I was flying with No. 617 and he said "Oh
> Benny, yes that was the 262 that was shooting at us and didn't hit us once, so he
> must have been a really new pilot, fortunately, and gone on after you."

It was a strange encounter that left a lasting impression on Goodman.

By the end of the war, Goodman had completed thirty operational sorties.
The odds of survival whilst serving in Bomber Command were against him, so
to make it through a tour of duty unscathed is something Goodman attributes
to luck. He remembers his last operational flight with the squadron:

> The last trip I ever did was Berchtesgaden, the Eagle's Nest and they certainly
> had flak there I can tell you, but it was right at the end and I think it was more
> of a token trip than anything else really, to show people that we could do it.

After the war, Goodman still wanted to fly. He served in Transport Command
flying Short Stirlings and later flew Handley Page Hastings with 51 Squadron.

The Battle of Britain Memorial Flight. (*Marcus Franklin, franklinphotography.co.uk*)

He was eventually posted to 604 Squadron that was equipped with the legendary Spitfire. It was a complete joy for Goodman who said that '...the Spitfire was the most beautiful, beautiful aeroplane to fly'. Goodman left the RAF in 1964 as a squadron leader. In 2008, he was still flying his own Comanche 250 private aircraft.

During the Second World War, RAF Bomber Command suffered astounding losses. 55,573 airmen were killed, 9,838 would become prisoners of war and a further 8,403 wounded.

Epilogue

In Wing Commander Tom Neil's fabulous book *Gun Button to Fire*, he describes what he believes was a turning point for Gerald 'Zulu' Lewis writing that after being mauled by Messerschmitt Bf 109s on one particular sortie and landing back at North Weald, Lewis was '…profoundly disturbed by the incident and unusually critical of the manner in which such sorties were being carried out. It was this engagement, (10 February 1941) I believe, that was a tipping point for him, as he never felt entirely comfortable on any such operations again.' Of Lewis' character Neil continues:

> Although we only served together for about five months, I grew to be very fond of Gerald. A shy and retiring young man, he was never at ease in mixed company especially and, despite his splendid physique, seldom took part in any overt display of horseplay… Later, I was told by friends serving with him, how he had gradually lost confidence in himself and that he was then keen "to get away from it all".[30]

It had been an exhausting war for Lewis in every way imaginable, but despite his desire 'to get away from it all' he continued to climb into a Hurricane cockpit and endure heavy burdens until the very end. Lewis found peace in later life with his faith and family, but his experiences were of the kind that one almost certainly could never forget.

The same could be said for Bobby Pearce, Alan Harker, Henryk Szczesny, Percy Beake and Benny Goodman. All had been lucky to survive the war but they were undoubtedly left with memories that are impossible for us to truly comprehend today. We must, however, remember their stories and the stories of those brave airmen who were not fortunate enough to have survived the tumultuous skies of the Second World War, paying the ultimate price for their country.

The ultimate sacrifice made by John Drummond, Jindřich Bartoš, Otto Hanzlíček, Wladyslaw Szulkowski, Ken Gillies, Stanley Connors, Don Cobden and Wally Churches should always be remembered for the noble cause for which they died. Without men such as these the world would undoubtedly be a very different place to live in.

> We do not want to be remembered as heroes, we only ask to be remembered for what we did... that's all.

Wing Commander Bob Doe, DSO, DFC*.

Acknowledgements

I apologise if this reads as if I am writing an Oscar award ceremony speech but there are a number of wonderful people that I would like to thank for their valued assistance in the making of this book and for those around me that have kept the fire burning. Firstly, I'd like to thank and acknowledge Mark Lewis, Gill and 'Tich' Palliser, Percy Beake, Tom Neil, Benny Goodman, Bobby and Dulcie Pearce, Keith Lawrence, Geoffrey Wellum, Terence Kane and Martin Doheney for the information they have kindly provided during the research of this work. I would like to thank David Pritchard for his dynamic paintings of the 'Few'. I would like to thank Eddie Nielinger, Eric Mombeeck, Chris Goss , Wojciech Zmyslony and the 74 Squadron Association for allowing me the use of their photographs. My thanks also extend to Brian Cull, Peter Cornwell and Geoff Simpson for providing additional information and details that have proved most helpful to this work. I am especially grateful for my lovely wife Kym who acts as my unofficial editor and never complains about the late nights or hours I spend doing what I love. I'm also grateful to my parents Bob and Beverley for their infectious enthusiasm and encouragement. My appreciation also extends to my brother David and his wife Sophia for their continued support. Last but not least I would like to thank Adrian for being a part of this project. It wasn't that long ago that we bumped into each other at a 'Rabbit Sqn' Battle of Britain veteran signing event. We eventually got to speaking because I kept darting in and out of the signing room to check the football scores. Both pleased that Liverpool were winning, we discovering that we had two interests in common and since then we became good friends. The rest, as they say, is history.

Christopher Yeoman

I would like to thank a number of people for their help and encouragement in writing this, my first book. Sadly, little is available on the pre-war lives of the Czech and Polish airmen so I'm indebted to Tom Dolezal of the Free Czechoslovak Air Force network for his assistance is researching Jindřich Bartoš and Otto Hanzlíček. In particular, members of John Drummond and Ken Gillies' families have been incredibly co-operative in sharing deeply personal stories and memories of what were shattering family events and allowing me to use them in this book. Peter Challis, Helen Adelsbury and Fraser Drummond could not have been more helpful in providing information and photographs about John. Mark Gillies, Ken's grandson, and John and Sue Gillies have helped so much in my research on Ken. But my most grateful thanks are reserved for Ken's sister-in-law Janet, for whom that summer is a living memory. She embodies everything that was great about that generation and it has been a privilege to get to know her. Finally, I would like to say thank you to my co-author Christopher Yeoman whose idea this project was and for giving me the opportunity to contribute to it.

Adrian Cork

Endnotes

1. Barclay, George, edited by Humphrey Wynn, *Fighter Pilot, A Self-Portrait*
2. Spurdle, Bob, *The Blue Arena*, p. 31
3. Wynn, Kenneth. G. *A Clasp for 'The Few'*
4. Spurdle, Bob, *The Blue Arena*, p. 85.
5. Cull, Brain, Bruce Lander, Bruce and Heinrich Weiss, *Twelve Days in May*
6. Bolitho, Hector, *Combat Report – The Story of a Fighter Pilot*
7. Cornwell, Peter D., *The Battle of France Then and Now*
8. Townsend, Peter, *Duel of Eagles*
9. Townsend, Peter, *Time and Chance*
10. Barclay, George, edited by Humphrey Wynn, *Fighter Pilot, A Self-Portrait by George Barclay*
11. Cull, Brian, *249 At War*
12. Neil, Tom, *Onward to Malta,*
13. Cull, Brian, *Bloody Shambles: Volume 2*
14. Tidy, D. P., *South African Air Aces of World War II, Battle of Britain Remembered #4*
15. Rall, Günther and Kurt Braatz, *My Logbook: Reminiscences 1938-2006*
16. Conners, S. D. P., 'Combat Report'
17. Hough, Richard and Denis Richards, *The Battle of Britain: The Jubilee History*
18. *1940* magazine, No 2, 2002, research by Stephen Bungay
19. Bungay, Stephen, *The Most Dangerous Enemy*
20. Tidy, Doug, *I Fear No Man,*
21. Franks, Norman, *Sky Tiger*
22. Willis, John, *Churchill's Few*
23. Doe, Bob, *Fighter Pilot*
24. Holland, James, Audio interview with Bob Doe, 12 March 2002
25. Willis, John, *Churchill's Few*
26. Simpson, Geoff, *Mortal Danger*

27. Iveson, Tony and Brian Milton, *Lancaster: The Biography*, p. 193
28. Iveson, Tony and Brian Milton, *Lancaster: The Biography*, p. 19
29. Iveson, Tony and Brian Milton, *Lancaster: The Biography*, p. 184
30. Neil, Tom, *Gun Button to Fire*

Bibliography

Manuscripts

Combat Reports from the National Archives

Published Works

Allen, H. R., *Battle for Britain: The Recollections of H. R. 'Dizzy' Allen, DFC* (Corgi Books, 1969)

Barclay, George, edited by Wynn, Humphrey, *Fighter Pilot, A Self-Portrait by George Barclay* (Crecy Books, 1994)

Bishop, Patrick, *Fighter Boys* (Harper Perennial, 2004)

Brooks, A. J., *Fighter Squadron at War* (Ian Allan Publishing Ltd, 1980)

Bungay, Stephen, *The Most Dangerous Enemy* (Aurum Press, 2000)

Cornwell, Peter D., *The Battle of France: Then and Now* (After The Battle Publication, 2007)

Cull, Brian, *249 at War* (Grub Street, 1997)

Cull, Brain, Bruce Lander and Heinrich Weiss, *Twelve Days in May*, (Grub Street, 1995)

Doe, Bob, *Fighter Pilot* (CCB Aviation Books, 1999)

Forbes, Athol and Hubert Allen, *Ten Fighter Boys* (Collins, 1942)

Franks, Norman, *Sky Tiger, The Story of Sailor Malan* (Crecy Books, 1994)

Gelb, Norman, *Scramble: A Narrative History of the Battle of Britain* (Michael Joseph Ltd, 1986)

Goss, Chris, *The Luftwaffe Bombers' Battle of Britain* (Crecy Publishing, 2000)

Hough, Richard and Denis Richards, *The Battle of Britain: The Jubilee History* (Guild Publishing, 1990)

Iveson, Tony and Brian Milton, *Lancaster: The Biography* (Andre Deutsch, 2009)

King, Richard, *303 (Polish) Squadron: Battle of Britain Diary* (Red Kite, 2010)

Mason, Francis K., *Battle over Britain* (Aston Publications Ltd, 1990)

Mombeeck, Erik and Jean-Louis Roba, *In the Skies of France: A Chronicle of JG 2 'Richthofen' Volume 1* (A.S.B.L. La Porte d'Hoves)

Neil, Tom, *Gun Button to Fire* (Amberley, 2010)

Neil, Tom, *Onward to Malta* (Airlife Publishing Ltd, 1992)

Oxspring, Bobby, *Spitfire Command* (Cerberus Publishing Ltd, 2004)

Rall, Gunther and Kurt Braatz, *My Logbook: Reminiscences 1938-2006* (NeunundzwanzigSechs Verlag, 2006)

Ramsey, G. Winston, *The Battle of Britain: Then and Now* Mk V (After The Battle Publication, 1989)

Robinson, Anthony, *RAF Fighter Squadrons in the Battle of Britain* (Weidenfeld & Nicholson Military, 1987)

Robinson, Michael, *Best of the Few* (Michael Robinson, 2001)

Shores, Christopher and Clive Williams, *Aces High* (Grub Street, 1994)

Shores, Christopher, Brian Cull and Yasuho Isawa, *Bloody Shambles: Volume 2* (Grub Street, 1993)

Spurdle, Bob, *The Blue Arena* (Crecy Books, 1995)

Tidy, Doug, *I Fear No Man, The History of No. 74 Squadron RAF* (Macdonald & Co., 1972)

Tidy, D. P., *South African Air Aces of World War II, Battle of Britain Remembered #4,* (The Battle of Britain Historical Society)

Townsend, Peter, *Duel of Eagles* (Weidenfeld & Nicolson, 1970)

Townsend, Peter, *Time and Chance* (Collins, 1978)

Walpole, Nigel, *Dragon Rampant: The Story of No. 234 Fighter Squadron* (Merlin Massara Publishing, 2007)

Wellum, Geoffrey, *First Light* (Viking, 2002)

Willis, John, *Churchill's Few* (Michael Joseph Ltd, 1985)

Wynn, Kenneth G., *A Clasp for 'The Few'* (self-published, 1981)

Wynn, Kenneth G., *Men of the Battle of Britain* (CCB Aviation Books, 1999)

Zielinski, Jozef, *Polish Airmen in the Battle of Britain* (Oficyna Wydawnicza MH)